The American Crisis Series
Books on the Civil War Era

Steven E. Woodworth, Associate Professor of H
Texas Christian University
SERIES EDITOR

D0745260

The Civil War was the crisis of the Republic's first century
—the test, in Abraham Lincoln's words, of whether any free government could long endure. It touched with fire the hearts of a generation, and its story has fired the imaginations of every generation since.
This series offers to students of the Civil War, either those continuing or those just beginning their exciting journey into the past, con-
cise overviews of important persons, events, and themes in that
remarkable period of America's history.

Volumes Published

James L. Abrahamson. *The Men of Secession and Civil War, 1859–1861*
(2000). Cloth ISBN 0-8420-2818-8 Paper ISBN 0-8420-2819-6

Robert G. Tanner. *Retreat to Victory? Confederate Strategy Reconsidered*
(2001). Cloth ISBN 0-8420-2881-1 Paper ISBN 0-8420-2882-X

Stephen Davis. *Atlanta Will Fall: Sherman, Joe Johnston, and the
Yankee Heavy Battalions* (2001). Cloth ISBN 0-8420-2787-4
Paper ISBN 0-8420-2788-2

Paul Ashdown and Edward Caudill. *The Mosby Myth: A Confederate
Hero in Life and Legend* (2002). Cloth ISBN 0-8420-2928-1
Paper ISBN 0-8420-2929-X

Spencer C. Tucker. *A Short History of the Civil War at Sea* (2002).
Cloth ISBN 0-8420-2867-6 Paper ISBN 0-8420-2868-4

Richard Bruce Winders. *Crisis in the Southwest: The United States,
Mexico, and the Struggle over Texas* (2002). Cloth ISBN 0-8420-
2800-5 Paper ISBN 0-8420-2801-3

Ethan S. Rafuse. *A Single Grand Victory: The First Campaign and
Battle of Manassas* (2002). Cloth ISBN 0-8420-2875-7
Paper ISBN 0-8420-2876-5

John G. Selby. *Virginians at War: The Civil War Experiences of Seven Young Confederates* (2002). Cloth ISBN 0-8420-5054-X
Paper ISBN 0-8420-5055-8

Edward K. Spann. *Gotham at War: New York City, 1860–1865* (2002).
Cloth ISBN 0-8420-5056-6   Paper ISBN 0-8420-5057-4

Anne J. Bailey. *War and Ruin: William T. Sherman and the Savannah Campaign* (2002). Cloth ISBN 0-8420-2850-1
Paper ISBN 0-8420-2851-X

Gary Dillard Joiner. *One Damn Blunder from Beginning to End: The Red River Campaign of 1864* (2003). Cloth ISBN 0-8420-2936-2
Paper ISBN 0-8420-2937-0

Gotham at War

Gotham in 1859 as seen from its East River side with Brooklyn in the foreground. From the Eno Collection, Miriam and Ira D. Wallach Division of Art, Prints & Photographs, The New York Public Library, Astor, Lennox, and Tilden Foundations. *Courtesy of the New York Public Library*

Gotham at War
New York City, 1860–1865

The American Crisis Series
BOOKS ON THE CIVIL WAR ERA
NO. 9

Edward K. Spann

A Scholarly Resources Inc. Imprint
Wilmington, Delaware

Scholarly Resources Inc.
104 Greenhill Avenue
Wilmington, DE 19805-1897
www.scholarly.com

Library of Congress Cataloging-in-Publication Data

Spann, Edward K., 1931–
 Gotham at war : New York City, 1860–1865 / Edward K. Spann.
  p. cm. — (The American crisis series ; no. 9)
 Includes bibliographical references (p.) and index.
 ISBN 0-8420-5056-6 (cloth : alk. paper) — ISBN 0-8420-5057-4
(paper : alk. paper)
  1. New York (N.Y.)—History—Civil War, 1861–1865. I. Title.
II. Series.

F128.44 .S72 2002
974.7'103—dc21   2002024515

About the Author

Edward K. Spann, emeritus professor of history and distinguished professor in arts and sciences at Indiana State University, is the author of five previous books: *Ideals and Politics: New York Intellectuals and Nineteenth-Century Liberalism* (1972; nominated for a Pulitzer Prize), *The New Metropolis: New York City* (1981; winner of the Dixon Ryan Fox Award in 1977), *Brotherly Tomorrows: Movements for a Cooperative Society in America* (1989), *Hopedale: From Commune to Company Town* (1992), and *Designing Modern America: The Regional Planning Association and Its Members* (1996). He is currently working on a biography of the artist-writer Gilbert Brown Wilson.

ACKNOWLEDGMENTS

In researching this work, I owe a special debt of gratitude to the keepers of our literary and archival treasurers, the librarians. My special thanks to the helpful workers at the Indiana State University, Columbia University, Cooper Union, and New York Historical Society libraries and also at the National Archives both in Washington, DC, and in New York. Working at the New York Public Library proved to be an often frustrating experience when it came to gaining access to its vast resources, but without that library this book could not have been written. My thanks also to Anthony Brentlinger in the Multimedia Support Services Division of Indiana State University for assisting with illustrations in this book. I owe another debt, of course, to the many scholars in the field of Civil War history—too many to be mentioned, except for James M. McPherson, whose insights and ideas have had a strong influence on my work.

CONTENTS

INTRODUCTION

TEACHING THE HISTORY of the Civil War period has convinced me that, despite the mountain of books produced by the Civil War publishing industry, there are important aspects of the war that have not been adequately explored. There is no shortage of books dealing with military engagements and with military units, but the complex relationship between the war and the civilian populations has yet to be fully detailed and analyzed. Over the last decade several notable efforts have been made to fill this gap, with varying degrees of success. J. Matthew Gallman's *The North Fights the Civil War: The Home Front* (Chicago: Ivan R. Dee, 1994) provides an excellent overview of this civilian world at war that at least partly supplanted Emerson David Fite's classic study, *Social and Industrial Conditions in the North During the Civil War* (New York: Macmillan, 1910). The design of Gallman's book, however, limits it to a general and occasionally frustratingly superficial discussion of complex issues and events.

Even before the publication of *The North Fights the Civil War*, Gallman had provided an illustration of how to deal with the subject in depth in his *Mastering Wartime: A Social History of Philadelphia During the Civil War* (New York: Cambridge University Press, 1990), a solid study that embraced the approach and techniques of the new social history to examine the war's impact on an important aggregation of people and industry. *Mastering Wartime* is one of several studies dealing with the contributions and experiences of the nation's major cities. Civil War Chicago is the subject of Theodore J. Karamanski's *Rally Around the Flag* (Chicago: Nelson-Hall, 1993), a narrative history that focuses on the more familiar elements of wartime society. Thomas H. O'Connor adopted a similar approach in his *Civil War Boston: Home Front and Battlefield* (Boston: Northeastern University Press, 1997).

These books are important studies of major cities, but they are no substitute for an insightful work on by far the biggest American city in population and overall power, New York City. Here, historical study has produced a more mixed result. There have been some notable articles on various aspects of the city, including my own study of one group that figures in every urban history of the war, "Union Green: The Irish Community and the Civil War" in Ronald H. Bayor and Timothy J. Meagher's edited volume, *The New York Irish* (Baltimore: Johns Hopkins University Press, 1996). Also, several works deal with the infamous New York City Draft Riots, including good narrative histories, such as James McCague's *The Second Rebellion* (New York: Dial Press, 1968) and Adrian Cook's *The Armies of the Streets* (Lexington: University Press of Kentucky, 1974). McCague's and Cook's books are important works, but both books had the unfortunate effect of greatly inflating the importance of the Draft Riots in the history of the city. Another work, Ivor Bernstein's *The New York City Draft Riots: Their Significance for American Society and Politics in the Age of the Civil War* (New York: Oxford University Press, 1990), attempts to place the subject in a larger context, as its subtitle indicates, but, although it is an excellent study of the riots, it provides few meaningful insights into the larger wartime experiences and developments of the city.

Only one work published in recent years attempts to provide a comprehensive history of wartime New York, Ernest A. McKay's *The Civil War and New York City* (Syracuse, NY: Syracuse University Press, 1990). McKay's book is the result of dedicated research that makes it a repository of information regarding most important events that took place in the city during the war. The "and" in the title, however, suggests a significant weakness: McKay made little effort to incorporate his findings into a coherent study of New York as an urban society. The result is an often discursive work in which the city tends to get lost in a plethora of wartime happenings. McKay gives much too little attention, for instance, to such matters as the central role played by the city as a supply center for the Union army and the influence of immigration on wartime society.

Although McKay's book partly filled an important gap in Civil War history, reviewing it convinced me of the need for a book on Civil War New York written from the perspective of an urban historian. When I completed my book *The New Metropolis: New York City, 1840–1857* (New York: Columbia University Press, 1981), I had no intention of writing a sequel that would carry the story forward into the Civil War era. Eventually, however, I could not resist the challenge of determining how a world-class metropolis responded to the greatest internal crisis in American history. What I have attempted to do here is to explore both the varied ways in which a great war affected a great city and the ways a great city affected the war. To this end, I give special attention to New York as a center of military supply, manpower, and naval shipbuilding and to key elements of its government, society, and economy. I begin with a discussion of the coming of the war from the presidential election of 1860 to the firing on Fort Sumter, presenting a background for conflict that should open new lines of thinking about its origins. I conclude with a discussion of the immediate postwar adjustments to a new time of peace and opportunity and with a brief overview of some long-term trends in Gotham's history.

It will not be long before the reader recognizes two opposing sides to New York's wartime involvements. On the positive side, the city's capacity to mobilize an enthusiastic albeit poorly trained military force during the first month of the war may have saved Washington, DC, from Confederate capture, and its strong financial support for the national government during a time of crisis may well have saved the Union. Materially, New York City became a major supply center for the Union military, providing, among other things, uniforms and equipment for soldiers and horses and hay for the horse-drawn army, and its shipyards created much of what became the world's most powerful navy. Medically, Gotham became a center of efforts to provide for sick and wounded soldiers, making for perhaps the noblest story of the war. Politically, the city's great Republican newspapers built public support for the Union cause, and such local leaders as William E. Dodge and Mayor George Opdyke made important contributions to the war effort. Overall, we have a picture of a great metropolis drawing on its national and international connections and on its organizational skills to help win a great domestic conflict.

On the opposing side, though, we have a highly insular city in its political and social outlook, a city that shared some of the same values that animated the Confederacy. New York was, in these terms, the most southern of northern cities, and therefore it was not surprising that it became a center of Copperhead opposition to the war effort. The hostility of many New Yorkers to conscription culminated in one of the greatest of all urban upheavals, the Draft Riots of July 1863. After a strong start in providing manpower for the war, Gotham's government increasingly used public money to buy exemptions for its citizens, a scheme that sunk to the level of bounty brokering and bounty jumping, helping to prepare the way for postwar corruption. Did the metropolis contribute its full share of manpower to the Union cause? Using the state census of 1865, I conclude that it did not.

The city was also strongly racist, hostile to the abolition of slavery and to any real freedom for black Americans. It was on matters of race especially that a deep ethnic cleavage was revealed between the rapidly growing number of Irish, whose antipathy to blacks reinforced the racist leanings of the local Democratic Party, and a much smaller but influential group of transplanted New Englanders who moved their Republican Party toward the dream of something like racial justice. The result of this interplay was a significant, although not entirely permanent, advance of civil rights.

CHAPTER ONE

THE ROAD TO WAR, 1860–1861

AT THE BEGINNING of 1860, New York City faced one of the most prosperous years in its history. It had recovered from the national depression of 1857 and could expect to get more than its share of the returning national prosperity. "What a golden era and bounteous land," enthused Horace Greeley's *New York Tribune* in welcoming the new year. "What a stately city—the third city of Christendom."[1] During the 1850s, New York City and its expanding metropolitan environs had become a world-class metropolis second only to London. The metropolis dominated the nation's commerce, handling more than one-third of American exports to foreign lands and nearly two-thirds of all American imports. Because of its overwhelming commercial strength, the city's financial institutions on Wall Street dominated the business of borrowing and lending money. Even though its special strengths were in commerce and finance, the metropolis was also America's leading manufacturer, producing a vast variety of goods ranging from steam engines to men's clothing.

During the 1850s the population of New York City had increased by nearly 60 percent, from 515,547 people to 814,254, and the ten-county area around it in the states of New York and New Jersey had grown even faster, from 380,000 to 690,000, an 80 percent increase. The total population of metropolitan New York was nearly 5 percent of the whole American population, a mass of people greater than that of all but four of the thirty-four states. In contrast, as the *New York Times* eagerly pointed out, Charleston, South Carolina—the cauldron of Southern secessionism—could boast of only 40,000 people, having experienced a 5 percent *decline* in population since 1850—a mere pip-squeak in the shadow of Goliath, or so it seemed.

The end of 1860, however, indicated that it was politics rather than economics that would rule the immediate future and that

Charleston, by leading the secession of the South, would shake the foundations of even Gotham. New York's commercial dominance had made it heavily dependent on the South, a condition illustrated by the fact that its single largest export was cotton, a fiber not grown within hundreds of miles of the city. For years, to protect its interests, Gotham had tried to moderate the developing political conflict between the North and the South with some success, but its efforts failed to prevent the national upheaval that began in December, when South Carolina seceded from the Union.

This revolutionary act was precipitated by the election of Abraham Lincoln a month before. Although Lincoln had no intention of attacking the slave-owning South, he had condemned slavery as an unworthy institution, leading anxious Southerners to the wrong-headed idea that his victory would bring the triumph of an aggressive abolitionism. It was a dangerous misconception that powerful voices in New York did much to support, chiefly for local political purposes. Although numerous factors were involved in the secession of the South, the city's special political arrangements had an ambivalent but strong effect on the unfolding of the great national crisis.

One basic fact of New York politics was the dominance of the Democratic Party over the city and the entire metropolitan region. The national party had long prided itself on being "the party of planters and plain people," making it the best hope for bridging the gap separating the North and the South. The Democratic Party's strong ties with the South reinforced its most characteristic policies. It stood for free trade—in opposition to the protectionism of the Republican Party—a position that appealed to local merchant and worker interests dependent on the import trade. Equally important for many New Yorkers, the Democratic Party stood for free behavior, in opposition to the intrusive tendencies of moral reform elements in the Republican Party—temperance men as well as abolitionists.

As such, the Democrats had the support of a substantial Roman Catholic Irish population hostile to the puritanical propensities of Yankee reformers. "It is a mistake to say that the fundamental idea of the Republican party is opposition to African slavery," declared the Catholic *New York Freeman's Journal,* "This is but one phase of Republicanism. The fundamental idea of that party is the claim to a right to determine by political legislation questions that, among a free people, do not belong to politics." The New York Democratic Party was also deeply racist, an openly white man's party hostile to freedom for black people in general. No better friend of the South existed in the North.[2]

Although it was virtually unbeatable in the metropolis, the Democratic Party had serious problems. For example, it was often badly divided by factional conflicts. Nationally, in 1860 it had split into two parties, each with its own presidential candidate, Stephen A. Douglas and John C. Breckinridge. In Gotham this division was complicated by a conflict between Tammany Hall and a rival political faction that met in Mozart Hall. Another problem was that the Democratic Party's political dominance was confined chiefly to the lower Hudson River valley, whereas the expanding areas of central and western New York ("upstate") leaned heavily toward the Republican Party. This division was a critical fact of political life for New York City, which seemed forever threatened by interference from a Republican-controlled state government. The conflict between upstate and downstate interests dominated politics for decades.

By October 1860, New York State appeared to be the likely president-maker in the race between Lincoln and the three candidates selected to oppose him. If Democrats could keep Republicans from winning New York's bloc of electoral votes, the largest in the nation, they might prevent Lincoln from getting a majority of the national electoral vote, throwing the final election into the House of Representatives, where Lincoln would likely lose. The critical question for both sides was whether the Democrats could turn out a sufficiently large popular vote downstate to overcome the upstate vote for Lincoln.

Republicans had some strength in the city, notably three influential newspapers, the *Tribune*, the *Times*, and the *New York Evening Post*, and the backing of reformers, businessmen, and others who, although not abolitionists, resented the "Slave Power" as an arrogant obstacle to progress. Early in October 1860 the party made its greatest effort, organizing a military-style mass demonstration of uniformed "Wide-Awakes" dedicated to the Republican cause. Hundreds of women labored for weeks to make uniforms for the demonstrators, who gathered by the thousands from the city and nearby counties to hold what the *Tribune* called a "Monster Torchlight

Parade—20,000 Lincolnites in Line—Seventy acres of Republicans—Over half a million spectators."³ It was one unplanned preparation for a war that was as yet unseen.

The great parade did much to attract favorable public attention, but it also spurred the Democrats to an even greater countereffort. On October 9 they held a mass meeting at Cooper Union, where they proclaimed themselves the "white man's party" and charged that Republicans were planning to abolish slavery regardless of the majority will of white America. Such partisan assertions served to reinforce Southern fears regarding a Republican victory. In response to the march of the Wide-Awakes, Democrats held their own mass torchlight parade: "Seven miles of 37,000 conservatives afoot," declared the *New York Herald*, "Over Half a Million Spectators in the Streets. The Wide-Awakes Completely Squelched. The City in a Blaze of Fire."⁴

In late October the young Democratic leader Samuel J. Tilden warned that Southerners would see a Republican-controlled government as an unacceptable "foreign government," a situation that was likely to bring a bloody civil war: "Defeat Lincoln and all our great interests and hopes are unquestionably safe." This warning was repeated by others sympathetic to the conservative cause, including the popular *Herald*. Although nominally nonpartisan, the *Herald* was violently anti-Lincoln and predicted the worst if he were elected. The secession of the South, it warned, would severely damage the economic interests of the many New Yorkers dependent on the Southern trade, not only merchants but ship carpenters, shoemakers, carriage makers, and other artisans. Elect Lincoln, the *Herald* predicted, and "one hundred thousand workmen and working women will be thrown out of employment." And that was not all: "Irish and German laborers! If Lincoln is elected today you will have to compete with the labor of four million emancipated Negroes."⁵

By election day the combination of scare tactics and mass demonstrations had excited voter interest, reflected in long lines at the polling places. In the evening the city employed the Police Telegraph to transmit vote counts from the various election districts to a central location where reporters were waiting. Lincoln polled 32,641 votes in Gotham, but his opponents won 59,728, defeating him in every ward of the city. They also did well in Brooklyn and elsewhere in the metropolis. However, the Democratic majority of 32,000 was not enough to outweigh the flood of Lincoln votes upstate.

Initially, many Republicans scoffed at Democratic warnings that Lincoln's election would lead to the secession of the South. As late as November 29, 1860, William Cullen Bryant, poet and owner-editor of the *Evening Post*, declared that "nobody but a few silly people expect it will happen." On the day before the election, however, George Templeton Strong predicted that at least four Southern states would secede if Lincoln were elected, although he voted for Lincoln anyway. Unfortunately for America, it was Strong and not Bryant who was proven to be the more accurate prophet. Two weeks after the election, George Opdyke, a prominent businessman and soon-to-be mayor, declared that "secession cannot take place, either peacefully or forcibly"—only to see South Carolina and six other states leave the Union between December 1860 and February 1861.[6]

The long-feared crisis of the Union had come. Now, what to do about it? On December 15, 1860, prominent Democratic politicians and merchants, including Samuel J. Tilden and William B. Astor, met privately on Pine Street in New York City. The meeting passed resolutions urging added protection for slavery to mollify secessionists and appointed a committee headed by former President Millard Fillmore to go to the South with assurances of support for the Southern cause. The Pine Street meeting was only the first of several efforts by conservatives to save the Union through concessions to slaveholders, most notably by amending the Constitution to provide permanent protection for slavery.

In early January 1861, however, these efforts were overshadowed by a more radical response to secession proposed by New York's mayor, Fernando Wood. Wood was the most remarkable mayor in New York's history, a man of bold ambitions and limited conscience who had built a strong power base, especially among the city's Irish population. Although he never received the support of a majority of New Yorkers, he was a powerful presence in the city's factionalized politics for more than a decade. After being ousted from office midway through his second term in 1857 by a state-imposed change in the city charter, Wood had won reelection in 1859. Strongly sympathetic to the South and equally hostile to Republican reformers, Wood was one of a number of Democrats prepared to accede to secession.

On December 12, Wood sent out invitations for a "meeting of gentlemen to consider the national crisis" in his office the next day. It was rumored, according to the *Times,* that he planned to "create the counties of Suffolk, Queens, Kings, Westchester and Richmond together with the city of New York, into an independent Sovereignty to be called the State or Kingdom of Manhattan." Whatever the doings of this meeting, in his annual message on January 6, 1861, the mayor actually proposed a scheme only slightly less audacious: the secession of the metropolis from the state of New York. Declaring that the city had closer ties with the South than with an intrusive and limiting state government, Wood proposed that New York become a "free city" that would continue to trade with the seceded states. Noting that import duties collected in New York yielded nearly two-thirds of the national revenues, he offered the prospect that New Yorkers could escape paying taxes.[7]

Although Wood argued that his scheme could be achieved peacefully, he won little support and much condemnation. The *Tribune* declared that the mayor "evidently wants to be a traitor," and the *Times* denounced him as issuing "an invitation to rebellion." Other New Yorkers agreed. Wood was not reelected when his term expired in December 1861. He continued, however, to exercise significant influence favorable to the South throughout the next years, and he was not alone. A week after his message, a group of his supporters publicly praised the South for upholding a "white man's government" and for defending "the holy cause of American liberty"—a bizarre contention from a more modern perspective but sensible for local Democrats.[8] In March 1861, A. H. Osborne won brief notoriety when he petitioned the legislature of Confederate Louisiana to invite the people of southern New York State to join the Confederacy. He was hung in effigy from a tree in Brooklyn's City Hall Square.

Probably, Wood expected that the economy of the metropolis would be so shaken by secession that his plan would be taken seriously. Southerners had long warned that New York would be devastated by the loss of its trade. In fact, several weeks before the election, anxieties about the future of a divided nation had disrupted the local economy and had brought the New York Stock Exchange to the verge of financial panic. Along with fears of losing the South's trade came a sharp decline in imports, especially of dry goods.

Southerners made the situation worse by raising fears that they would not repay the millions in debts owed to New York merchants for the goods that they had purchased. As a result, the last three months of 1860 saw an unusually large number of business failures and thousands of job losses in businesses connected with the Southern trade.

Times often were bad, but they did not become bleak enough to drive the city into the South's embrace. Fortunately, the important dry goods trade had largely completed a profitable season before the panic began. Even better, in partial compensation for diminished Southern trade, New York benefited from a prospering Northwest, whose breadstuffs were much in demand in Europe. Grain exports from New York City in the last three months of 1860 were 30 percent larger than in the same period of any previous year. Moreover, the South failed, despite its boasts, to break its own dependence on the metropolis. Throughout early 1861 cotton continued to flow north for export and orders continued to arrive from Southern merchants. Expanded exports and the arrival of large shipments of gold from California enabled financial New York not only to support a faltering economy but also to provide much needed loans for the beleaguered national government. In mid-January the *Times* was able to boast that the "economy was too rich and too diverse" to be seriously shaken by the loss of Southern trade.[9]

Not that there was a sustained recovery. The economy continued to be perplexed by political uncertainties. On January 12, 1861, the *Tribune* noted that the stock market had recovered much of its buoyancy, a development that it attributed to renewed hopes for a peaceful settlement of sectional differences. Three weeks later, though, it reported a panic on the exchange—which was soon replaced by renewed hopes when elections in Virginia ran against the secession of that state. Soon after, the *Herald,* which had earlier reported signs of recovery, again returned to gloomy prophecy, warning that the North would face "a calamitous commercial crisis" unless it recognized the new Confederate nation. In late February the *New York Observer* reported that New York hotels had fewer patrons than usual, especially from the South, but also that there were hopes for a recovery.[10] Up or down, however, the situation was educating New Yorkers to the confidence that even the greatest political calamity could not overturn mighty Gotham.

That confidence perhaps explains the favorable reception that New York gave to the man whose election it had opposed. In February 1861, on his way to his inaugural, Lincoln scheduled at least a short stop in every important town on his route, and he chose to spend extra time in New York in mid-February. When he arrived by special train, an express pulled by two powerful locomotives often at a mile a minute between stops, he was accompanied by representatives of the city council, who had gone to Albany to meet him. In preparation for his arrival, ships at the wharves and in the harbor displayed red, white, and blue banners, pennants, and flags, with the conspicuous exception of the East River docks that served Southern shipping; vessels there were barren of patriotic colors. The captain of one ship hung Lincoln's effigy from a masthead and refused to take it down. The presidential procession, however, was cheered as it moved down a flag-bedecked Broadway to the Astor house, where the Lincolns were to stay. The Metropolitan Police delegated 1,300 members of the force to control the crowds.

The next day, Lincoln was officially greeted by Mayor Wood, a tableau of opposites: the compactly suave advocate of secession and the 6'4" gangling defender of the Union. In his welcoming speech, Wood stressed the commercial interests of New York, noting that "her commercial greatness is endangered. She is the child of the American Union," a Union that he said could be maintained only by "peaceful and conciliatory means." In his reply Lincoln observed that, although New York had not voted for him, it had welcomed him, and then he got to his main point: "There is nothing that can ever bring me willingly to consent to the destruction of this Union, under which not only the commercial city of New York but the whole country has acquired its greatness." After seeing some of the sights and visiting with Republican leaders, Lincoln left the city on February 21, taking the ferry to Jersey City for his trip by railroad to Washington and to destiny.[11]

At the time, few knew that the New York police were concerned about a possible attempt to assassinate the president-elect. Even before his election, rumors had surfaced that a group of Southerners were planning Lincoln's death, and his arrival was accompanied by reports that "poisoned honey and suspicious boxes" had been sent to him. Police Superintendent John A. Kennedy warned that the police had picked up rumors of a possible assassination plot in the city, and the *Herald* reported that Lincoln barely escaped death while attending a performance of Verdi's opera *A Masked Ball* at the Academy of Music: "It is stated that Lincoln was to be assassinated at the same moment that the tenor falls by the hand of the baritone, but some leaky vessel informed the police, and the president left the Academy precipitously."[12] In fact, Lincoln did leave the opera after the first act, but otherwise there seems to be nothing to confirm this story. However, such rumors led the New York police to send several detectives to Washington, DC, and Baltimore to help protect him.

Whether real or not, these concerns were linked in New York to several only half-hidden hints of the violence soon to erupt in the Civil War. A few days after Mayor Wood presented his free city idea, reports circulated that there were Confederate agents in the city with intentions to stir up trouble. "The programme is," wrote an anxious Strong in his diary, "a nocturnal insurrection by an armed mob, taking possession of the armories of the several militia corps, breaking into banks, and sacking the houses of conspicuous Republicans."[13] A few days later, the *Herald* warned of a plot to seize government forts and other installations as a step toward making the metropolis an independent nation.

Such concerns were soon quieted. When Strong suggested to Police Superintendent Kennedy the idea of forming citizens into a "special police corps" to deal with the plot, Kennedy assured him that the regular police were enough. Kennedy was far more concerned about local support for the armed rebellion that was being formed in the South itself. In mid-January came rumors of an effort to organize a "Southern regiment" of New Yorkers to fight for the secessionist cause. Of more substantial concern was the shipment of arms and munitions to the South. As early as November 1860 the *Tribune* reported that four of the cotton states had been purchasing large orders of rifles and pistols; one brig alone sailed from New York with 60,000 weapons aboard.

Actual secession brought efforts to stop this trade. In early February the New York Police Department seized thirty-eight cases of muskets about to be shipped on the steamer *Monticello* to Savannah; two policemen had followed a cart bearing these "secession muskets" to the docks, where they had alerted headquarters by telegraph. In defense of this action the *Times* charged that "ships are every day leaving our wharves loaded with arms and munitions for the open and avowed purpose of waging war upon the Government of the United States."[14] The *Tribune* agreed, warning that one steamship en route to Charleston, South Carolina, was virtually a floating arsenal of weapons intended for the Confederacy.

Arms seizures evoked controversy. The *Herald* denounced them as an infringement on the "indefeasible right" of everyone to possess guns and applauded when the police were unable to prevent the sailing of the steamer *Montgomery* for the South with a cargo of arms. The governor of Georgia demanded that the arms seized from the *Monticello* be released and, when the New York police refused to comply, retaliated by twice seizing New York ships in Savannah harbor. Superintendent Kennedy, however, refused to back down and, instead, seized a shipment of ammunition destined for Charleston. Southerners looked to Mayor Wood for help, but he could only reply that he had no control over the Metropolitan Police, which had been created by the state during his first term as an entity removed from local control.

Early in 1861 trade with the South continued despite these controversies. In fact, late February brought an upsurge of shipments to Southern ports. This increase in business, however, resulted not from an easing of underlying tensions but from efforts to get goods into the Confederacy before that rebel nation imposed tariffs on "foreign" imports. After that, some Southerners boasted, European trade would be diverted from New York to Southern ports because Confederate tariffs were lower than those of the old Union. In mid-March the *Charleston Mercury* gloated that soon in New York "pauperism and general distress will be so great that uprisings and riots will take place."[15] The metropolis did experience new difficulties. Several dry goods firms were forced into bankruptcy, largely because debts owed to them by Southern buyers were not paid. Despite earlier assurances that Southerners were too honorable to dodge their obligations, New York businessmen were left holding the bag for an estimated $160 million in debts, and numerous business, including shipbuilding and horse trading, suffered from the loss of Southern patronage.

Concerns over the future led some merchants to revive the idea of making New York a free city. In early April the *Herald* reported that various prominent citizens had launched an effort to form Manhattan, Staten Island, and Long Island into a city-state. By then, however, it was evident that no grass was likely to grow in the streets of the great city. To the contrary, New Yorkers were beginning to recognize that cotton was not their king, that they were not as dependent on the South's trade as they had thought. New York's financial power remained intact, to be strengthened by large imports of California gold. In February, Wall Street had no trouble taking 30 percent of an important $8 million Federal bond issue that strengthened the national government at a critical time. In addition, compensation for the loss of the Southern trade came from the prospering grain producers in the Northwest.

Overall, the metropolis was learning that it had a diverse basis for its prosperity, much of it close to home in the Northeast. "This city is the commercial center of eight neighboring States," declared the *Tribune,* "all hives of human activity whose annual products, not including consumable food, amounts to $900,000,000." [16] The manufacturing, mining, and craft work of the industrial North was the real source of wealth and power on which the metropolis could expect to draw in the future. The work of manufacturers, mechanics, miners, merchants, and bankers would prevail over the boasts and delusions of the agrarian South.

While Gotham continued to hope for peace, by early 1861 it also had begun to help the nation prepare for war. By then attention had come to focus on a few remaining points of Federal military control in Confederate territory: forts that had yet to be seized in Florida and South Carolina. New York had a special interest in them because its port was their principal source of supply and because its Governors Island was then headquarters for the entire American army. In February headquarters ordered reinforcements to be sent from New York to Fort Pickens near Pensacola and to Fort Jefferson in the Florida Keys; both forts were to be important bases for Union military operations in the war. The men were to be sent on a chartered steamer, the *Daniel Webster.* Even earlier, an abortive attempt had been made to reinforce Fort Sumter in Charleston Harbor, using the chartered New York steamer *Star of the West.*

In March military preparations in New York took a serious turn. On March 7 the *Tribune* noted that men were being gathered on Governors Island, and the next day it reported that the government was sending unusually large quantities of arms through New York Harbor to unspecified points in the South. In mid-March the *Herald* observed that several warships were being readied along with chartered vessels for a secret expedition, allegedly to Texas but also possibly to South Carolina. Soon after, a report arrived from Charleston that the Fort Sumter garrison was to be evacuated to New York on the steamship *Columbia,* but this information was quickly followed by the news that the *Columbia* had sailed without the garrison and that the fort was strengthening its defenses.

Preparations escalated in early April when a sizable force of soldiers was loaded on the steam frigate *Powhatan* and the transport *Atlantic.* This event and the rumors surrounding it were widely reported in the New York press. The *Times* said in a front-page article on April 4 that "intense excitement" could be seen at Governors Island, Fort Hamilton, and the Brooklyn Navy Yard, all key Federal installations. What was happening was clear; why it was happening was not. Although the Lincoln administration apparently intended only a supply expedition, at least one influential newspaper saw much more: On April 8 the *Herald* used a provocative heading, "Invasion of the South—Inauguration of the Civil War," for a report on these preparations:

> Ships of war and transports, with troops, provisions, stores, ammunition and arms, large and small tools; stalls for horses, boats . . . for landing, and "all the circumstances of war" cleared this port, with sealed orders, for ports unknown. The city was like a camp, and the excitement was intense. Some of the officers of the army, knowing the bloody mission [of] the *Powhatan* and *Atlantic,* are said to have resigned rather than mingle in the fratricidal conflict.[17]

The *Herald* denounced the idea of using force to restore the Union as "the wildest chimera that ever entered the brain of man." It followed this with a warning on April 12 that New York would suffer severely from a Civil War and urged New Yorkers to hold a mass meeting for peace. On the same date the conservative *Journal of Commerce* used the expedition as the basis of a warning that any effort to force the Confederate states back into the Union would lead to a "perpetual alienation" of the South.[18] Whatever the chances for peace, however, they were virtually ended by the exaggerated reports of the character and intentions of the mission.

Although the *Herald* was no more certain of the destination of the force than any other newspaper, it surmised that at least part

The public loading of troops and supplies at the Collins Line dock, Canal Street, on April 6, 1861. The stated intention was to resupply Fort Sumter, but on April 8 the *New York Herald* reported on the expedition under the headline "Invasion of the South," perhaps influencing the decision of the Confederacy to attack the fort and thus precipitate the war. From *Frank Leslie's Scenes and Portraits of the Civil War* (New York: Mrs. Frank Leslie, 1894), 33.

of it was headed for Charleston Harbor as an invasion force. In fact, the Lincoln administration advised the Confederate government on April 6 that it was sending a peaceful mission to resupply Fort Sumter. The expedition left New York Harbor on April 9, but by the time it reached the entrance to Charleston Harbor, Fort Sumter had been bombarded into surrender by the Confederacy, possibly convinced by the news reports that it faced an armed invasion. On April 19 one of the lead ships of the expedition, the *Baltic,* returned to New York carrying the men of the Fort Sumter garrison.

The news of the April 12 Confederate attack reached New York with the shock and speed of a lightning bolt. The response of the mass of people was an unprecedented outburst of patriotism, an eruption of emotion that focused on a patriotic symbol, the American flag. The Star-Spangled Banner was displayed on nearly every public building, and carts and omnibuses were decorated with red, white, and blue bunting. The Broadway Bank raised a large silk flag with a declaration of its importance: "Traitors—rank traitors have laid violent hands upon it—trailed it in the dust—fired upon it." Children quickly picked up the fever, and the boys of Ward School Number 44 paraded through the streets carrying a mass of flags. Churches and synagogues displayed flags, leading one Southern Catholic to warn that the practice would "bring down the curse of God."[19]

Not everyone went along with the tide. The *New York Daily News,* owned and managed by the mayor's wealthy brother, Benjamin Wood, resisted the demands of a mob that it raise the flag. When an office above the newspaper unfurled a flag, some members of the *Daily News* staff went up to remove it, only to meet resistance and to be "tumbled down the stairwell." More than a few New Yorkers agreed with the *Freeman's Journal* when it said that the real traitors to the Union were not the secessionists but the Republicans: "We call them doubly traitors because, led by the abominable instincts of Puritanism, they are walking roughshod over the letter and spirit of the old Constitution."[20] Hostility to abolitionism and to New England was to survive throughout the war.

In April 1861, however, these sentiments were overshadowed by the eruption of patriotism. Reluctantly, even Mayor Wood went along with the tide, appearing at the city's first war rally, where he declared "I am with you in this contest. We know no party now."[21] He soon actively supported the organization of a military effort to "conquer the peace." Not to be outdone, Tammany Hall Democrats approved a series of resolutions supporting the Lincoln administration. Most of the merchants, who before had striven for peace, now came to support the war, if only because they had concluded that only a Union victory would enable them to collect the money owed to them by Southern debtors. In general, they expected a short war, but at least one of them, William E. Dodge, warned in May that Confederate military preparations were far stronger than generally believed.

Such warnings were ignored, for the attack on Fort Sumter ignited a firestorm of military zeal. For a brief time the manhood of the metropolis was eager to participate in war. How could this raw energy be organized into an effective military weapon? That was a question for which there was only a complicated and hardly satisfying answer.

NOTES

1. *New York Tribune* (hereafter cited as *Tribune*), January 2, 1860.

2. *New York Freeman's Journal* (hereafter cited as *Freeman's Journal*), October 6, 1860.

3. *Tribune*, October 1 and 4, 1860.

4. *New York Herald* (hereafter cited as *Herald*), October 24, 1860.

5. Samuel J. Tilden, "The Union! The Dangers! And How They Can Be Avoided," Tilden Papers, New York Public Library. *Herald*, November 4 and 6, 1860.

6. George Templeton Strong, *Diary* (4 vols.), ed. Allan Nevins and Milton H. Thomas (New York: Octagon Books, 1974), v. 3, 56–59. William Cullen Bryant to John H. Bryant, November 29, 1860, Bryant-Godwin Papers, New York Public Library.

7. Samuel A. Pleasants, *Fernando Wood of New York* (New York: Columbia University Press, 1948), 113–14. *New York Times* (hereafter cited as *Times*), December 12, 1860, and January 8, 1861.

8. *Tribune*, January 1, 16, and 18, 1861. *Times*, January 8, 1861.

9. *Times*, January 14, 16, and 19, 1861.

10. *New York Observer* (hereafter cited as *Observer*), February 26, 1861. *Herald*, February 13, 1861.

11. Abraham Lincoln, *Collected Works* (8 vols.), ed. Roy P. Basler (New Brunswick, NJ: Rutgers University Press, 1953), v. 4, 232–33. *Herald*, February 18, 19, 20, and 21, 1861.

12. *Times*, February 18 and 21, 1861. *Herald*, February 27, 1861.

13. Strong, *Diary*, v. 3, 89–90.

14. *Times*, February 25 and 26, 1861. *Tribune*, January 18, 21, 23, 25, and 28, 1861.

15. *Tribune*, March 22 and 25, 1861.

16. *Tribune,* January 4 and 8, 1861, and March 8, 1861.
17. *Times,* April 4, 1861. *Herald,* April 8 and 9, 1861.
18. *Herald,* April 12, 1861. *Journal of Commerce,* April 12, 1861.
19. *Herald,* April 17, 18, 19, and 24, 1861. Letter to James A. McMaster, June 6, 1861, McMaster Papers, Notre Dame University.
20. *Freeman's Journal,* April 20, 1861.
21. *Herald,* April 16 and 17, 1861. Jerome Mushkat, *Fernando Wood: A Political Biography* (Kent, OH: Kent State University Press, 1990), 116.

Chapter Two

Patriotism in Action, 1861

News of the fall of Fort Sumter brought popular support for the Lincoln administration and for war. Richard O'Gorman, Irishman and Democrat, said that although Lincoln had not been the city's choice for president, he should be supported "as the President chosen under the Constitution and laws." The *Herald* described the popular mood on the first Sunday after the fall of Fort Sumter: "The sound of church bells, calling the multitude to worship the Prince of Peace, was drowned by the roll of drums, calling soldiers to march to the wars. Men, women, and children who ordinarily attend places of worship, thronged the streets, to bid goodbye and God speed to their relatives and friends, who were marching to defend their country." Never was New York more a united community than in its early dedication to war. In July, observing this "glorious uprising," the British reporter William H. Russell concluded that it refuted Southern hopes, encouraged by some of the New York press, that the metropolis would side with the South. "If they had always spoken, written and acted as they do now," said Russell of New Yorkers, "the people of Charleston would not have attacked Sumter so readily."[1]

A combination of patriotism and thirst for military glory fueled a spontaneous mobilization of the city's manpower—and womanpower as well. The will to fight, however, needed training and organization. Although it had been governed more by money than by militancy, New York City was not entirely unprepared for war. In previous years many men had formed themselves into volunteer military companies, primarily for parades, target shooting, and the opportunity to wear dashing uniforms. Some of the companies had a political angle. In October 1860, for instance, the F. I. A. Boole Musketeers, named after an important Democratic politician, paraded its 300 men to target practice in Jones's Wood, after which they were reviewed by the city council in front of City Hall. Time was soon to prove that these amateur soldiers were unprepared for real war, but they did help ignite the near spontaneous creation of military units after the attack on Fort Sumter.

A slightly more reliable force was the First Division of the New York State militia, charged with the defense of the metropolis. Earlier, the First Division had provided an example for the future military when it shifted from an emphasis on company units to larger organizations, especially regiments and battalions, and so helped lay the foundations for the organization of the Union army during the war. The division was long commanded by Major General Charles W. Sanford, too long in the eyes of many of his subordinates, who viewed him with contempt. In 1860, Sanford commanded four brigades with a total of sixteen regiments; the extent of their preparedness can be gauged by the fact that their total enrollment was 5,242 men, an average of 330 men per regiment when the ideal regimental number was 1,000. In general, discipline was negligible. At the annual inspection of the division in October, many men simply declined to attend, believing it was cheaper to pay the $6 fine for nonattendance than to lose a day's pay. Such weaknesses were not unexpected, because the First Division was intended not so much to fight on the battlefield as to maintain internal order against urban mobs.

The First Division, however, did have two exceptional regiments. One was the Sixty-ninth, an all-Irish regiment headed by its popularly elected colonel, Michael Corcoran. Under its regimental banner, a green flag with an Irish harp, its men drilled with more than the usual intensity, moved by hopes of learning the military expertise needed to redeem their homeland from English rule. This regiment evoked much controversy when in October 1860 it refused to participate in a parade honoring the visiting Prince of Wales, an act that made Colonel Corcoran a hero in Irish eyes but also led to his court-martial—an action that was quashed when Fort Sumter was attacked and Irish American recruits became much in demand.

The other regiment occupied the high end of the social spectrum. The Seventh Regiment was New York's "Kid Glove Regiment." Many of its members came from New York's wealthier classes, and its commander was Marshall Lefferts, an engineer with interests in telegraph companies. The Seventh was especially intended for riot control. It was the best drilled and, with the help of its money, the best equipped regiment in the First Division. Its quarters above Tompkins Market on Third Avenue was described in 1861 as "the finest one appropriated to the use of volunteer soldiers in the world, with carpets and elegant works of art."[2] Nearby, it had a gymnasium and rooms for boxing and fencing. The Seventh Regiment was the undoubted pet of the city's upper classes, in part because its regimental band frequently performed for the public.

The Seventh Regiment responded to Lincoln's call for volunteers to suppress the insurrection with alacrity. Supported by money collected from its members and admirers, it quickly embarked on what proved to be its most important mission, the defense of Washington, DC. The nation's capital was vulnerable to Confederate attack, because neighboring Virginia joined the rebel cause the day after Lincoln's call for volunteers. The Seventh marched down Broadway on April 19, an orderly column of 945 men dressed in trim gray uniforms, cheered by thousands of spectators. The *Times* declared that "New York loves the Seventh. It has distilled all its best blood into it."[3]

Because rebels had disrupted rail traffic in Maryland, the regiment had to take a circuitous route to get to the capital, arriving four days after departing from New York. Its experiences on the way were given the full attention of the New York press. If the Seventh was the most noticed, it was also the least damaged by war, because its term of service to the nation was limited. After a month defending the capital, the Seventh Regiment returned to Gotham, where it was welcomed by the great bell of Trinity Church and the cheers of multitudes. In the future it would see two brief terms of military engagement outside the city, but throughout most of the war the regiment was at home, safe from the bloody mayhem that was to be inflicted on the Sixty-ninth Regiment.

That, however, was not the whole story of the Seventh. It might have disappointed the promise of the *Tribune* that "though the Seventh may wear kid gloves, the South will find that it has beneath them hands of iron," but many of its men went on to become officers in an officer-starved Union army. As early as June 1861 it was said to have furnished four colonels, two majors, twenty captains, and thirty-eight lieutenants to various other regiments. Before the war

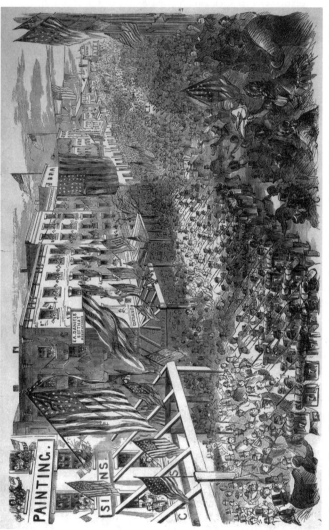

Gotham's elite Seventh Regiment marching down Cortlandt Street on April 19, 1861, on its way to defend Washington, DC, from Confederate attack. The march elicited a patriotic frenzy among New Yorkers complete with an unprecedented display of the American flag. The regiment returned a month later without fighting a single battle. From *Frank Leslie's Scenes and Portraits of the Civil War* (New York: Mrs. Frank Leslie, 1894), 19.

ended, it had earned a reputation as the "West Point of the National Guard," with over 600 of its members serving in ranks from major to major general. Moreover, the Seventh Regiment had provided a rapid defense of the nation's capital at a critical time. Washington, DC, surrounded by slaveholding territory, was vulnerable in April to capture even by a small rebel force. Although the regiment saw no action, it was, said its historian, "the first regiment in the county to pitch its tents in front of the enemy."[4]

The Seventh Regiment was soon joined by other regiments rushing to the defense of the capital. Among them were a significant number of units from the metropolis. New York City had both a ready pool of manpower and access to the means to transport troops by land or by sea. The actual extent of the manpower pool was uncertain. In 1860 there were 225,000 men over 20 years of age in New York City, or 27 percent of the population, but this likely was an undercount because there was a large floating population of males in the city, most of them of military age, who escaped the census taker.

Whatever the real extent of the male population of military age, the number who volunteered for action was inflated because numerous enlistees in regiments formed in New York City actually came from rural areas upstate. One military recruiter from the city said that in 1861 he had gone as far west as Elmira to enlist men, only to discover that many had already volunteered for Gotham units "thinking that they filled up quicker and by joining them they could get sooner to the scene of war." Another observer claimed that in 1861 "not a regiment left the city which had not men from more than a dozen counties, and some of them nearly all recruited from the country." All in all, the actual manpower contribution of New York City itself remained unclear throughout the war.[5]

In the early months of hopeful patriotism, however, there was little doubt that Gotham was vitally involved. By early May the metropolitan area had furnished nearly half of the 16,000 troops gathered to defend Washington, five regiments from New York City itself, one from Brooklyn, and another from Hudson County, New Jersey. The New York regiments included the Eighth militia (the Washington Grays), which the *Herald* described as mostly skilled workers with families to support. They were generally well equipped with new muskets and bayonets from the Springfield (Massachusetts) Arsenal. The Eighth Regiment was accompanied by the Irish Sixty-ninth, which had to leave behind many eager recruits because its regimental roster was full. The *Times* gloated that the patriotic zeal shown by the Sixty-ninth Regiment had disappointed Confederate hopes that the Irish would support the South. The near simultaneous march of the two regiments down Broadway on April 25 evoked another outpouring of popular enthusiasm.

And this was not all. Throughout the month following the attack on Fort Sumter, Gotham saw the formation of dozens of volunteer military organizations outside the framework of officially organized regiments. The city was full of former soldiers, aching for the chance to lead men into glorious combat, who published numerous advertisements in the newspapers urging men to join their units: the Garibaldi Guard (to be formed from the city's European, especially Italian, population), the Citizens Guard, Company D (to be drawn from the Nineteenth through Twenty-third Wards), the First Regiment New York Legion (to be formed from the "mechanics, laborers, and able bodied men of every nation" along with "four colored servants"), the First Regiment New York Light Infantry, the New York Invincibles, the Scott Life Guard, the Jackson Guard, the Imperial Zouaves, and a unit to consist entirely of men with the last name of Smith—myriad would-be units marched through the military notices of the *Tribune* in early May.

This military mania achieved its most dashing expression in the form of various "zouave" units, modeled on special French units that had won world notice in the 1850s. Introduced into New York by Colonel Elmer E. Ellsworth, the zouave style attracted much popular attention for its unique method of drill and for its colorful uniforms. "By this method of drill," said the *Times*, "mobility and power of adaptation is obtained to a degree not possible . . . in the old school of discipline."[6] In the rush to mobilize, not all went well. One zouave unit was fashionably dressed in the approved style of red caps, blue jackets with red trimmings, and red trousers but lacked such campaign essentials as canteens and overcoats. The most noticed of these units was the First Regiment New York Fire Zouaves, formed from the city's volunteer fire companies under the leadership of Colonel Ellsworth. In theory, the firemen's experience with emergencies and hardships promised to make them ideal soldiers, but they also brought with them a contentiousness and disregard for discipline drawn from decades of conflicts among their various companies.

The first weeks of the Fire Zouaves were not auspicious. First, they failed to receive their weapons on time, leading them to declare that they would not go "till they have something better than bare fists to fight with." Finally, they were able to leave, bearing "two magnificent banners" presented to them by a group of ladies headed by Mrs. John Jacob Astor Jr.[7] A few days later, they reached Washington, DC, where some of them made the regiment notorious for what a reporter called "their very free and easy ideas about property," taking boots from a shop without paying for them and knocking down a passing waiter to feast on the food he was carrying. "Today," wrote the reporter, "they have been ransacking the Capitol like so many rats, breaking open doors, ripping cushions, and tearing carpets, knocking down the guards, and chasing imaginary Secessionists through the streets."[8] The firemen soon revealed a better side when they helped save the Willard Hotel from being destroyed by fire, but further trouble lay ahead, this time on the battlefield.

If the first month of patriotic enthusiasm produced an inchoate and poorly equipped military mass, it also brought the beginnings of efforts to organize that enthusiasm into a capable armed force. By late April, for instance, New York State had erected a large barracks complex in City Hall Park for the use of troops being sent to war. The Park Barracks were soon accommodating thousands of men in the center of the city. The municipal government was even more active. Ten days after Fort Sumter was attacked, Mayor Wood proposed that the city appropriate $1 million to support local units organizing for war, and the City Council quickly passed an ordinance providing that sum. Some of that money went to equip regiments, but another part met the needs of the families of volunteers left without adequate support. This contribution was an important one made by the city throughout the war. Keeping the wives and children of soldiers from starving was both good politics and a way to encourage enlistment.

In this first chaotic month of war, New York's businessmen provided critical financial support to an ever needy national government. August Belmont, a Democrat and a banker with important European connections, volunteered to use his influence to promote loans from Europe, but this soon proved unnecessary because the city's banks were able to back Union loan efforts with their own money. After making a trip to Wall Street, Secretary of Treasury Salmon P. Chase announced in August that he was satisfied that the

The German Steuben Volunteer Regiment receiving the American flag along with regimental colors on May 24, 1861, in front of City Hall. The park in front of the building soon became the site of a massive barracks complex. From *Frank Leslie's Scenes and Portraits of the Civil War* (New York: Mrs. Frank Leslie, 1894), 20.

government would be able to finance the war. Early in 1862 he estimated that of the first $260 million lent to the government, $210 million had come from New York State, mostly from the city. These early loans came with one important requirement adopted by the banks: that the war be prosecuted with all the energy needed to bring about the early defeat of the rebels.

Most businessmen believed that their interests were intertwined with the effort to restore the Union, not least because they wanted some way to collect the millions in debts owed to them by Southerners. They helped awaken the New York Chamber of Commerce to play an active role in the war. On April 19 the Chamber approved a proposal by William E. Dodge to raise money to help equip departing regiments, and within 10 minutes $21,000 had been pledged. By the end of the month the Chamber had raised over $100,000 for the military.

Along with money, the Chamber also provided much of the leadership behind an effort to organize the city for war. On April 17 a large group of prominent businessmen held a war meeting at the Chamber. Among those attending were many who would head virtually every such effort over the next four years, most notably Dodge, Moses H. Grinnell, Robert B. Minturn, Moses Taylor, Hamilton Fish, Peter Cooper, C. H. Marshall, and George Opdyke. Determined to rally popular support for the government, on April 20 they convened a "Monster Meeting" in Union Square that attracted an enthusiastic crowd estimated at more than 100,000 people. Among those who spoke was Mayor Wood, who urged support for the Union, the Constitution, and the flag.

Aside from fanning patriotic fires, the rally led to the creation of a central organization to give direction to mass mobilization, the Union Defense Committee (UDC). The UDC got off to a fast start with the help of the $1 million appropriation from the city government. Over the next months it supplied, equipped, and armed ten state militia regiments and twenty-six volunteer regiments. It chartered a ship to carry a gang of workers to Annapolis for the repair of the strategic railroad from there to Washington. After having helped get the first desperately needed regiments to the capital, the committee chartered and armed an oceangoing steamer, the *Quaker City*, to guard military transports sailing from New York southward. It also spent more than $200,000 to assist 6,700 needy families of the volunteers and distributed 2,000 bags of flour provided by the flour merchants of the city, each bag bearing the motto "God Bless Our Volunteers."

The UDC helped make Gotham a major factor in the early Union war effort. In early May the *Tribune* estimated that the city had contributed $2,173,000 to the war, nearly 10 percent of all the non-Federal money raised for that purpose and far more than any other Northern city. In addition, by the summer of 1861, New York had officially provided 30,000 men to the defense of the Union. If the quantity of the contribution was impressive, however, its quality had yet to be tested. In late May the UDC boasted that it had been able to organize a fully armed and well-led force for the defense of Washington "in a shorter time and with less expenditure than any act of mobilization before," but it could not assure everyone that the money was well spent. Some critics complained that the UDC had wasted thousands of dollars on paper regiments that never went off to war. In June the *Herald* charged that some of the volunteer units raised by the UDC had fallen under the command of New York lawyers "who know as little of fighting as they do about shoemaking."[9]

If there were doubts about leaders, there was also uneasiness about the men under their command. In May reports had surfaced that some of the regiments had inflated their actual enrollments by lending men to each other for counting purposes and also by having the same men "drill over and over again." One regiment, which had less than 400 men, was drawing rations for twice that number. Whatever the numbers, the absence of systematic physical examinations led to the enlistment of numerous incapable men: At least one-tenth of all recruits, recalled one soldier, "were unfit for service the day they entered it." Moreover, the patriotic enthusiasm of the men was worn away by delays in receiving their pay, uniforms, and equipment, often their first exposure to what was to be a frequent irritant designated by a newly fashionable phrase, "red tape." When they were supplied, they sometimes discovered that both their uniforms and their equipment could best be described by another newly fashionable word, "shoddy." Add the inept leadership of inexperienced officers and the result was a serious morale problem in some of the regiments.[10]

The most serious weakness was inherited from the backgrounds of officers and men alike: Many of them were city boys who came from a commercial rather than a warrior culture. Although slave-holding society tended to breed soldiers, the metropolis bred a diverse mix of personalities oriented toward peaceful pursuits. Even the often brawling firemen inhabited an urban world a long ways from any real battlefield. On May 1 the *Times* made this point in giving "A Word to Volunteers": "The first reply to a call to arms brings patriotism and enthusiasm to the service; but not experience and not skill. Our young men eagerly take the field with some knowledge of military tactics and evolutions, but none of active duty in actual warfare, none of the startling terrors of battle, very little practice in marksmanship and in the use of the bayonet."[11] For the New York units that had rallied so eagerly to the defense of Washington, the next ten weeks brought virtually no experience with actual warfare and much with the debilitating idleness of camp life.

Finally, however, the battlefield test came on July 21 near a muddy little stream in northern Virginia called Bull Run. In the metropolis an impatient public applauded the first and what they hoped would also be the last campaign against the rebel nation. Under the head "A Short War," the *Tribune* observed that the stock market "went crazy" with anticipations of victory: "It seems to be the universal and joyful conviction that this is 'the beginning of the end.'"[12] The Battle of Bull Run, however, proved to be only the beginning of an increasingly grim and bloody war. Confronted with the smoke, the sounds, and the bloodshed of real war, New York's citizen soldiers often fought nobly, but in the end they and their compatriots retreated in disorder. The brave march to victory that had begin in April ended in a humiliating rout. Two of the regiments experienced the defeat, however, in very different ways, ways that affected their reputations and futures.

One was the Irish Sixty-ninth Regiment commanded by Colonel Corcoran. The "gallant Sixty-ninth" won public esteem for its courage, first capturing three Confederate artillery batteries before the rout set in and then helping to cover the retreat. It suffered heavy casualties, including the death of one of its officers, whose body, when found, reportedly revealed that his "throat had been cut from ear to ear, and his ears and nose were cut off," perhaps the first atrocity story in an atrocious war. The Sixty-ninth also produced two heroes: Colonel Corcoran was captured by the Confederates and held for over a year before being returned to a cheering New York. The other was Thomas Francis Meagher, whose bravery was dramatized by the *Times:* "He rode a splendid white horse. He lost his cap, and was remarkable in his bare head, urging his men forward."[13] The regiment returned to the city in August to a hero's welcome and was mustered out, having completed its three months of duty, but many of its men soon reenlisted in the famous Irish Brigade organized by Meagher. Over the next two years the city's Irish soldiers won much acclaim for themselves and for their community, but at a dreadful cost in deaths and injuries.

No such heroic future lay ahead for the First Fire Zouaves Regiment, which had once seemed so sure of demonstrating the courage of New York's volunteer firemen. The Fire Zouaves went into battle dissatisfied with the treatment they had received in Washington, poorly disciplined, and badly led. Their commander, Colonel Ellsworth, had been killed nearly a month before by a Confederate sympathizer when he had ripped down a rebel flag in Alexandria, Virginia. Although the first reports from Bull Run indicated that the Fire Zouaves had fought heroically with many casualties, later accounts painted a more complex picture of individual acts of courage amid inept and cowardly leadership. "It is a singular fact," wrote a reporter for the *Herald*, "that, although the Fire Zouaves sustained such heavy losses, not a single one of the company officers was killed or injured."[14]

To make matters worse, after the battle, many of the regiment's members refused to reassemble with their broken unit, including some of its captains, who reportedly fled back to the city. With or without the permission of their officers, hundreds of the men straggled back to New York, one of them explaining that at the battle he had been ordered to retreat and had "never gotten the word to halt"![15] Eventually, most of the regiment was reconstituted in New York, only to be treated as little better than deserters and mutineers. The last blow to the unit's reputation came in September, when it was reported that the battle flags that had been presented to it by the women of the city had been found "in a pile of trash" in Virginia. Although other firemen were to volunteer and fight, the experience of the Fire Zouaves instilled a disaffection with the war within the New York Fire Department that had serious implications for the future.

The bold and brash patriotism of April ended in defeat and disillusionment in July. Hopes of easy heroism and dramatic victories gave way to increasingly opposing attitudes in the metropolis. On the one side, the experience planted the seeds of opposition to the war, benefiting Mayor Wood and others opposed to the Lincoln administration. On the other side, the experience brought a grim determination to learn the lessons of defeat, to get beyond a mobilization based on precarious popular enthusiasm to a more disciplined and organized effort to win a long war. Much of that effort was heartened in the months following the Battle of Bull Run by successes where the metropolis could do the most good, not on the land but on the sea.

NOTES

1. *Freeman's Journal,* April 27, 1861. *Times,* May 14, 1861. *Herald,* April 21, 22, and 24, 1861. Bayrd Still, *Mirror for Gotham: New York as Seen by Contemporaries from Dutch Days to the Present* (New York: New York University Press, 1956), 180–81.

2. City of New York, *Manual of the Corporation* (1861), 221.

3. *Times,* April 20, 1861.

4. John F. Carroll, *A Brief History of New York's Famous Seventh Regiment* (New York, 1960), 8.

5. *Times,* April 19, 1861. *Tribune,* August 22 and 25, 1863.

6. *Times,* May 1, 1861.

7. *Herald,* April 30, 1861, and May 25, 1861. *Times,* April 29, 1861.

8. *Times,* May 8, 9, and 13, 1861.

9. *Tribune,* May 26, 1861. *Herald,* June 15, 1861.

10. *Times,* April 22, 1861. *Journal of Commerce,* May 2 and 11, 1861. *Herald,* April 21 and 26, 1861, and January 13, 1862.

11. *Times,* May 1, 1861.

12. *Tribune,* July 19, 1861.

13. *Times,* July 24 and 26, 1861.

14. *Herald,* July 25, 1861.

15. *Tribune,* August 9, 1861. *Times,* August 11, 16, 21, and 22, 1861.

CHAPTER THREE

WAR ON THE SEA

AFTER THE BATTLE of Bull Run, New York was to long await a dramatic victory on the land, but it soon took heart from important triumphs in which its seaport played a vital role. Most of this pride developed out of one of the greatest Union successes in the war, the blockade of the southern coast, one of the first acts of the Lincoln administration. The blockade was intended to weaken the rebel war effort by preventing trade between the industrially backward Confederacy and the outside world. The blockade also demanded some control over New York's trade, because the metropolis was a logical source of war matériel needed by the South. In April 1861, for instance, the federal marshal seized a vessel carrying a thousand barrels of gunpowder for New Orleans, and ships were assigned to both the Narrows and Throgs Neck to board every suspicious ship leaving the port. Despite such efforts, however, some New York merchants continued a clandestine trade with the Confederacy throughout most of the war, using Nassau in the Bahamas and Matamoros in Mexico as transfer points.

If it occasionally defied the blockade, however, Gotham had a far greater interest in maintaining it. Before the war began, it had to consider the possibility that the Confederacy would entice foreign trade away from it through a combination of its cotton exports and low tariffs, a threat that could be nullified with an effective blockade. Another reason was fear that the city's shipping would be devastated by privateers operating from Southern ports; of particular concern were shipments of gold from California, which came to Gotham by sea by way of Central America. A week after the attack on Fort Sumter, the New York Chamber of Commerce unanimously approved a resolution demanding that the government blockade every Confederate port to protect commerce against privateers.

The Lincoln administration was quick to respond in ways that brought significant benefits to the entire metropolis. Even to begin to cover a coast as long as that of the South demanded a rapid increase in the size of the Union navy. By the fall of 1862 the navy had grown from about 90 ships to 266, one-third of which were assigned to blockade duty along the Atlantic seaboard. These figures underestimated the actual extent of the expansion because they did not include ships temporarily leased by the government. The rapid increase in the demand for ships was a boon to New York shipowners, who profited from chartering or selling their vessels to a desperately needy government. In 1862, Commodore Cornelius Vanderbilt made a gift to the government of one of his best ships, the 5,000-ton steamer *Vanderbilt,* but most shipowners exacted the greatest compensation possible. One ship, the *Stars and Stripes,* originally built at a cost of $35,000, was leased for an indefinite period at $10,000 a month. In a sarcastic reference to the "remarkable patriotism of government contractors," the *Herald* charged that prominent war supporter Marshall O. Roberts had sold two ships for $82,000 more than their actual cost; one ship foundered and sank on its first voyage. By December 1861 the government had purchased 133 ships, 104 of them in New York.[1]

To bring some order to this business, in the summer of 1861, Secretary of Navy Gideon Welles appointed George D. Morgan, a New York merchant, as naval purchasing agent in New York. In less than two months Morgan had spent nearly $3 million to buy more than seventy vessels of various kinds—sailing ships and steamers, barks, brigs, schooners, side-wheelers, propellers, and tugs. Morgan raised some eyebrows when he purchased the steamer *Stars and Stripes* for $20,000 more than its original cost, but he explained that it was still cheaper than leasing it at $10,000 a month. During the war the government also bought twenty of the harbor's ferryboats, using them either as troop transports or as gunboats, losing four in combat. The Staten Island ferry *Clifton,* purchased for $90,000, had the distinction of serving on both sides. She participated on the Union side in the capture of New Orleans, only to be seized later by the Confederacy and used as a blockade runner; in 1864 she was recaptured by the Union and destroyed by fire.

Overall, both the government and the shipowners benefited from such transactions; the owners were able to rid themselves of ships during a period of slack trade, and the government was able to acquire a fleet, which soon proved highly useful. The conversion of these ships and their preparation for war brought more benefits, not only profits to businessmen but also employment to workers. The conversion of a fast Hudson River steamer to military use, for instance, created much work: Its entire upper deck was removed, eight cannons were installed, and its engines were lowered below decks to protect them from enemy fire. Many of the more than 100 ships purchased by the government by the end of 1861 required some kind of refitting for war.

Much of the refitting was done by the government itself at its Brooklyn Navy Yard, commanded by Rear Admiral Hiram Paulding. Before the war this facility on the East River had been overshadowed by the Norfolk, Virginia, yard, but in 1861 the Virginia installation fell into Confederate hands, increasing the workload of the other navy yards in Washington, DC, Philadelphia, Boston, and especially Brooklyn. At the height of its activities in 1864 the Brooklyn Navy Yard employed 6,000 men and generated business for hundreds of others; 200 men alone were employed in its foundry, producing, said the *Tribune*, "death-dealing shot and the bursting shell."[2]

The Brooklyn Navy Yard had several distinctive functions. It was the permanent base for the receiving ship *North Carolina*, which introduced new recruits to life in the navy. It was a supply station for ships on duty and for other bases, buying large quantities of provisions to be distributed southward by the hardworking ships *Relief* and *Supply*. It was heavily involved in the regular overhaul and repair of naval vessels. As the war expanded, the yard also became increasingly involved in the construction of new war vessels. In the beginning, however, its greatest role was to produce an instant fleet from the various civilian ships acquired by naval agent Morgan and the often broken-down vessels of the regular navy. In the early summer of 1861 men worked night and day, seven days a week, to overhaul and arm twenty-six warships and thirty transports; special gas lines were installed to provide nighttime lighting.

Even with a much strengthened fleet, the blockade was never fully successful. In October 1862, for instance, the *Times* complained that there were weekly reports of blockade runners reaching Charleston with vital supplies and then leaving with shipments of cotton. Failures were virtually guaranteed, because the attempt involved 3,500 miles of Southern coastline with numerous harbors and river openings. The blockade was successful enough, however, not only in limiting trade with the South but in sending numerous captured blockade runners to New York to be sold at auction, 141 of them in the first two years of the war alone. These sales produced more than $2 million in prize money, which was distributed among the various crews responsible for the captures, and made New York an important market for the sale of property confiscated under the blockade. At least one ship, the *Memphis,* with its cargo of cotton and turpentine, was sold for over $500,000 and then was converted into a blockader itself, eventually capturing at least one blockade runner.

Moreover, the blockade fleet assembled in 1861 played another and more dramatic role that produced perhaps the most important Union victories of the year. It did not take long for naval authorities to realize that the best way to effectively strangle the South was to seize portions of the southern coast. In late August, motivated in part by concerns about Confederate privateers, the Union took possession of Hatteras Inlet in North Carolina, and over the next months it extended its control southward as far as Roanoke Island and New Berne. One of the ships involved in the attack on Roanoke Island was a converted Staten Island ferryboat, the *Hunchback.* It was riddled with Confederate shot, but, said Walt Whitman's brother George, a member of the expedition, it "stuck it out like a good fellow."[3]

The occupation of more than half the North Carolina coast was a major victory, but it was overshadowed by a remarkable triumph along the South Carolina coast. In October 1861 rumors circulated that a great naval expedition was being prepared in the harbor to attack the South. Several regiments encamped around Gotham suddenly disappeared into transport ships. The force was well planned, including surfboats to land the troops on the shore managed by experienced surf men and 200 stage drivers from New York City to help handle the mass of wagons and horses included in the expedition. Where were they headed? The answer came in November when a large Union force attacked the coast south of Charleston and seized Port Royal and Hilton Head Island in the largest American military landing before D-Day more than a century later. Gotham supplied many of the 10,000 men as well as the ships. In an attacking force of three brigades New Yorkers formed three of the five

The landing of Union troops at Fort Walker in Port Royal, South Carolina, on November 7, 1861. This attack, the most massive military landing before D-Day in World War II, was partly organized in New York City and vicinity. Port Royal became a major Union naval base and was supplied principally from Gotham. From *Frank Leslie's Scenes and Portraits of the Civil War* (New York: Mrs. Frank Leslie, 1894), 63.

regiments in the First Brigade, commanded by General E. L. Viele, formerly head engineer in the development of Central Park.

Conquest resulted in the development of the Port Royal area into a massive military complex, with much of the work being done by a special New York Unit, the First Regiment of Engineers, headed by Colonel Edward W. Serrell. Assisted by skilled workers and laborers drawn from the city, the Engineers regiment built fortifications, a railroad, and a 940-foot pier to accommodate deep-draft vessels; most of the timbers and other building materials came from New York. In less than a year Port Royal became a major Union naval base, supplying the South Atlantic Blockading Fleet with needed coal and food and thus enabling the ships to remain on station for long periods. Because the area included numerous plantations, it soon provided the conquerors with their first direct exposure to slavery and cotton, raising hopes in New York that freed slaves could be persuaded to grow cotton for the city's benefit. Although little of this hope was realized, New York did develop a profitable trade with Port Royal throughout the remaining years of the war.

The coastal victories in the Carolinas demonstrated the importance of sea power in the war, and the next years brought a tremendous increase in the size of the Union navy, this time in the form of new ships: "Never have so many ships been built and fitted in so short a space of time," said the *Herald* in 1862.[4] A revolution in naval power was underway, one in which New York played a major role. Before the war the shipyards on both sides of the East River had achieved a wide reputation for the quality of their ships. With the help of various mechanical devices, such as steam derricks and sawmills, they could turn out good ships in short order. Although the shipyards produced few of the nation's wooden sailing craft, they were America's leading producers of ocean steamers, a logical extension of the city's dominance of foreign trade. The shipyards were interconnected with several firms specializing in the construction of big steam engines. The Allair, Fulton, Neptune, Delamater, Novelty, and Morgan works constituted a major concentration of technical talent and equipment capable of turning out masses of powerful marine engines in a short time. Significantly, the East River shipyards were experienced in building warships for foreign navies, one being the 4,600-ton steam frigate *Ocean Admiral* for the Russian navy.

Wartime need was an immense stimulus to shipbuilding in the metropolis, not only along the East River but also in Jersey City. By September 1862 over 5,000 men were employed by private shipbuilders, aside from those working at the Brooklyn Navy Yard. Including ancillary industries, shipbuilding provided jobs for nearly 20,000 men. Although the shipyards continued to construct many vessels for peaceful uses, much of their work was for the rapidly expanding navy. In June 1861, New York shipbuilders won contracts to build six of a new fleet of twenty-three wooden gunboats, each 158 feet long and powered by two engines, intended especially for the blockade. In less than two months the Engles and Westervelt shipyards on the East River each completed one of the 550-ton boats, and shipyards in Brooklyn, Williamsburg, and Greenpoint soon finished the other four. By the fall the Novelty, Morgan, and Allair works had built a dozen sets of the engines needed to power these and similar boats built elsewhere.

Wooden ships were important, but by 1862 the shipyards had become deeply involved in producing radically different vessels destined to revolutionize naval warfare: ships made of iron. Iron ships were a logical outcome of the Industrial Revolution, and the idea of building them had surfaced in America and in Europe before the war. For many years Edwin A. Stevens of Hoboken had advocated the construction of iron ships, and in 1854 he began what proved to be one of the greatest failures in naval history, the *Stevens Steam Battery*. By 1861 he had sunk more then $200,000 of his own money along with $500,000 from the national government into this ship without completing it. On paper, the *Stevens Steam Battery* was the most powerful ship of its time, a 6,000-ton, 420-foot iron screw steamer sheathed in a nearly 7-inch-thick iron skin and carrying five 15-inch guns. The outbreak of the war raised hopes that Stevens would get another half-million dollars from the government, which he said would finish the work. Although he won some support, most noticeably from the *Times*, which enthusiastically supported his cause for several years, he was denied the government money he needed, and his dream remained incomplete, to be decisively overshadowed by another naval creation that had government support.

By 1861 Stevens was not alone in advocating iron vessels. Soon after the outbreak of war, the *Times*, in urging the need for a crash program to build a blockade fleet, declared that the East River ironworks were capable of producing iron gunboats of 150 tons each at the rate of four to six each month. In June the New York Chamber of Commerce urged the government to begin the construction of "iron-plated steamships," and Congress responded by appropriating $1,500,000 for ironclad warships. Under this program, in October a contract was given to John Ericsson for an entirely new kind of iron vessel of his design, with the ship to be completed in 100 days. By the end of October a sense of urgency began to develop over reports that the Confederacy was building an ironclad, the *Merrimack.* George Templeton Strong recorded in his diary a warning that such a ship could "steam up the Narrows and lay this city under contribution," the first of a succession of fears during the next three years.[5]

Ericsson's radically new design for what became the *Monitor* was transformed into reality by the Continental Iron Works of Greenpoint, which employed a thousand men working night and day to build the iron hull. The ship was launched on the last day of January 1862. The *Monitor's* unique turret was constructed by the Novelty Works and its powerful engines were built by the Delamater Works. The *Journal of Commerce* reported that three large rolling mills in the city were used in providing the iron plating. Because ordinary cannonballs were expected to shatter against the armor of the *Merrimack,* the Novelty Iron Works forged 400 wrought-iron shots, each weighing 184 pounds, for the *Monitor's* 11-inch guns.

Early in March, after having been prepared for battle at the Brooklyn Navy Yard, the "Ericsson Battery No. 1" took one last test run on the East River—at about 8 knots—and soon went south to battle the *Merrimack* and to open a new era of naval warfare. "All the fleets of the world—thousands and thousands of ships," declared the *Times* after the battle, "must be laid up, or rebuilt, or plated."[6] Actually, even before the battle, the United States Navy Department had advertised for bids to build "iron-clad steamers of three kinds" for rivers, harbors, and coasts, and 1862 saw a frenzy of iron construction in northern shipyards, especially in New York. Some ships were simply converted wooden vessels, "mailed" with iron: The Brooklyn Navy Yard worked around the clock in the spring of 1862 to turn the frigate *Roanoke* into an ironclad. Other ships were entirely new constructions. At least one iron battery, the *Keokuk,* was built on a plan proposed as early as May 1861 by the New York merchant C. W. Whitney; it was launched in December 1862, only to be

The Union ironclad *Monitor* engaged in battle with the *Merrimack* off Newport News, March 9, 1862. This revolutionary naval vessel, designed by John Ericsson, was built at the Continental shipyards in the New York suburb of Greenpoint. From *Frank Leslie's Scenes and Portraits of the Civil War* (New York: Mrs. Frank Leslie, 1894), 189.

sunk four months later during an attack on Charleston. Numerous ships were built along the lines of the *Monitor*, with iron hulls and revolving turrets, in most cases even bigger and more powerful than the original.

In December 1862 the Continental Iron Works in Greenpoint, the nursery of the new ships, completed its fourth *Monitor*-class man-of-war, the 200-foot-long, 1,800-ton *Montauk*, which soon proved itself in an attack on a rebel fort: "Thirteen ponderous missiles struck the vessel's turret and deck," wrote a New York reporter, "doing as much damage as the pattering of so many rain drops."[7] The engines for the *Montauk* and others of its class were built by the Delamater Works, which itself was engaged in building an even larger ironclad, the 320-foot oceangoing *Dictator*. Most of the ironclads were built in the East River shipyards, but Jersey City's Secor and Company also constructed three ironclads. One of these, the *Monitor*-class *Comanche*, was designed to be disassembled so that it could be shipped by sea to San Francisco, and so, thanks to the work of Jersey City, the United States became in 1864 the first nation to put an ironclad into the Pacific Ocean.

By 1864, however, "*Monitor* fever" had begun to subside as the weakness of Ericsson's design became apparent. In the summer of 1864, Captain Charles H. Marshall, an influential shipowner and pillar of the Chamber of Commerce, published a letter criticizing the Ericsson batteries as being too slow and unseaworthy, unsuited for much beyond harbor defense. Attention turned back to more conventional hull designs ranging from light-draft ironclads for river use to oceangoing iron ships. The most ambitious of the post-*Monitor* vessels was already being constructed at the East River shipyard of William H. Webb. Billed as "the greatest engine of naval warfare that has ever yet been set afloat," this was the 378-foot, 7,000-ton *Dunderberg*, which mounted four 15-inch and fourteen 11-inch guns.[8] Construction on it, however, was delayed by a shortage of skilled labor, especially in the iron foundries, and it was not completed until the war was over.

The *Comanche* and the *Dunderberg* exemplified the concentrated skills and technological prowess of naval shipbuilding in the metropolis. Big ships meant heavy industry. The work of iron-sheathing the frigate *Roanoke*, for instance, involved plates of iron weighing as

The Dictator, an advanced *Monitor*-class ship, being constructed at the Delamater Works on the East River. At 320 feet, the ship was 50 percent longer than the original *Monitor* and was designed for ocean service, unlike the rather unseaworthy original. It took nearly 1,000 men to complete it in 1864. From *Battles and Leaders of the Civil War,* ed. Robert Underwood Johnson and Clarence Clough Buel (New York: Century, 1887).

much as 4 tons each. They were pounded out of scrap iron by huge steam hammers at the Franklin Forge on First Avenue near 25th Street. Moving the plates required a powerful crane, and bending them demanded that they first be heated in a large furnace and then shaped by a special hydraulic press. The *Roanoke's* gun turrets were built at the Novelty Works, where rivet holes were drilled through inch-thick iron and where the plates were bent into the proper curves by a press exerting 3.5 million pounds of pressure.

The cannons installed on the *Monitor*-class ships were equally awesome. The 15-inch cannons mounted on the *Montauk* and its sister ships were capable of throwing 450-pound shots over a mile. In December 1862 the *Montauk* steamed up the Hudson River to the favorite testing area for such guns, the Palisades, and fired three hollow shots, two solid ones, and two shells at the rocky cliffs. "They actually shook the entire shore for hundreds of yards," wrote an observer, "and where the solid shot fell, rocks and gravel for nearly a quarter of a mile rolled into the river." The revelation of such brute power led the *Herald* to say that no ironclad in the world could withstand the shock of "such terrible projectiles."[9]

In many ways Gotham helped to make the Union the world's greatest naval power. By January 1863 its shipyards had built fifteen of the Navy's forty-nine ironclads along with an assortment of other vessels. Not every part of every vessel was built in New York. Wooden hulls were often constructed in New England and then floated to the city to be equipped with engines by one of the local ironworks. In one unusual case the hull and engines of the torpedo boat *Stromboli* were constructed in Connecticut, its torpedo equipment in Schenectady, and its deck and pilothouse at the Secor shipyard in Jersey City. Because the boat was viewed as a revolutionary design employing "the submarine torpedo," the government had decided to conceal the project by dividing its construction work among the three areas.

Military shipbuilders provided employment for thousands of workers, who were often among the highest paid in the metropolis. To accommodate the much expanded work force at Greenpoint, builders constructed blocks of new houses, thereby creating more jobs for skilled labor, and so went the chain of buying and selling. By the end of 1861 the metropolis was beginning to realize that the war was of great benefit to its economy. Shipbuilding was a major factor in the new prosperity, but it was only a part of a much larger metropolitan economy that found numerous ways to profit from the increasingly bloody conflict.

NOTES

1. *Herald,* July 27, 1862.
2. *Tribune,* July 26, 1864.
3. George Washington Whitman, *Civil War Letters,* ed. Jerome M. Loving (Durham, NC: Duke University Press, 1975), 41–42.

4. *Herald,* August 10, 1862.

5. George Templeton Strong, *Diary* (4 vols.), ed. Allan Nevins and Milton H. Thomas (New York: Octagon Books, 1974), v. 3, 187, 191.

6. *Times,* March 16, 1862.

7. *Times,* February 11, 1863

8. *Times,* February 19, 1863.

9. *Herald,* November 16, 1862. *Times,* November 19, 1864.

Chapter Four

The Business of Supply

Two days after the attack on Fort Sumter, the *Herald*, which had been predicting economic disaster for New York, abruptly changed its tune, declaring that with war "New York City will be a central point from which the troops and ships of the federal government will be fitted out and dispatched." Soon after, it estimated that the war would cost at least $150 million, with much of the money being spent in the metropolis.[1] Like nearly everyone else, the editors of the *Herald* underestimated the magnitude of the war, but they were right in their predictions that the New York metropolitan area would prosper from meeting the ever-expanding demand of the conflict for services and materials. From the start the level of military spending was high, thanks especially to the willingness of New York bankers to take up Federal loan issues during the first months of the war. By November 1861 the *Times* estimated that, nationally, the Lincoln administration was spending almost $2 million a day: "War is a costly business—more costly now than it was before railroads, rifled cannon, and shell were invented."[2] Most of the money was spent outside the metropolis, but military expenditures in New York City alone during one week in November reached nearly $3 million.

The shower of government dollars, said the *Times*, "cannot fail to give a decided impulse to business," and so it did, as New York businessmen leaped to meet military needs. Accustomed to dealing in large volumes of goods, the merchants and manufacturers were well qualified to meet the massive needs of war, and the vast diversity of their skills promised that they could deliver almost any product. The first months of enthusiastic patriotism were also months that saw great confusion in the effort to create an effective system of military supply. Much of the trouble arose simply from the rapid mobilization of a citizens army that had no precedent, but it was

compounded by the inefficiencies of several poorly coordinated
public agencies working with dozens of volunteer regiments and
myriad private businesses. To add to the confusion, initially local
volunteer units often depended on money provided by voluntary
donations or by local government. By August, as both popular enthusiasm and resources dwindled, this local effort had largely
ended, leaving control over military spending to New York State
and Federal agencies headquartered in the city.

During the first frantic months after Lincoln's call for volunteers, the state was especially active in providing for its military, especially when it discovered that the Federal government was not yet
ready to supply needed arms and uniforms. In the rush to provide
for the defense of Washington, DC, the State Military Board spent
most of the $3 million appropriated by the legislature. Among other
things the Board contracted for 20,000 Enfield rifles (from England),
over 200 gun carriages (from the Althouse ironworks at Houston
and Greene Streets), and 50 military ambulances (from Wood and
Company at Broadway and Walker Street). The greater part of the
Board's purchases involved clothes and subsistence for the state
troops. This was done under the direction of State Assistant Quartermaster Chester A. Arthur (the future president). Arthur, a lawyer,
had gotten his post chiefly as a reward for helping to elect Republican governor Edwin E. Morgan in 1860, but he soon learned how to
cope with a pressure-driven situation.

Much of Arthur's work involved providing every volunteer with
the state-mandated articles of clothing: one jacket, one pair of
trousers, one overcoat, two flannel coats, one pair of shoes, one blan-
ket, and various other necessities. Early in May, Arthur made a contract with Brooks Brothers Clothiers to produce 12,000 sets of uniforms and by the end of the month had awarded new contracts for
15,000 sets to various competing firms, mostly from the city. This
hasty effort got off to an unfortunate start. In their rush to meet dead-
lines and to maximize profits, Brooks Brothers resorted to the use of
"shoddy" (ground-up rags) in their uniforms, making "shoddy" a
term of reproach when some of the uniforms fell apart after a few
days. "Men are constantly crowding in at the Commissarial Department and coming out a few moments later with their arms full of
uniforms," said the *Tribune* in July, "probably unconscious that the
coat and trousers . . . will hardly hold together a week."[3] Reports of

nearly naked, shivering soldiers, victims of "shoddy" contractors, were long remembered by critics of government policies.

It was not long, however, before General Arthur created an orderly system, tightening the inspection of military goods supplied by contractors and providing for the warehousing of reserve supplies. Arthur's office issued rations, uniforms, underwear, blankets, tents, and weapons to more than half of the 30,000 men mobilized by the state during the first year of the war. To protect soldiers from inclement weather, he ordered the construction of 200 wooden barracks. To save both money and time, he leased special trains to carry men and supplies.

Not everything ran smoothly. Disappointed contractors complained that the firm that had received a contract to supply 15,000 military caps at $11 a dozen was not a capmaker and had subcontracted the work to a firm that made the caps for $6 a dozen. Arthur had trouble with the Fire Zouaves before they left for Bull Run, bringing in the police when they refused an order to unpack and clean the muskets distributed among them. Furthermore, he had trouble with the regiment when they came straggling back and began raiding local restaurants for food. On the whole, however, Arthur did organize an effective procurement program, allowing him to boast on his retirement in January 1863 that his office had "completely clothed, . . . equipped, supplied with camp and garrison equipment, and transported . . . sixty-eight regiments of infantry, two battalions of cavalry, and four battalions and ten batteries of artillery."[4]

What eventually became the much larger Federal procurement program got off to a stumbling start in the early chaos of the war. The problems faced by the Federal government were complicated by the suspicion that, as Lincoln put it later, "the several departments of the government at the time contained so large a number of disloyal persons that it would have been impossible to provide safely through official agents."[5] To get around a possibly treasonable bureaucracy, the administration temporarily resorted to private agents to help supply the rapidly expanding Union military. Soon after the attack on Fort Sumter, Secretary of War Simon Cameron empowered Alexander Cummings, a friend and editor of the *World* newspaper, to spend up to $2 million on military procurement in New York. Neither Cummings nor his associate, George D. Morgan (brother of the governor), had experience with military purchasing, which might explain why they bought, among other items, 75,000 pairs of shoes at the inflated cost of $2.20 a pair. The shoes came from the firm of Benedict and Hall, which later admitted making "loans" to Cummings of $500 or more. Adjustments to an unexpectedly long and massive war were often slow, leading the *Times* to complain that the program was conducted as if the army still consisted of 15,000 men rather than the 750,000 it had become and that it was tied up "in the fatal windings of red tape."[6]

By September 1861, however, Federal authorities had begun to respond to the new situation, creating several agencies in New York to maintain a direct system of supply. The Medical Purveying Depot on Grand Street, under the direction of Dr. Richard S. Satterlee, for instance, was soon attempting to meet the rapidly growing need for medical supplies. The Commissary of Subsistence, under Major A. B. Eaton, was reported in October to have "an immense amount of business to attend to, as most of the army supplies are purchased here." Secretary of War Simon Cameron authorized the Ordnance Department in the city to contract for whatever arms were needed, vowing that he "would rather have a million guns in excess of our needs, than to have a single regiment without arms in a battle that might decide the fate of the nation"—a bit of piety that did not protect him from charges of corruption.[7]

The largest share of Federal procurement fell to the United States Quartermaster Department, especially through its New York Clothing and Equipage Depot, headed by Colonel D. D. Thompkins, one of four such depots in the nation. Thompkins and his successor, Colonel D. H. Vinton, directed a miniature bureaucratic empire scattered among several buildings on Broadway. Vinton reported in early 1863 that his staff consisted of twenty-one clerks of various ranks, fourteen inspectors of clothing and materials, five inspectors of boots and leather, one inspector of hardware, one inspector of hats, one inspector of harnesses, knapsacks, and Indiana rubber goods, one inspector of tent poles and other wooden articles, one inspector of tents, four watchmen, and one hundred twenty laborers.

The bureaucracy was large in order to handle the demands created by a growing military for mass purchasing, inspection, and shipment. In 1863, for instance, Quartermaster General M. C. Meigs ordered the New York depot to have a reserve stock sufficient to clothe 150,000 men. Early in 1864 Colonel Vinton reported the following quantities either on hand or soon to be received: 85,000 uniform coats, mostly for the infantry but also for the cavalry and engineers; 253,000 field coats for the infantry; 270,000 pairs of trousers; 530,000 shirts; 515,000 hats and caps; 142,000 pairs of boots; 135,000 ponchos; 123,000 canteens plus thousands more each of at least 30 other items. It was experience with such quantities that led Vinton to estimate that, to equip an additional 600,000 men in the army, it would cost over $48 million. He was confident that, if given the time, he could find enough suppliers to meet even that need.

Not all the contracts for these items went to New York businessmen, but the superior resources and location of the metropolis gave them the advantage in most bidding. In October 1861 the *Tribune* reported that million dollar contracts for clothing had been given to four New York firms: Payne & Carhart, Hanford & Browning, Cole & Hopkins, and Seligman & Company. Among other lines, Albert Jewett and Company, hardware dealers of lower New York, provided a steady supply of mess pans, kettles, and various implements, and Benedict Hall and Company provided 80,000 pairs of shoes in one contract. Fewer than twenty firms supplied most of the depot's needs.

The most interesting of the contractors was George Opdyke, who was elected mayor of New York in 1861 to replace Fernando Wood. Opdyke had been in the business of manufacturing and selling clothing for decades; much of his product was cheap clothing intended for Southern slaves. In August 1861 he won a contract to supply 4,884 blankets to the clothing depot; this was soon after he had given approval, in his capacity as a state clothing inspector, to the shoddy uniforms provided by Brooks Brothers. This contract proved to be only the surface of his involvements. Thurlow Weed, a political enemy, in 1864 charged that Opdyke "had made more money out of the war by secret partnerships and contracts for army clothing, than any fifty sharpers in New York."[8] At the consequent libel trial initiated by Opdyke against Weed, it was revealed not only that Weed was right but also that Opdyke, while mayor, had owned a gun factory where he produced more than 1,000 carbines for the government at $25 apiece, a price that by one estimate was $10 above the cost of manufacturing each weapon.

Opdyke was certainly not alone in shady dealings. A government

investigator charged that outright fraud was common among
contractors:

> There exists a large class of men who, for the sake of making them-
> selves rich, have taken advantage of the present confusion of af-
> fairs, and robbed the country to the extent of many millions of dol-
> lars in the most shameless way. They have put our cavalry on
> diseased horses, armed them with sheet-iron sabres, and pistols
> that would not revolve; given our infantry arms that would not
> shoot, our artillery powder that would not burn; supplied the navy
> with worthless iron boilers, with pot-metal for armor, with worm-
> eaten timbers for hulls, and fittings for ships of such quality that
> no merchant with any sense of shame would dare to palm them off
> upon private customers.[9]

Even with rigid government regulations to prevent such shod-
diness, contractors in New York and elsewhere were able to bribe
inspectors into passing their goods. At the Brooklyn Navy Yard
contractors allegedly bribed officials to sign receipts for naval hardware, paints, nails, and other materials that were never delivered—
perhaps as much as $1 million fraudulently diverted into the pock-
ets of crooked officials and corrupting suppliers.

Undoubtedly, there was corruption, but that was not the whole
story. What was more important was the ability of New Yorkers to
meet the suddenly expanded needs of the government for a vast array of goods. In September 1861, for instance, the Althouse ironworks completed 100 gun carriages for the state and expected to
produce 113 more. In October it was reported that Orison Blunt, a
prominent Republican politician, was about to open a large gun factory that would employ 500 men to manufacture rifles for the war.
Two weeks later the *Tribune* reported that New York firms had made
at least three batteries of artillery (cannons, carriages, and caissons)
for the War Department.

Other companies produced ammunition, generally in obscurity
until explosions attracted public attention. In January 1863 three explosions in local percussion cap factories killed at least two men. A
few months later a large factory that produced cartridges for the
government blew up. This "terrific" explosion, on 78th Street near
the East River, was so powerful that it damaged the Workhouse and
Lunatic Asylum on Blackwell's Island and shook houses 15 miles
away. The factory itself was obliterated, but fortunately the explo-

sion took place at night, when the 300 factory workers were at home. These disasters occurred north of 62d Street, an area where the city allowed the production and storage of explosives.

Gotham displayed its share of ingenuity in meeting the needs of war. Abram H. Hewitt, the partner and son-in-law of Peter Cooper, set out to produce a superior kind of gun iron, in response to the all-too-frequent bursting of muskets when they were fired. By early 1863, after experimenting extensively with various mixtures of iron ores from New Jersey mines, Hewitt had found a way to produce gun barrel iron equal to the best in the world. By the end of the war, the firm of Cooper & Hewitt had produced 5,000 tons of the iron, enough to make a million rifles and muskets.

In other ways New Yorkers devoted themselves to more and more powerful weapons: In August 1861 J. G. and J. Edge, "Pyrotechnists of Jersey City," announced that they had developed a variety of military rockets and incendiary shells. One shell was designed to burst into a ball of fire 4 feet in diameter on landing and then to explode into fragments, which flew "in all directions with great force."[10] One month in 1862 brought reports of two other military inventions that had implications for the future. One was the steam "tractomover" that Simon Stevens was building to haul heavy artillery over roads. The other, developed by the firm of Requa & Billinghurst Gunsmiths, was a rapid-fire "rifle battery" of twenty-five barrels that they claimed could hit targets more than a mile away. In a test they at least succeeded in firing 3 shots in 11 seconds at a target 500 yards away.

In early 1863 the Brooklyn Navy Yard witnessed two experiments described as "destined to have great influence on naval warfare."[11] One was a submarine battery designed to fire shots under water, a project so secret that no details were provided. The other experiment was an inflatable life raft invented by John Rector of New York City and made of gutta-percha cylinders. It was a logical response to the limited space of the *Monitor*-class ships, themselves compendia of wartime inventiveness, although they were among the least seaworthy of vessels. To test the life raft, officers ordered men from the frigate *San Jacinto* to crowd on it while it bobbed in the frigid waters of the East River. It did not sink.

Although these inventions often anticipated later developments, their practical significance was small compared with the few adjustments made in the metropolitan industry most affected by the war, the clothing industry. In the months before the war the more than 300 clothing manufacturers in New York City and surrounding areas confronted a depression resulting from the loss of their Southern market. With war they faced a rapidly escalating demand for their services to clothe an expanding military. To complete an estimated $2,500,000 worth of work for the government in 1861, clothing contractors resorted to large-scale organization of production involving the extensive use of cutting and sewing machines. In the four floors of their building on Broadway, for instance, Brooks Brothers used 125 cutters and 1,800 sewers to fulfill their first contract for military clothing. Among other firms, Seligman and Company followed the same path, employing 2,500 hands to turn out thousands of garments a day. In front of the clothing establishments lining a portion of Broadway, wrote one observer in November 1861, "tables groan beneath piles and stacks of uniforms."[12]

Large-scale production was also evident in another important New York industry, baking. The needs of both the army and the navy generated big contracts for bread. In March 1863, seventeen firms had contracts to produce over 2.5 million pounds of bread per month under exacting government standards. In 1862, Spear, Ball and Company responded to the demand by erecting a mammoth bakery on Cedar Street capable of turning out 400 barrels of bread a day. Another baking firm, using much "ingenious machinery," turned 200 barrels of flour a day into bread and crackers for the military. "The recent introduction of machinery into our bakeries," said the *Tribune*, "have so changed the making of hard bread that thousands of dollars have been saved for the government during the last few weeks."[13] Intensive mass production was not without its perils: In February 1863 the large bakery of Godwin & Company was run night and day to the point that it caught fire and burned to the ground, one of five bakeries destroyed by fire in a two-month period.

Not all contracts for food were filled in the metropolis, but the city's commercial skills and economic dominance and its great population made it a natural center of supply for items produced far beyond its borders. New York City was, for instance, a major supplier—and consumer—of beef. During the war the number of beef cattle sold in the New York market rose to as high as 7,000 head a week. Although most of the beef went for local consumption, the military took a notable share. In July 1861, when the New York market was overstocked, the *Tribune* urged the government to shift the feeding of soldiers from salt pork to "cheap fresh meat," and by September the newspaper was able to report large military orders. During the war Gotham provided at least 25,000 head of cattle to a meat-hungry military.

The city played an even larger role in providing the most essential of all animals to the army, horses. The horse was a necessary part of any army, not only for the cavalry but also for artillery units and supply transports. New York and its associated cities had established access to the nation's horse supply to provide the power needed to move omnibuses and street railway cars as well as carts, wagons, and various kinds of private vehicles. By one estimate there were 70,000 horses in the city in 1862. Most New Yorkers found what they needed at the great Horse Market on East 24th Street between Second and Lexington Avenues, where as many as a thousand horses of various kinds could be found at any time.

The expanding army needed many horses, and its need was increased by their high casualty rate; 11,000 horses died from disease or battlefield injuries in the first 14 months of the war alone. In the first 18 months the government bought about 150,000 horses from various sources, a great many either directly in the Horse Market or through New York horse dealers who roamed through the North looking for animals to sell. Big battles brought increased demands. In preparation for one military expedition in late 1862, "a long line of blue coats marched into the street, clanking their steel scabbards of their sabers upon the pavement," having come to New York to claim a "regiment" of horses for the expedition.[14]

Especially during the early hasty months of the war, the government often found itself with diseased and broken-down nags. Because no one had bothered to determine whether some horses had been broken for riding, charged the *Herald*, "the lives of many cavalrymen had been sacrificed."[15] Eventually, though, a system with reliable agents and effective inspectors emerged, and the army continued its extensive purchases in New York, on the average paying $150 for cavalry horses and $180 for the more powerful animals required to pull heavy artillery. By mid-1864 the war's needs had driven prices so high that the horse-drawn street railroads in the city were starting to think of converting to steam power.

After July 1862 responsibility for this horse traffic rested with the quartermaster's depot on State Street in New York, headed by General Stewart Van Vliet. In April 1864, Van Vliet reported that he had spent over $1 million in recent months for horses and that much more spending was to follow. Aside from horses the New York depot also was responsible for providing a large share of horseshoes. Army agents in the city also took on the responsibility of providing the fuel for the vast hordes of hayburners that they had helped assemble. The feed for masses of horses in the field could not be found on the spot and had to be shipped in from supply centers such as New York. Contracts for hay were often large; one in 1861 was for 5,000 tons, which could only be met by contractors in the city. Profits were equally large; the 1861 contract was awarded to a New York supplier for $110,000. At times, the demands of the army in the South grew desperate: "It is very important that the loading of forage should go on *night* and day," wrote Van Vliet in 1864 regarding a government hay ship being loaded in Brooklyn. "I consider it of very great importance that every exertion should be made to push forward forage." [16] And so Gotham became a major supplier of the most rural of all products for war.

Hay, horses, cattle, rifles, cannons, bread, and uniforms—the metropolis drew on its vast reservoir of skills and facilities to meet virtually every military need. It was also to make a notable if flawed contribution to the preparation and deployment of the most essential ingredient of all for war, the soldier himself.

NOTES

1. *Herald,* April 14, 1861.
2. *Times,* November 18, 1861.
3. *Tribune,* July 15, 1861.
4. Quoted in George F. Howe, *Chester A. Arthur* (New York: Dodd, Mead, 1934), 24.
5. Abraham Lincoln, *Collected Works* (8 vols.), ed. Roy P. Basler (New Brunswick, NJ: Rutgers University Press, 1953), v. 5, 242.
6. *Times,* August 27, 1862.
7. *Times,* October 5, 1861. Simon Cameron to Horace Greeley, January 15, 1862, Horace Greeley Papers, New York Public Library.
8. *Times,* December 15, 1864.

9. *Times,* June 19, 1864.

10. *New York Daily News* (hereafter cited as *Daily News*), August 31, 1861.

11. *Times,* February 21, 1863.

12. *Times,* November 10, 1861.

13. *Tribune,* June 16, 1862.

14. *Tribune,* December 17, 1862.

15. *Herald,* June 21, 1863.

16. Stewart Van Vliet to Captain S. L. Brown, January 28, 1864, Quartermaster Depot, New York, "Letters Sent, January–November 1864," National Archives, Regional Center, New York City.

CHAPTER FIVE

MOBILIZATION FOR REAL

BY THE AUTUMN of 1861 the enthusiastic patriotism that had animated New York's first chaotic mobilization in the spring had withered under the shock of the Battle of Bull Run. For some New Yorkers, doubts about the prospect of victory would soon ripen into a movement for peace under the leadership of such men as Fernando and Benjamin Wood. For many more, however, the dominant response was a grim resolve to shape a disciplined army that was able to conduct a long campaign. "Nothing but war—strenuous, energetic and resolute, which shall develop our strength and give us victory will meet the necessities," proclaimed the *Times* in August 1862.[1] Out of such thinking would eventually come a total mobilization to fight a total war.

A year later the *Times* advocated the creation of a million-man army, estimating that 100,000 men could be found in Gotham alone. The problem was to recruit, discipline, and organize such a mass into effective fighting units. This task was made both easier and more difficult by the first mass rally of men after the attack on Fort Sumter. In mid-1861 thousands of men had encountered their first military experience, but many of them gained that experience in poorly organized regiments whose terms of engagement expired after three months of service. The Battle of Bull Run had cooled much of their earlier ardor. Could the men be persuaded to reenlist for periods long enough to make them effective soldiers? One of the bright spots was the heroic Sixty-ninth Regiment, whose men reenlisted en masse to become the nucleus for the famous Irish Brigade under the charismatic Thomas Francis Meagher. The Irish Brigade, three regiments of which were from New York City, compiled a noble but bloodied battle record during the war.

The effort to create a disciplined army was handicapped by the continued presence of volunteerism. Although the regular army stepped up its recruiting efforts, it faced strong competition from a host of would-be colonels eager to form their own regiments. By August, fifty-three different military units, bearing names such as the Anderson Zouaves and the Yates Rifles, had set up recruiting stations. Most of their stations were in lower New York, but they could also be found in Brooklyn, Jersey City, Hoboken, and elsewhere in the metropolis. This military entrepreneurism did serve to stimulate enlistments—at least on paper. George Opdyke estimated that in 1861, New York City alone contributed over 60,000 volunteers to the military, but, if so, they were often hard to find. When the Federal government ordered what it thought were twenty-six New York City regiments readied for service, it found that only eight were fully formed. At least a dozen "regiments" were little more than fictions; one, the Fremont Rifles, could muster only fifteen men.

New York State soon tried to correct this situation. It required that all self-proclaimed officers be examined for their fitness to serve in the field and that all file reports on the real number of men in their units. To make fighting units out of military mushrooms, Governor Edwin Morgan ordered the consolidation of undersized regiments into ones at least close to the standard of 1,000 men. As regulation replaced enthusiasm, the authorities also gave more attention to monetary rewards as a way to entice enlistment. Pay was increased—to $13 a month minimum—and by the summer of 1862, $90 worth of Federal and state bonuses, or bounties, were being offered to enlistees.[2]

From the beginning much attention was paid to a major impediment to volunteering: the concern of men for their families. The loss of the breadwinner to the military was especially important in cities such as New York, where families depended on wages for the barest necessities. In December 1861 some soldiers' wives rioted on the Lower East Side over the lack of assistance, and one woman warned that she would get her husband to desert from his unit rather than see her family starve. The pay given even at the lowest ranks was often better than what the unskilled could earn in civilian employment, but at the beginning of the war there were delays in actually paying the men, who, when they did receive pay, often wasted it on alcohol and gambling.

As early as July 1861 the *Tribune* urged the city to increase soldiers' base pay to $15 a month, with two-thirds being sent home through local disbursing agents. Soon, Mayor Wood proposed that the city comptroller be authorized to handle the distribution of allotments among the families of soldiers so that the money would find its way to New York rather than "into the pockets of camp-followers and Army speculators."[3] The real heroes in this matter were three New Yorkers, William E. Dodge, Theodore Roosevelt, and Theodore Bronson, who first lobbied Congress to pass the Allotment Act of 1861 and then spread out through some eighty New York regiments in the field to persuade their paymasters to regularize allotments. By July 1862 the new system had funneled more than $400,000 in military pay to families in the city.

Some early supporters of the allotment system had hoped that it would head off a program of direct public relief for the poor families of volunteers, but a relief program had already gained momentum, becoming one of the foundations of military participation throughout most of the war. At the start, relief funds were often provided by volunteer efforts organized to support particular units. In August 1861, for instance, the Irish community held a great festival at Jones's Wood to raise money for the families of soldiers in the Sixty-ninth Regiment who had been killed, wounded, or captured at Bull Run. The first general source of aid was the Union Defense Committee (UDC), which used public and private money to provide assistance for the families of volunteers. By late August the UDC had paid out $230,000 to 2,500 families, developing a system of distribution that included a blacklist of 500 people who were to be denied assistance. Soon after, however, the UDC suspended its operations, and private efforts proved inadequate, leaving it up to local government to fill the gap.

Over the next years the city spent millions of dollars to provide for its military poor, paying out approximately $4 a week per family to as many as 15,000 families. There were serious doubts over the legal power of cities to make such appropriations, but soldiers' relief was a necessary program. When New York was slow to distribute relief money in December 1861, the Irish wife of a volunteer soldier spoke for many when she said, "You have got me man into the soldiers, and now you have got to kape us from starving."[4] When one appropriation ran out in May 1862, a mob of angry, desperate women gathered outside City Hall; they were met by the police to keep them "from interrupting the mayor in his business." By this time the mayor was Opdyke, elected as a Republican at the end of 1861. When he was presented with a new relief appropriation for his signature in 1862, he considered vetoing it because it would win votes for the heavily Democratic city council. In the end, though, Opdyke signed the bill, moved perhaps by memories of those women who had gathered at the gates of City Hall. Overall, the city borrowed more than $4 million to provide relief for the families of its soldiers.

By the summer of 1862 it was proving easier to sustain poor families than to find volunteers to fight in the war. On paper, Gotham's manpower contributions were impressive. In August 1861 the *Tribune* estimated that New York City had contributed nearly 50,000 men to the war, proportionately more than any other place. By 1862, however, a powerful undertow against serving in the military had developed. The decrease in enlistment resulted in part from the growing prosperity of the wartime metropolis, which reduced the unemployment that had moved men to join the army the year before. In addition, the decline resulted from the prolonged and bloody character of the war itself. As lists of the killed and wounded grew and as the handicapped victims of war appeared, most of the old enthusiasm was extinguished. Reversing its optimistic assessment of two years before, the *Tribune* in August 1863 charged that New York County and the other counties associated with it had contributed only eight volunteers for every thirteen contributed by the largely Republican counties upstate. In 1865 the state census found that only 11,974 New Yorkers were serving in the military along with 11,326 from Kings, Queens, Richmond, and Westchester Counties. The total of these five metropolitan counties, with one-third of the state's population, was only 18 percent of the 123,000 enlistments for the state at large.

How could the North meet the rapacious needs of a bloody war? The question became a pressing one in mid-1862. In May, when it seemed that Washington, DC, again would be the target of a Confederate attack, the Seventh Regiment and half a dozen other National Guard regiments of the city were called into active service for three months to defend the capital. In July the national government issued a call for another 300,000 men from the states. In the middle of July supporters of the war effort held a giant rally in Union Square to revive the enthusiasm of the previous year. "Bands of music, playing national tunes, gave the scene the air of a gala day," wrote one observer, "while the thunder of cannon seemed echoes of the [Fourth of July] celebration that had just passed."[5] Mayor Opdyke urged his listeners to give their all in the great struggle against treason, and Judge Charles P. Daly told his listeners that the South had outdistanced the North in mobilizing its population: "If we fail in this crisis, then, the South are, as they claim to be, our masters. They will triumph in the consciousness that they have chafed into submission these artisans, tradesmen, and laborers of the North."[6]

To help in the recruitment process, the head of the Metropolitan Police instructed his men to actively engage in finding recruits, offering prizes of $50, $40, and $30 for the three policemen who enlisted the largest number, and the *Times* urged employers to replace their male clerks with women: "There are thousands of putty-faced, dainty-fingered gentry in our large cities who should forget the mysteries of silks and muslins for a while, to grow familiar with knapsacks and bayonets."[7] In support of this idea, Frederick Law Olmsted proposed that New Yorkers petition shop owners to send their young clerks off to war and to hire women in their place.

The main concern was to find some way to prevent the collapse of the volunteer system, or to put it another way, to avoid a compulsory draft. By mid-1862 states and cities faced manpower quotas, which were to be met by outright conscription if necessary. Regardless of the efforts to excite a patriotic response, the enlistment campaign came increasingly to depend on money, something that the now prospering metropolitan economy could well afford. The chief result was a rush to provide bounties to enlistees. The Grocer's Association raised a War Fund of $21,000 to encourage enlistment, and a group of "patriotic Germans" raised $3,000 to provide bonuses for men joining German military units. Irish enlistments received some special attention: A war committee created by Democrats raised money to reward those who joined the newly formed Corcoran Legion. In addition, a skirt manufacturer offered $10 to each of the first fifty men to volunteer for the Irish Brigade.

Much more of the bonus money came from the city government. In Gotham the response was complicated by two distinct considerations regarding enlistment. Private bonus money had done much to encourage the formation of new regiments, but this system increasingly competed with another need: replenishing the depleted numbers in existing war-experienced regiments. To prevent them from collapsing, the city council urged Governor Morgan to give special priority to enlistments in the old regiments in the distribution of state bounties, but Governor Morgan decided not to do this. The council then enacted its own $50 bonus for those who enlisted in the old regiments, arguing that this would ensure that recruits would be prepared for war by the veteran members of their units. The amount soon proved to be too small to be effective, but for a time, it did enable the city to attain its quota, in part because it continued to attract recruits from other parts of New York State.

Although the new mobilization was wrapped in patriotic colors, the importance of money was all too obvious. "The substitution of cupidity for patriotism as the activating motive for enlistments," said the *Times* military reporter, "is at best less bitter a humiliating confession of our weakness than a draft." Others thought that it was not even marginally better than a draft because it had some of the weaknesses of the volunteer system. In part, the problem was that numerous weak regiments that likely would never see battle continued to be produced. These regiments contributed to the abundance of uniformed officers seen parading with showy uniforms and swords on Broadway, many of them, said the *Herald* in November 1862, "with a company not yet organized."[8] Even more, it seemed that the old system was nearing the bottom of the military barrel, finding not only increased reluctance to serve but also some disposition among the recruits to take their bounties and run, thus beginning the practice of bounty jumping that was to trouble the city throughout the rest of the war.

Anticipation of the draft highlighted the nature of the problem. Some men enlisted in the fire department in the belief that its men would be exempt; others formed draft insurance companies to provide money for substitutes should they be drafted. Some men reportedly took to wearing military uniforms in the belief that the risk of being arrested for desertion was less threatening than the draft. Gray-haired men abandoned the use of hair dye, and other men declared foreign citizenship. "We have cowards and traitors in our community," grumbled the *Tribune*, in warning that false exemption papers could be found in the city.[9] Whatever the recourse, there was widespread reluctance to serve, partly screened by the success of the metropolis in filling its quotas from outside its limits. Other problems also had to be solved to produce a powerful military force. One problem was simply to ensure that recruits were physically qualified to be soldiers; this was not easy because the early system of medical examination often missed basic defects. After observing troops sent to Virginia to fight in 1862, a *Times* correspondent estimated that as many as half the enlistees were physically incapable of being soldiers, weakening the army and filling military hospitals. Another essential problem was simply to prepare a disciplined force for battle—a need glaringly revealed by the Bull Run disaster.

After making a careful study of that fiasco, Olmsted concluded that the men were victims of a "terrible mental disease, under which all manliness was lost to the utmost cowardice, unreasonableness and fiendish inhumanity." [10] To immunize against that disease in the future, Olmsted advocated improved physical care of the soldiers, more professional leadership, and especially better training for all. Memories of the rambunctious, runaway Fire Zouaves underscored the need for discipline. How could the character of enlistees be improved? Given the shady backgrounds of many of the recruits, that was no simple question.

Some answers to the problem of discipline came from outside the military. One involved the city's large public school system. In January 1862, the Republican governor proposed that every student in the state above age 12 be given some military training, an idea that was soon taken up by the city school board. Supporters claimed, with good reason, that it had been the neglect of military training that had caused Union failures on the battlefield. In March 1862 a committee of the school board reported a plan to prepare one male teacher in each school to provide training, arguing that it would soon "produce an army of intelligent men well versed in drill and discipline." The plan was never implemented, but individual schools did organize military drills on their own, leading one parent to complain that the idea had become "the mania of the times" that was pushed to extreme by overcompetitive schools. [11]

Another attempt to resolve the discipline problem came from New York's well-organized world of evangelical religion, which offered to instill character and commitment in the men. In May 1861,

Henry Ward Beecher, at his Plymouth Church in Brooklyn, declared that it was the duty of a Christian people to see that the men in military camps received adequate moral and physical care, especially to work against the drunkenness and disease that threatened to disable the army. New York was well prepared for this work. The dynamic center of the evangelical world was the Bible House on Third Avenue and 9th Street, a national center for religious publications and missionary activity. During the first year of the war, the New York Bible Society distributed 85,000 Bibles along with various religious tracts to the army and navy, and its female branch distributed many more Bibles and tracts, all in the hope of maintaining the religious faith of soldiers under the adverse conditions of camp life.

Some of the most important work was done by the New York Young Men's Christian Association (YMCA), which from the beginning carried out a well-organized effort through its Army Committee not only to provide religious materials but also to send missionaries to the various military training camps around the city. In November 1861 the YMCA hosted a national meeting at the Bible House to "consider the United States Army as a field of Christian Usefulness." Out of such efforts came the New York Christian Alliance, which in early 1863 became the New York Christian Commission, the most important branch of the United States Christian Commission.

The New York commission was headed by the seemingly ubiquitous William E. Dodge, a man so pious that he resigned as a director of the Erie Railroad when it insisted on running its trains on Sunday. The commission took as its special province the military ships, forts, camps, and hospitals not only of the metropolis but also of the entire Atlantic coast to the Gulf of Mexico. Its aim was "to render our soldiers and sailors more and more intelligent, resolute, conscientious, and devout," to make them capable of fighting a truly Christian war.[12] Over the years the commission tried to carry on what Beecher termed a campaign of enlightened Christian solicitude by bringing both food for the soul and a concern for the physical health of the men in camp, not only injunctions against drunkenness and other debilitating practices but also clothing, blankets, and books. Supported by an army of 5,000 generally unpaid delegates, the United States Christian Commission distributed more than $3 million in supplies along with its tracts and Bibles.

The New York YMCA also played another and even more direct role in the effort to give the military a Christian character by appealing to the churches of the city to help organize "a regiment of earnest, loyal God-fearing men." The call evoked what the *Times* called a grand uprising of the churches, a widespread effort in New York and Brooklyn to organize an Ironside Regiment. Prominent local leaders, for example, Horace Greeley and William Curtis Noyes, supported the movement, which was widely advertised, as was a $10 extra bounty offered to the first 100 recruits. Finally, in January 1863 the Ironside Regiment left the city for the war, "between eight and nine hundred of the best men who have ever been enlisted in this state."[13] The regiment (the 176th New York) served until the end of the war, with 240 casualties.

A select regiment was one way to ensure the right character, but it did little to discipline the mass of recruits, especially those who needed discipline the most. The larger picture was an uneven one drawn by numerous officers and drill sergeants in the scattered camps of the volunteer units. By late August 1861 the eruption of volunteer units had produced about thirty camps around the city. Staten Island, because of its presumed isolation, was a favorite location. One of the most political units, the brigade of the notorious Daniel E. Sickles, occupied what became Camp Scott; the men lived in part in a large circus tent acquired from P. T. Barnum. Another unit, the Scott Rifles, camped at Silver Lake; they were described rather hopefully as "daily undergoing the routine of camp life, and a uniform system of drill and discipline" under officers who were "gentlemen of education." In Westchester County a camp at Scarsdale was depicted as being a "camp of instruction," set in romantic woodsy surroundings, for 1,300 men intended to be the "nucleus of twenty-seven regiments."[14] The only flaw in this little paradise seems to have been the First Fire Zouaves Regiment, who were moved to Scarsdale in September to get them away from the city. The Fire Zouaves soon got into a fight with men from some of the other units. It was reported that recruits were being armed to protect themselves from these renegade zouaves.

By the fall of 1861 romance was beginning to give way to the reality of serious warfare. Early in August, Brigadier General Charles Yates, commander of the state military depot in the city, instructed each company, as soon as it was encamped, to "divide into squads, and assign competent persons to drill the men in the school of the soldiers."[15] Responding to the inexperience of the men in relating themselves to units larger than their own regiments, a critical failure at the command level at Bull Run, Yates also instructed regimental commanders to prepare their men to fight as a part of divisions, anticipating the later importance of these larger units. This training plus the new state requirement that all officers pass a military examination offered some hope that New York's soldiers would be able to participate effectively as integrated units in the large armies required by the war.

Progress, however, was slow. A major problem was simply isolating the men in camp from the influence of civilian society. When it was proposed that training camps for as many as 75,000 men be concentrated on Staten Island, the *Times* objected that even that island was not far enough away to exclude "the numberless hangers-on and the vile temptations which infest the quarters of troops in or near a great metropolis." Access to liquor was a factor in several riots among new regiments. In August and September 1862 the Empire Brigade twice rioted at its camp in east New York because soldiers, enraged by a failure to get their bounty payments and fueled by liquor from nearby shops, attacked their officers until suppressed by the Seventh Regiment, the riot specialists. In September the Metropolitan Police were called in to end a riot of the Fifty-third Regiment at their barracks in downtown New York, where they had made the night "hideous with bacchanal songs, dances and gymnastics performances."[16]

Such incidents lent support to the conviction that the volunteer system had to be replaced by a national army raised by national conscription and subjected to uniform discipline. In 1863 the *Times*, an advocate of conscription, expressed hopes for "one army with one hand, and one law and one soul."[17] That was a dream never to be completely realized, but the trend was distinctly in favor of a national system to raise and discipline troops. By September 1864 the state had turned over its training facilities on Staten Island to the national government.

Even at the height of state recruitment the regular national army played a major role in the local military scene. It was recruiting its own men to be trained at its own camps, especially on Rikers, Davids, and Hart Islands and at Forts Schuyler, Richmond, and Hamilton. As early as August 1861 the army began to build barracks on the islands with the intention of isolating the men from the physical and moral dangers of the city. Early in 1864 a Federal officer estimated that the local Union camps could accommodate about 2,700 men plus another 2,000 in a complex being built at Willets Point. Such facilities along with the navy receiving ship *North Carolina* made New York a significant staging area for enlistees.

From the beginning the city played a major role in the movement of troops not only from the metropolis but also from New England. This involved providing temporary shelter for the men on the move, at first in the City Park Barrack, a hastily built 400-foot-long building in front of City Hall. In May 1861 a reporter described the barrack as being "a little world of busy activity only inferior to the outside routine of city life." Capable of accommodating as many as 2,000 men at a time, the barrack was often a hodgepodge of various units from the city, from upstate, and from New England on their way to training camps or, increasingly, on the way to war. During its first year, the City Park Barrack provided shelter and food for 70,000 men, but the setup became increasingly unsatisfactory, and in 1863 the barrack was replaced with a new complex capable of housing 5,000 troops at the Battery, close to shipping points. All told, a city official estimated that during the summer of 1864 "some 40,000 soldiers were encamped in our city and in our public parks."[18]

Most of the responsibility for moving and feeding this military mass fell on the shoulders of Stewart Van Vliet, head of the Union Quartermaster Depot in New York. In late 1864, Van Vliet estimated that he had arranged for the transportation of 218,513 soldiers to and from New York over the previous three years. More than one-third of these men were sent by sea on what one of his aides called "our large fleet of ships," mostly chartered vessels costing the government as much as $900,000 a month. In general, government shipments by water were handled cheaply and with some efficiency, but ships were too slow for the rapid deployment of troops, and so Van Vliet sent tens of thousands of men by railroad—130,706 in the year ending in June 1864 alone.

Rail transport was certainly much faster than sea transport, but for most people it was not fast enough, thanks to the stubborn inefficiency of the rail system between New York and Washington, DC. Part of the problem was that troops from New York City had to

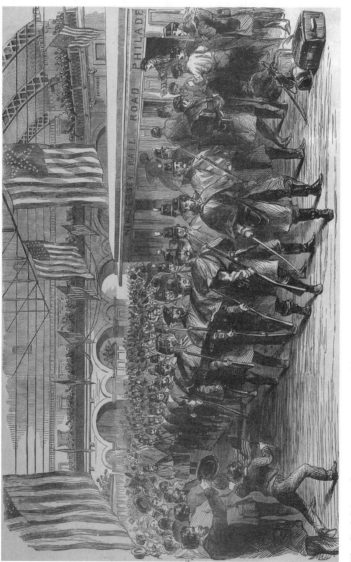

The Sixth Massachusetts regiment assembled at Jersey City en route to war. Gotham was an important way station for regiments from both New England and upstate New York, many of which were ferried across the Hudson River to the Jersey City railroad depot. From *Frank Leslie's Scenes and Portraits of the Civil War* (New York: Mrs. Frank Leslie, 1894).

be ferried to rail terminals in New Jersey, but that was relatively minor compared with the nuisances posed by the railroads themselves. The reality was that no good direct route existed between the two cities. In 1861 the New York Chamber of Commerce complained that it took at least twelve hours to get to Washington, a distance of 240 miles, when it might have been done in half that time on a normal railroad. Much of the delay resulted from two breaks in the route, at Philadelphia and at Baltimore, where in each place freight and passengers had to be trucked from one rail terminal to another.

As the volume of military traffic grew, this system raised a growing volume of complaints. Washington, DC, said the *Herald*, had been transformed by secession "into a frontier city, beleaguered and threatened," and it needed an efficient link with New York, the "great emporium of wealth and power." [19] New Yorkers campaigned to get Congress to support an entirely new double-tracked "airline" road that would eliminate dependence on the existing railroads, and a bill to that effect was introduced in 1863. The bill was defeated, but it did help produce some improvement in the situation, especially in closing the gaps between the stations in Philadelphia and in Baltimore. By December 1863 the railroads boasted that improvements had reduced travel time to less than nine hours. The inaugural run, however, took ten hours, and complaints continued until the end of the war. Although the rail link between the Union's political and financial capitals was imperfect, it was still good enough to help carry masses of men to war. In early 1864 the *Daily News* estimated that the city was sending reinforcements to the army at the rate of 3,000 men a week.

The important traffic in supplies and reinforcements was southbound, from the centers of production and population to the battlefronts. Inevitably, though, there was also a growing northbound traffic, much of it a grim reminder of the costs of war in the form of sick and wounded soldiers. What sprang up to deal with this aspect of the militarized world became one of the noblest chapters of an all too often bloody and brutal story.

NOTES

1. *Times*, August 2, 1861.
2. *Times*, October 2, 1862.

3. *New York Weekly Caucasian* (hereafter cited as *Weekly Caucasian*), December 21, 1864.

4. *Tribune,* July 16, 1862.

5. *Times,* July 16, 1862. *Herald,* July 16, 1862.

6. *Times,* July 14, 1862.

7. Times, August 27, 1862.

8. *Times,* August 24, 1862. *Herald,* November 20, 1862.

9. *Tribune,* August 12, 1862.

10. Frederick Law Olmsted, *Defending the Union,* ed. Jane Turner Censer, vol. 4 of *The Papers of Frederick Law Olmsted,* ed. Charles Capen McLaughlin and Charles E. Beveridge (Baltimore: Johns Hopkins University Press, 1977–), 167–68.

11. New York City Board of Education, *Journal* (1862), 67–68, 141–42. *Times,* March 1, 1862.

12. *Tribune,* January 29, 1863. *Observer,* January 29, 1863.

13. *Times,* August 23, 1862. *Tribune,* January 15, 1863.

14. *Times,* August 2, 1861, and September 10, 1861.

15. *Times,* August 4, 1861.

16. *Times,* May 21, 1861, and September 13, 1862.

17. *Times,* March 21, 1863.

18. *Herald,* May 4, 1861. *Tribune,* January 25, 1864.

19. *Herald,* April 30, 1862.

CHAPTER SIX

TENDER MERCIES

IN DECEMBER 1862, Walt Whitman, already on his way to becoming
New York's greatest poet, went south to Virginia to find his brother
George, a soldier in Brooklyn's Fifty-first Regiment. Walt finally located George, and he found something else that would redirect his
life. It was the sight of "a heap of feet, arms, legs, etc. under a tree"
outside a military hospital, bloody evidence of the realities of war.
For the next two years, Whitman would dedicate his life to nursing
sick and wounded soldiers in the military hospitals around Washington, DC. There he found a vast array of hospitals, which even as
early as the first months of 1862 had as many as 50,000 patients. It
was, as he wrote in March, a life-stirring experience: "These thousands and tens and twenties of thousands of young men, badly
wounded, all sorts of wounds, operated on, pallid with diarrhea,
languishing, dying with fever, pneumonia, etc., open a new world to
me, giving closer insights, new things, exploring deeper mines than
any yet, showing our humanity."[1]

Whitman was one of many New Yorkers whose sense of humanity arose to minister to the human remnants of war. Gotham itself had long moderated its materialism with a well-organized commitment to meeting the needs of the unfortunate. Especially among
those businessmen with roots in New England, making money was
often deeply connected with a felt obligation to do good. Doing
good among the masses of the metropolis required more than individual dedication. Dealing with the needs of the many required rational organization, a mating of mind with heart, giving benevolent
New Yorkers the experience needed to deal with the large-scale
challenges of a massive war.

New York was well prepared, within the limitation of its times,
to deal with the medical emergencies of the conflict. Its more than

1,000 physicians and their uncounted assistants formed a major pool of medical talent, and its medical colleges, such as the one at New York University, and its hospitals, such as Bellevue, made it a center of medical skill. Its medical dispensaries, which ministered to the health needs of 125,000 poor people in 1860, provided a valuable experience for dealing with the mass medical problems of war. In May 1861 the Eastern Dispensary, having vaccinated thousands of the city's children against smallpox, performed the same service for the military units of the state. At the same time, New York General Hospital opened an unused wing for the treatment of sick and disabled volunteer soldiers, who were placed under the care of some of the hospital's leading physicians.

To be fully effective, these agencies required organized citizen support, much of it from the women of the city. For decades benevolent-minded ladies had helped to fight poverty, drunkenness, vice, and disease, learning much about the means and the virtues of organization. Although benevolence was still basically a man's world, it did provide women with some executive experience. In 1860 women were the principal officers of the Ladies Home Missionary Society, the American Female Guardian Society, the Society for the Education of Young Deaf Mutes, the House and School of Industry, the New York Woman's Hospital, the House of Mercy, and ten other societies.

The outbreak of war and the excitement of mobilization stirred the hearts of women as well as of men. In April one woman watched the departing Seventh Regiment parade off to war down Broadway: "It was an effort to keep from shouting. I was never so excited. Oh! I did wish I was a man, but I am a *woman, and can do woman's work.*" For her and for many others the nature of woman's work was already defined. Benevolence stereotyped women as the gentler sex, more nurturing than men, and so it seemed logical that women would be the ones to patch up the results of men's brutal havoc. A week after the attack on Fort Sumter, the *Times* published a letter from "Nightingale," in which she volunteered "to nurse the sick, bind up the wounds and render all those little attentions and mercies which a woman loves to do." By then, women's groups had started to spring up all over the city, setting an example that was publicized nationally. "They are our most zealous patriots," wrote William Cullen Bryant of women's efforts. "They make shirts for the wounded in the hospitals; they send on boxes of jellies and other little comforts for the sick." Time soon proved that women were willing to do much more.[2] The womanly energy was there, but how could it be coordinated for maximum effect? The answer came at the end of April 1861, when 2,000 women gathered for a meeting at Cooper Institute to form the Woman's Central Relief Association (WCRA), the purpose of which was to "enlighten, methodize, and make efficient the practical benevolence of the women of the country." The new association soon evolved into a powerful national effort for the care of the sick and wounded. The WCRA Board of Managers was headed by men, including the famous surgeon Dr. Valentine Mott as president—no surprise in an age when leadership was presumed to be the field of men—but most of the WCRA's executive committee members were women, including the energetic Louisa Lee Schuyler, a great-granddaughter of Alexander Hamilton. No figurehead, Schuyler provided her growing cadres of volunteers with the leadership needed to sustain an efficient national organization that, in her words, contributed to "the patriotic education of the people."[3]

The WCRA raised money for medical care and organized shipments of much needed medical supplies and food items to frontline hospitals. It also recruited and trained women to be army nurses, not an easy task at a time when nursing was dominated by men. "The nurses that have been trained under this association," the executive committee declared in August 1861, "notwithstanding the many difficulties arising from the novelty of their position, have made themselves so useful to surgeons and patients, that they are now recognized as indispensable."[4] By establishing branches in other cities, the WCRA was able to organize large-scale support for its mission. In New York City alone, during the fall of 1861, "bands of fair workers" shipped an average of 3,500 articles a week—bandages, clothing, blankets, dried fruit and vegetables, coffee, sugar, and even wine and whiskey. Although persistently short of the money needed to sustain its ambitions, the WCRA continued to be an important source of medical necessities throughout the war.

The WCRA was the helpmate and to some degree the progenitor of an even more important organization, the male-dominated United States Sanitary Commission (USSC), probably the most important agency produced by the war. Two members of the WCRA's board, Henry Whitney Bellows and Frederick Law Olmsted, helped to organize the USSC, in part because they discovered that army medical officers were unwilling to work with women. Although officially formed in June 1861, the USSC had been proposed more than a month before at a meeting of the WCRA. Despite its name, the USSC was a private voluntary organization, another product of the benevolent world, whose policy it was to direct government agencies toward better health care without seeming to preempt their responsibilities. The USSC, like the New York Christian Commission, grew out of Gotham's benevolent world and strove to improve discipline in the military, but its means and ends were fundamentally different. Whereas the Christian Commission used Bibles and missionaries to work on the moral character of soldiers, the USSC used health science and bureaucratic organization to strengthen their bodies and their physical capacity to win the war.

From the beginning the USSC benefited from the determined leadership of three New Yorkers: Henry Whitney Bellows, George Templeton Strong, and Frederick Law Olmsted. Bellows, the president, lent the influence of his highly respected Unitarian ministry, and Strong, the treasurer, gave the USSC connections with upper-class New York. The USSC's essential character, however, bore the special stamp of its general secretary, Olmsted, the great landscape architect. Fresh from a losing battle with local politicians over the development of Central Park, Olmsted was determined to create a tightly disciplined national organization that could work effectively with the national government and lessen the influence of localism on military decisions. He was suspicious of women's sentimentalism. "Even the care of the sick & wounded of war," he wrote in August 1861, "is not a feminine business. It must have masculine discipline." He recognized, however, the worth of women's practical service, noting that some WCRA members working on hospital transports "beat the doctors all to pieces. I shall have sunk the ships in despair before then if it hadn't been for their kindness and good nature."[5]

The USSC strove, with much success, to channel the wealth and energies of the benevolent world into one unified campaign guided by science and reason. "How shall this rising tide of popular sympathy," said Bellows in reference to the early months of the war, "be rendered least hurtful to the army system, and most useful to the soldiers themselves." He hoped that men of wealth in New York would recognize, as Strong put it, that it would "save the nation thousands of men and millions of dollars within the next three months" if wasteful duplication of effort was avoided and if the death rate in the military was reduced.[6] Although the wealthy proved to be somewhat less than farsighted, the USSC did become a successful fund-raising organization. It collected nearly $4 million for its New York branch alone, without counting more millions of dollars in the form of donated supplies. It received some of its earliest financial support from New York life insurance companies, which had a stake in reducing deaths in the expanding military. Later, much of the money came from California, through San Francisco, with which New York had strong economic ties.

Under Olmsted's dedicated leadership, the USSC pushed for an efficient national army to replace the ramshackle system of volunteerism of the early months. For Olmsted the Battle of Bull Run demonstrated the necessity of setting a model of discipline for inexperienced men. A careful investigation of the disaster also persuaded him of the importance of uniting discipline with care for the physical well-being of the men, because he found that forced marches and lack of food exhausted many regiments even before the battle began. The most essential goals of the USSC were to strengthen the army by improving health conditions and medical treatment in the camps and to radically reform the Army Medical Bureau.

Progress, as in most areas, was slow and uneven. Ten months after its formation, the USSC found that 10 percent of the 600,000-man army were sick each day and that of these, seventy-five would die, the equivalent of twenty-seven regiments lost during a year. Over the years, however, the USSC expanded two successful efforts. One was essentially preventive: to improve sanitary conditions and the soldiers' diet to reduce the extent of disease in military camps. The other effort was restorative: to improve the care of the sick and wounded in military hospitals. Working through a cadre of 200 paid inspectors and many more volunteers, the USSC could claim at the end of 1862 that it had helped produce the healthiest army in history with a death rate of 5.5 percent, about one-third the mortality rate of European armies during the Crimean War.

In support of the USSC and otherwise, the women of the metropolis continued their mission of tender mercies throughout the war. They were, said a grateful Bellows, "more united than the men, because their moral feelings and political interests were not so affected by selfishness and business, or party considerations."[7] Numerous women's church groups collected or made clothing for soldiers, much of which was distributed through the channels of the USSC. In the fall of 1862 about eighty churches in Brooklyn and elsewhere on Long Island formed their own Woman's Relief Association, eventually raising a half-million dollars in money and supplies.

Women also contributed their time and skills to provide for the masses of soldiers passing through the city. Almost from the beginning the City Park Barrack had accommodated troops headed south for war. Soon, however, came the less romantic flow of men northward: growing numbers of soldiers on furlough or released from hospitals and Confederate prisons—tired and sick and crippled men. For such soldiers, deprived of the protection of their units, the city was often a heartless place where they were cheated by cabmen or threatened by thieves and thugs who looked on them not as heroes but as potential prey.

Earlier in 1862 a group of New England residents of Gotham formed the New England Soldier's Relief Society, which opened a home to care for men on their way to New England or to upstate New York. Located on Broadway a few blocks from the Hudson River, it was capable of accommodating as many as 300 men. In its first eight months, the home helped at least 8,000 weary veterans, with the generous assistance of its women's auxiliary. New York State soon followed this lead, appropriating $200,000 to establish the Soldiers' Depot on Howard and Mercer Streets, where the returning warriors received food, lodging, clothing, and hospital care as well as the facilities of a library and game room. From the moment they arrived in the city, the men got special care, especially from the depot's Ladies Visiting Committee, which did much of the work, including the laundry and the cooking. In addition, "the system of Station Agents and Train Couriers," wrote the head of the depot, "protects the returning soldiers from robbery, imposition, and vice."[8]

As the war ground on, benevolent-minded Gothamites considered new ways to help the growing numbers of wounded and sick men. In March 1863 a group of New Yorkers began to lobby the government for the creation of a United States Ambulance Corps, with an ambulance company of 250 men attached to every division to reduce the time it took to get the wounded to hospitals. Early in 1864 several women organized the Association of Army Nurses to recruit and train women for work in military hospitals. As part of the training, the association arranged a series of free lectures by well-known surgeons on such subjects as gunshot wounds. Almost simultaneously, another group, the Ladies' National Relief Association, was organized to hire nurses and to arrange for their placement in camps and hospitals.

Like the USSC, these efforts were designed to deal with the sick and wounded at a distance, but by 1862 the metropolis had to confront more directly the casualties of war. In April the New York Surgical Aid Association fitted a part of the City Park Barrack as a "medical infirmary" and recruited local physicians to provide medical treatment. In the same month the New England Soldier's Relief Association announced that it had gotten "the best surgical skill of the city, free of cost, for the relief of wounded soldiers," after having decided that this service would not be limited to the soldiers of New England.[9] These efforts, however, proved to be only a modest prelude to what was soon to come.

By the late spring of 1862 the primary military hospitals around Washington were being crowded with casualties from General George McClellan's bungled campaign to capture Richmond. In April the secretary of war asked Governor Morgan to provide hospitals in New York City for some of the expected overflow, and on May 19, Ellen Collins of the WCRA warned that the sick and wounded had filled Washington hospitals to capacity. In response, the USSC acquired hospital ships and otherwise arranged for the transportation of the sick and wounded to Northern hospitals. Olmsted took the lead in preparing the *Daniel Webster*, a small coastal steamer, and the *Ocean Queen*, a 2,800-ton transatlantic steamer, to convey disabled soldiers, many of them the victims of pestilent fevers common to tidewater Virginia. By May he could boast that the new system was working well, "every man knowing his place," and soon New York was made aware of it. On May 10 the *Ocean Queen* reached the port with 800 sick and wounded soldiers from eastern Virginia, and a few days later the *Daniel Webster*, staffed by ten doctors (six from New York), brought hundreds more. Olmsted was particularly pleased with the women nurses on the ships, who he thought had saved the men from "the narrow incompetence of the surgeons."[10]

By May 23, 2,000 men had arrived and many more were to follow, brought chiefly by USSC steamers but also by railroad, some in specially equipped hospital cars; on one day alone, 408 men arrived by rail. "During the past three months a sufficient number of sick and wounded men have passed through this city to form an immense army," declared the *Tribune* in July, "and they continue to come here by hundreds and thousands from every point of the compass." Arrivals depended not only on actual casualties but on anticipated but not yet fought battles. In June 1863, Walt Whitman, working as a nurse in Washington, noted that inmates from the great hospital complex there were being sent northward to open space for expected new casualties because "it is pretty certain that there is to be some severe fighting, maybe a great battle." Indeed, the great battle of Gettysburg was soon to come.[11]

The first waves of sick and wounded soldiers overwhelmed existing hospital space in New York, forcing some men to be sent elsewhere. Gotham responded by creating a military hospital complex of its own. The City Park Barrack was converted to hospital use, and in July, Mary Todd Lincoln, the First Lady, visited the place to observe how casualties were being treated. Some space was found in existing civilian hospitals. New York's famed Bellevue Hospital took care of 700 military patients, and hospitals in Brooklyn, Newark, and Jersey City had equivalent numbers; even the tiny Jewish Hospital in New York took thirty-three men. All told, an estimated 30,000 patients were distributed throughout the metropolis.

New facilities were created to meet the emergency. As early as May 1862 a group of benevolent women, headed by Mrs. George Opdyke, opened the Ladies' Home for Sick and Wounded Soldiers at 51st Street and Lexington Avenue, at first using some of the rooms of the Northeastern Dispensary and then expanding until they could accommodate as many as 450 patients. Eventually, the home was able to mobilize a force of six surgeons, five "medical cadets" from the army, and a staff of male and female nurses. The home also had the direct support of numerous volunteers, not only women but also male "watchers" from the YMCA who sat with patients during the night.

Another distinctly different hospital was opened in the old St. Vincent's Convent building in Central Park. By 1863 this military hospital, renamed St. Joseph's, had expanded to thirteen wards for

250 patients, much of the expansion being done under the supervision of Stewart Van Vliet, the Federal quartermaster in New York. At one time the patients there included seventeen men, each of whom had lost a leg, a need that was met by "a celebrated manufacturer of artificial limbs." St. Joseph's Military Hospital was unique in that it included in its staff more than a dozen "nursing nuns" drawn from the Roman Catholic Sisters of Charity and received strong support from the local Catholic community. This was part of a broader effort by Gotham's Catholics. In June 1862 the *Freeman's Journal* reported that "the Sisters of Charity and the Sisters of Mercy, with members of other active Religious congregations of Catholic women, are hurrying to scores of Hospitals" in Virginia.[12]

Such benevolent enterprises were important both in providing care for patients and in serving as a link between the people of the metropolis and the war. However, by 1863 they were overshadowed by much larger national military hospitals. In the beginning the national government used facilities such as the Ladies' Home and St. Joseph's, but it soon was forced by the magnitude of the problem to build several new hospital complexes at a distance from the city. The goal was to return men to their regiments as quickly as possible, thereby reversing what was becoming a threatening depletion of manpower. The new hospitals were built on a massive scale in response to the extent of the casualties. The hospital complex near Fort Schuyler at Throgs Neck, for instance, centered on a main building accommodating more than 2,500 patients in 50 wards; it had 116 male and 16 female nurses and a kitchen capable of feeding 3,000 men. This hospital, along with others on Davids, Rikers, Bedloe's, and Governors Islands, were in place to receive not only many Union casualties from Gettysburg but also 2,000 sick and wounded Confederate soldiers captured in that battle. In 1864 in response to the growing casualties from Grant's Wilderness campaign, a new hospital for 2,000 or more patients was planned at Willets Point, to be called, probably without irony, Grant's Hospital.

The government hospitals, with their high degree of professional organization, had less room for benevolent women volunteers. Even they, however, could not entirely dispense with the cooking, the comforts, and the special tenderness that women could provide. At Fort Schuyler, "lady visitors" prepared cakes, pies, and other desserts on a regular basis, and various groups, such as the

Rose Hill Ladies Soldiers' Relief Association, helped soften conditions in the wards with their visits. Some volunteers played a more vital role. In late 1862, Emily Elizabeth Parsons, a volunteer nurse, worked as much as sixteen hours a day caring for sixty soldiers at the Fort Schuyler Hospital until her failing health forced her to leave.

In April 1864 women made another significant contribution to the war effort through the great Metropolitan Sanitary Fair. The idea of a fair had first been tried in Chicago in 1863. Inspired by the Chicago success, the *Tribune* proposed that New York City take the lead in promoting a national movement for a fair in "every City, County, and considerable township" to raise money for the USSC.[13] Brooklyn beat its bigger neighbor to the punch, holding a fair in March 1864 that raised about $100,000 for the USSC, but this was to be overshadowed by Gotham's metropolitan fair a month later.

Planning for the great fair began in January with the appointment of a Ladies' Association, headed by Mrs. Hamilton Fish, and a twenty-five-woman executive committee composed of the wives of prominent merchants and millionaires. The overall aim was to hold what the *Herald* called the Greatest Charitable Enterprise of Modern Times. To make the fair truly representative of the awesome variety of talents and people constituting the metropolis, the planners organized exhibitions of everything from machinery and hoopskirts to art and agriculture. Two large buildings in the area of Union Square were made ready, and a long list of businessmen, manufacturers, artisans, artists, and agriculturists were persuaded to stock them with a great diversity of goods. In line with their ambitions to provide substantial assistance to sick and wounded soldiers, the organizers of the event declared that it was no mere fair in the conventional sense but a magnificent gathering of "all the material resources of the great city of New York, and of the regions directly tributary to it."[14]

On April 4, 1864, the fair began with a military parade accompanied by "the musical thunder of half a hundred bands" and the opening of the two buildings to thousands of eager people willing to pay the $1 admission fee. Patrons saw a profusion of displays of dresses, lingerie, hats, furs, porcelain, pianos, machines, and, among many others, the "mammoth ox" valued at $1,000. They bought items on display in the Floral Temple (fruits and flowers), the Art Gallery (donated works of local artists), and the Jewelry and Silver

Department. And they ate either at the restaurant (30,000 oysters consumed before 2 P.M. on the first day) or at the Knickerbocker Kitchen, where teams of women volunteers served coffee, doughnuts, and other light fare amid 200-year-old furniture.

During its three-week run the fair was a broad mirror of the metropolis at its workaday best, and it succeeded where it counted most. The *Tribune* noted that the fair reflected the diversity of the city in that the Germans, Irish, Swiss, and Welsh were conspicuously involved. Many of the city's schoolchildren were induced to participate. With the help of crowds from the cities and suburbs around New York, the fair produced more than $1 million to support the work of the USSC. It was a culmination of the work of women and others on their mission of tender mercies, a reflection of the organizing genius bred in the world of reform. Even the skeptical Strong was impressed by the fair's large-scale manifestation of patriotism and benevolence: "Thank God for the hearts and heads He has given the women of this country."[15]

Unfortunately, as Strong was all too aware, neither the benevolence nor the relative efficiency of the fair was matched by other strivings in the metropolis. One of the least benevolent and least efficient of all was also the most common of all, that tangled world of muddled ideals and half-revealed self-interest called city politics. Here, women played virtually no role, because politics was still the domain of the almighty male.

NOTES

1. Walt Whitman, *Correspondence, 1842–1867,* ed. Edwin H. Miller (New York: New York University Press, 1961), 59, 75, 79, 81.

2. William Cullen Bryant, *Letters,* ed. William Cullen Bryant II and Thomas G. Voss (New York: Fordham University Press, 1975–80), v. 4, 225–26. *Tribune,* May 4, 1861. *Times,* April 22, 1861.

3. Frederick Law Olmsted, *Defending the Union,* ed. Jane Turner Censer, vol. 4 of *The Papers of Frederick Law Olmsted,* ed. Charles Capen McLaughlin and Charles E. Beveridge (Baltimore: Johns Hopkins University Press, 1977–), 626n. *Tribune,* May 6, 1861.

4. *Tribune,* August 7, 1861.

5. Olmsted, *Papers,* v. 4, 148, 351.

6. H. W. Bellows, "The Sanitary Commission," *North American Review,* 98:179 (1864). George Templeton Strong, *Diary* (4 vols.), ed. Allen Nevins (New York: Octagon Books, 1974), v. 3, 162.

7. Henry W. Bellows, in the introduction to L. P. Brockett, *Woman's Work in the Civil War* (Philadelphia, 1867).

8. S. V. Talcott to S. J. Tilden, July 1863, Samuel J. Tilden Papers, New York Public Library.

9. *Times*, April 1 and 12, 1862.

10. Olmsted, *Papers*, v. 4, 351.

11. *Tribune*, July 9, 1862. Whitman, *Correspondence*, 110.

12. *Freeman's Journal*, June 28, 1862.

13. *Tribune*, November 10, 1863.

14. *Herald*, April 4, 1864. *New York Observer*, January 14, 1864.

15. Strong, *Diary*, v. 3, 429.

CHAPTER SEVEN

A DEMOCRATIC WORLD

THE GREAT NEEDS of a great war worked against the system of volunteers and volunteerism that had sprung into chaotic action in April 1861. Under stress that system gave way to increasingly bureaucratic organizations that could deliver the masses of men and matériel required by a large-scale conflict. In military procurement and recruitment and even in benevolence, system and command replaced enthusiasm and good intentions. This was not an unfamiliar trend in the metropolis. To reduce corruption and inefficiency resulting from political meddling, bureaucratic systems had been created in the 1850s to manage New York's great Croton Water System, its Central Park, and especially its police. The Metropolitan Police, under the command of its superintendent, John A. Kennedy, had performed well in maintaining order during the uncertainties of secession days. The benevolent world had also developed its own form of bureaucratic organization to deal with the masses of needy people. In these organizations scientific rationalism prevailed over shortsighted political concerns.

If wartime New York was already familiar with bureaucracy, however, it was also steeped in the contrary traditions of a more democratic world, one more sensitive to the will of the people and also one strikingly more prone to corruption and inefficiency. Its politics was chaotically organized around two distinct poles. On one side was a persistent minority, first the Whigs and then the Republican Party, each of which functioned as the channel for the wishes and discontents of those who claimed to be the taxpaying, law-abiding business elements of the city. There was a significant ethnocultural leaning in that Republicans tended to be upper- and middle-class Protestants from New England and British backgrounds, morally oriented toward the Protestant ethic, benevolence, and reform. As a

83

minority of great influence, they often found support for their interests outside the Gotham, in the state and national governments. It
was from the Republican ranks that most of the war leaders in the
city came.

In a world of great and shifting diversity, however, no distinc-
tions were wholly clear-cut, and this was especially true of the other
political pole, the Democratic Party. Although the Democrats depended heavily on Irish Catholic votes, their largely native-born
Protestant leadership found diverse support. Before the war Democrats had included numerous men of wealth and respectability, such
as businessmen Moses Taylor and Peter Cooper, and even after the
war had led such men into an alliance with Republicans, the Democratic Party retained some affluent supporters, for instance, the international banker August Belmont. More broadly, the Democratic
Party drew loyal support from a vast array of individuals, poor and
not so poor, who shared a common devotion to individual and local
freedom against what they saw as the meddlesome intrusion of
"abolitionists and moral reformers and of outside governments, national and especially state."

The Democratic Party, or as it often called itself, the Democracy,
generally could count on substantial electoral majorities not only in
Gotham but also in Brooklyn and Jersey City and elsewhere in the
counties along the Hudson River. In theory, it had, with the support
of the people, effective control over local government. The reality,
however, was very different. In the first place, local control of some
significant public functions had been lost to state control, most notably the police. Moreover, the party suffered from deep internal divisions. Whereas the Republicans sought bureaucratic efficiency,
Democrats stressed personal loyalty, forming networks that bound
them to a variety of big and little political chiefs, leaders often divided among themselves by self-interest, personal animosities, and
half-forgotten differences over matters of principle.

In New York City the most conspicuous political chief was Fernando Wood, who could command the loyalty of his followers no
matter what he did. Although many of his supporters were Irish, he
also appealed to others who admired his bold ideas and defiance of
state interference in city affairs. Confronting his personal Mozart
Hall organization, however, was the even more powerful Tammany
Hall. Tammany was a coalition of political chieftains who collec-

tively commanded the loyalties of the largest number of voters in the city. When it was united, Tammany easily dominated local politics, but a reliable unity was hard to achieve among a group of ambitious politicians. To ensure its dominance, the coalition needed a dominant boss. By 1863 such a boss appeared in the semigargantuan form of William M. Tweed, who was elected Grand Sachem of the Tammany Society without a dissenting vote. Less than five years later Tweed became boss of the entire city.

Secession and the war had a wrenching impact on the Democratic Party. Before the war, New York Democrats could expect to have influence through the national party, but that depended heavily on support from the South, most of which vanished with secession. The Civil War created even more problems for the Democratic Party. As in most wars, the conflict strengthened the party in power: It was the Republican Party that could command the upsurge of patriotic feeling evoked by the attack on Fort Sumter, when numerous Democratic businessmen joined with their Republican counterparts to support the war.

Overall, in 1861 the Democratic Party faced a perplexing future. In the first months after the attack on Fort Sumter, it had been swept up in the patriotic furor. Even Wood announced his support for the war to restore the Union, and both Mozart and Tammany Halls fielded regiments, each of which served with some distinction throughout the conflict. After the defeat at Bull Run, however, numerous Democrats began to have second thoughts about supporting the Republican war government. The most open critic was Wood's brother, Benjamin, who used his *Daily News* ("the cheapest and best New York newspaper") to blast the Lincoln administration as the real cause of the war and to argue for the recognition of the Confederacy if reunion could not be achieved peaceably. The aggressiveness of this stand led the Federal post office to ban the *Daily News* from the mails in September 1861, forcing the paper to suspend publication for most of the following year.

The war had become a long-term issue in New York politics by September, but then and later it was shadowed by local issues, especially those relating to corruption within the city government. As in the past, concern focused on the Democrat-controlled city council, which by the time of the war had fallen under the control of what reformers called a ring of skilled manipulators. How could the ring be ousted? Reformers tried to rally support by identifying the Democratic Party not only with corruption but also with support for the treasonable South. In September a group of prominent citizens of both major parties, including Taylor, Cooper, Horace Greeley, and Moses H. Grinnell, organized a new "grand Union political movement" to combine support for the war with governmental reform. Before the end of September mass meetings launched the new Union Party in both New York and Brooklyn. Within a month, however, the movement found itself confronted by three other supposed parties bearing the "Union" name—a favorite trick of politicians to undermine promising reform movements by confusing the field. The result was to compound one major failing of New York's politics: a profusion of parties that worked against any kind of meaningful political order.

This confusion flowed toward two important local elections. One election, in November, involved the selection of a new county sheriff, an important functionary with both power and patronage. The fragmented system produced five candidates, but only two really counted. Tammany Hall, which had proclaimed its support for the war, nominated Tweed, and rival Mozart Hall backed James Lynch. Lynch was the more controversial candidate. He had commanded a volunteer unit that immediately before the Battle of Bull Run had refused an order to advance and had, in the words of General Irvin McDowell, "moved to the rear to the sound of the enemy's cannon." Lynch's supporters claimed that he had a right not to fight because the term of enlistment for his unit had expired; opponents warned that his election would be viewed by the Confederacy as a sign that Gotham was not supporting the war. In what the *Tribune* called a languid contest, however, Lynch was an easy winner.[1]

Unionists had better luck with the mayoralty election in December. Despite the controversies surrounding him, Wood decided to stand for reelection as mayor. In September he announced his position: "One God, one Government, and one destiny boldly flung to the breeze." He resorted to a principal theme of his past campaigns, that the people needed him to preserve their individual freedoms, warning in particular that temperance-minded Republicans would interfere with the right of New Yorkers to drink as they chose: "I am for the largest liberty consistent with the safety of the community. I am opposed to dictating to any man whether he shall drink water, lager beer, or rum." He also declared himself the champion of the ordinary white man against "abolition fanaticism." Without hesitation, Wood played the race card, warning that Republicans were determined to use the war to free "the black slave to compete with the white labor of the North." To forestall such a threat, he promised that, if reelected, he would use the great power and prestige of the metropolis to end the war through compromise with the South.[2]

Wood had reason to hope for reelection, because he faced a divided opposition. Tammany Hall nominated C. Godfrey Gunther, a businessman and former member of the fire department who was expected to appeal to German and Irish voters, and the Republican Unionists ran George Opdyke, a businessman and strong supporter of the Lincoln administration. Opdyke had the backing of most of the merchant community, including various government contractors. His supporters denied that he was an abolitionist and ran a campaign designed to play on patriotic feelings, making it a contest primarily between their Unionist candidate and Wood, whom they identified with both political corruption and the Confederacy. The *Times* went so far as to call Wood "an open sympathizer with the traitors of the South."[3]

The election results in December indicated that New York was a deeply divided city. Wood came in third, but he lost to Opdyke by only 1,200 votes out of the 74,300 cast for the three candidates; Opdyke polled little more than one-third of the votes, winning only because of the divisions in the ranks of the Democrats. Apparently, many New Yorkers swallowed the *Herald's* charge that Opdyke supported the "diabolical schemes" of the abolitionists, meaning not only emancipation but the use of blacks in the military, producing "crops of nigger lieutenants, captains, majors, generals and major-generals."[4] As slim as it was, however, Opdyke's victory was important because it denied the Confederacy the hope of winning the support of the Union's largest city.

When he took office, Opdyke determined to be a strong mayor in the interest of both reform and the Union. He was a man of the world, a successful clothier, merchant, banker, and government contractor who also had some prior experience in politics. His reform objectives generally left him at odds with the Democrat-controlled city council, especially on matters of spending. The system of local representation tended to favor the election of legislators who had

little interest in thrifty, orderly government. To control their tendency to spend the taxpayer's money, the mayor made abundant use
of his veto power during his two years in office—fifty-nine vetoes of
acts by the Board of Aldermen and forty vetoes of acts by the
slightly more cooperative Board of Councilmen.

Whatever its limitations, the council made a substantial contribution to the war effort, especially through its Joint Committee on
National Affairs. The committee represented the city in dealings
with state and national government, but most of its work involved
the local needs of New Yorkers. It received requests from some of
the volunteer regiments for money to replace uniforms and equipment—a matter that, after calculating the costs for all the city's regiments ($3 million), it recommended be redirected to the state legis-
lature. Its grimmest task was to arrange for the free burial of local
soldiers at the Cyprus Hills Cemetery, where it had been able to negotiate the purchase of 200 lots for $80 each. When the committee
was also offered free burial plots in the Calvary Cemetery, it hesitated over a requirement that burials there be limited to Roman
Catholics, only to recommend that the offer be accepted in the hope
that this would encourage other cemeteries to provide free ground,
"each endeavoring to outbid the others" in honoring those who had
died in defense of the Union.[5]

The city council and Mayor Opdyke came closest to agreement
on two important matters where its spending propensities and his
Unionism converged. One was relief for the poor families of volunteers, a concern from the beginning to the end of the war because
relief had a direct effect not only on enlistees but also on families.
During Opdyke's administration the city appropriated more than
$1 million to provide 15,000 poor families with up to $6 a month in
relief money. The program was both a necessity of war and good
politics. The second matter of agreement involved encouraging enlistment in the army. A series of Union defeats in Virginia in the summer of 1862 precipitated new calls for men. The question was how
to promote volunteering in order to avoid a compulsory draft. In
July, Opdyke urged the council to appropriate money for a $25 city
bounty to each enlistee. At the time the Joint Committee on National
Affairs rejected the idea of bounties as inviting fraud, but when enlistments declined, it changed its mind and appropriated $500,000
for $50 bonuses.

In such ways the city council seemed to confirm hopes that a bipartisan coalition of Republicans and Democrats would place New York's power and population solidly behind the war effort. At the end of his first year in office, Opdyke could boast that the city had given critical support for a conflict that "now embraces a larger force and covers a larger area than any other war in modern times." Moreover, this had been done without any "apparent inconvenience or diminution in the capital employed in trade and commerce." The city was able to have prosperity as well as its guns and also was able to experience "an universal exemption from disease and crime."[6] It had all of this without any notable increase in taxes or public debt, despite the money spent for relief and bounties—happy days in the midst of tumultuous, bloody times.

By the summer of 1862, however, the political dynamics behind policy had already begun to change the situation for the worse. Military defeats in Virginia introduced a note of war weariness among many New Yorkers, and feelings of disillusionment were often intensified into outright hostility to the war by the prospect of conscription. The prospect of a radical change in the objectives of the war was leading to spreading anger and dread. A war in defense of the Union was a war that only a small minority of peace advocates rejected, but by the late summer of 1862 it was increasingly likely that the conflict would become a war to abolish slavery, a victory for the hated abolitionists.

The idea of emancipation was already familiar to some New Yorkers. It had been introduced as early as September 1861 from a surprising source, the conservative *Knickerbocker Magazine,* whose editor, Charles Godfrey Leland, predicted that the war would soon be making abolitionists in the North by the millions. In January 1862, Cooper, an industrialist and philanthropist but no abolitionist, publicly urged President Lincoln to warn the rebels that, if they persisted in the war, the nation would confiscate "the slaves and other property of all persons found in arms against the laws and Government of the country."[7] William Cullen Bryant, editor of the influential *Evening Post,* was soon advocating the emancipation of slaves held by rebels, and by the summer the logic of war was driving a reluctant Lincoln administration down the same road. In September 1862, Lincoln issued his "Preliminary Emancipation Proclamation." This did no more than warn that he would be forced into emancipation unless the Confederacy stopped the war, but Lincoln's critics attacked the proclamation as if it were emancipation itself.

This development deepened the prejudiced conviction of Peace Democrats, such as Fernando and Benjamin Wood, that Republicans had wanted to use the war to abolish slavery from the beginning. Early in July, what the *Times* called the anti-Negro-Submission Party held a mass rally at the Cooper Institute, where speakers with great regularity attacked New England, a favorite target of Democrats. The meeting approved a set of resolutions expressing support for the Union, the army, and the Constitution but condemning abolitionism: "This is a government of white men, and established exclusively for the white race." Fernando Wood again condemned the abolitionist "traitors" of the North, charging that they were planning to flood the city with black workers. To that he added the warning that white children would soon be crowded into schools with black children, who would be favored over them.[8]

This was only the beginning of a long campaign to convince the people of the metropolis to abandon their support for the war in the interests of peace and the restoration of the nation as it was. Many New York Democrats refused to follow Wood's lead, but they had to face the problem of disassociating their support for the war from support for abolitionism. By autumn both Tammany and Mozart Halls, sensing the possibility of a backlash against Republicans, had worked out an alliance to support Horatio Seymour for governor in the November elections; Seymour's position regarding the war was sufficiently vague for both factions to support him; his chief campaign charge was that the Lincoln administration was too incompetent to deal effectively with a national crisis.

"The Union as it was; the Constitution as it is" served as the general slogan of the Democratic campaign, but it barely concealed the anti-abolitionist and racist views of many of its supporters. The November election was basically a referendum on the Lincoln administration, emancipation, and freedom for black Americans. Some of the most extreme attacks came from the respectable *Journal of Commerce*, long hostile to Republicans and now almost paranoid in its views. It charged that "a secret society consisting of radical abolitionists and their political tools, existed in New York," which was planning an armed overthrow of the government in the interests of racial equality.[9] Hostility to radicals and blacks was a powerful combination, especially when harnessed to disillusionment with the war and resentment of conscription.

The November results indicated clearly where New York City stood: In the governor's race, Seymour won more than 70 percent of the votes cast in the city over his Republican opponent, James S. Wadsworth, and he was elected statewide. In addition, Democrats won all six of Gotham's seats in Congress, sending to Washington both Fernando and Benjamin Wood among others. The election was less a victory for Peace Democrats than for the Democratic Party in general, but it alarmed supporters of the war and encouraged their opponents. By late 1862 antiwar Democrats could claim the support of three influential newspapers, the *Express,* the *World,* and the *Journal of Commerce,* as well as the Catholic papers, the *Metropolitan Record* and the *Freeman's Journal.* This combination was expanded with the rebirth of Benjamin Wood's *Daily News,* which claimed that four of every five New Yorkers rejected war in favor of conciliation and concession.

What could be done to reverse the peace trend? One answer came from Frederick Law Olmsted. The day after the elections, he unveiled a plan to form an exclusive club of American "aristocrats" who would use their influence to support the nation and the war. He wanted men of substance and wealth and "clever" creative men in the arts and literature with the addition of "promising young men" who could be educated to a strong devotion to the Union cause.[10] Olmsted's idea of creating a power above the reach of Democratic politics appealed to many leading Republicans, and in March 1863 they formed the Union League Club, an elite organization of 500 select individuals, with initiation fees, dues, and membership standards. Like the United States Sanitary Commission, with which it was closely connected, the Union League Club became an effective lobby of talented supporters of the war and, with that, also of emancipation and black rights. In May 1863 it opened its clubhouse in a renovated mansion on Union Square.

The Union League Club was to have a long and distinguished history as a quietly strong voice for national unity, and it was soon joined by other Union organizations in the effort to shape public opinion. In mid-April 1863, on the second anniversary of the great patriotic response to the attack on Fort Sumter, Unionists organized a large rally in Union Square. There were six speaker's stands, with the usual profusion of patriotic colors, booming cannons, and brass bands. The aim was to revive the enthusiasm of two years before, to restore the "great uprising" of patriotism that had produced the first mass mobilization. Similar rallies were held throughout the metropolis, all with the intention of reversing what seemed to be the growing trend toward peace and of building new support for the Lincoln administration.

To some extent, these efforts succeeded, but the hope of recreating the patriotic spirit of the war's first months was disappointed by the profound changes that had occurred over the two years. Enthusiastic mobilization was giving way to conscription and organization; the war for the Union was becoming a war not to restore but to radically change the old white nation, to set the black man free. These changes were bitterly resented by many New Yorkers. The most dramatic result of this trend was to come in July, three months after the Union Square rally, when New York was shaken by a "great uprising," one very different from the one that the Unionists had hoped to ignite.

NOTES

1. *Times,* November 4, 1861. *Tribune,* November 6, 1861.
2. Quoted in Samuel A. Pleasants, *Fernando Wood of New York* (New York: Columbia University Press, 1944), 127–30. *Tribune,* September 10, 1861. *Times,* November 23 and 28, 1861.
3. *Times,* December 1, 1861.
4. *Herald,* November 28, 1861.
5. "Records of the National Affairs Committee" (April 1862), Municipal Archives, New York City.
6. *Official Documents, Addressess, Etc. of George Opdyke Mayor of the City of New York during the Years 1862 and 1863* (New York: Hurd and Houghton, 1866), 148–49.
7. *Times,* January 27, 1862.
8. *Times,* October 9, 1862.
9. *Journal of Commerce,* October 6, 1862.
10. Frederick Law Olmsted, *Defending the Union,* ed. Jane Turner Censer, vol. 4 of *The Papers of Frederick Law Olmsted,* ed. Charles Capen McLaughlin and Charles E. Beveridge (Baltimore: Johns Hopkins University Press, 1977–), 466–70.

CHAPTER EIGHT

RIOTS AND RELIEF

IN THE FIRST week of July 1863 the metropolis had cause to celebrate what the *Tribune* called the Great Victory at Gettysburg and then, soon after, the capture of Vicksburg in the west. Months of gloom yielded to hopes that the war would soon end with the defeat of the Confederacy. A week later, however, optimism was shattered by a great social explosion in New York City, when mobs rioted through the streets of many areas for five days beginning on July 13 in a frenzied opposition to forced service in the war. The Draft Riots had a shattering effect on the city in the short run, but, like the eruption of some great volcano that releases great natural tensions, they were not to be repeated during the remainder of the war.

Riots were nothing new. The city had been shaken by two earlier social explosions, the Astor Place Riot of 1849 and the Dead-Rabbit Riot of 1857. Even more than most great cities, New York had the prime ingredient for violence: a large floating population of unattached males, many the habitués of the barrooms of the city. They were responsible for most of the drunken assaults and knifings and shootings that enlivened the inside pages of the newspapers. They were part of an aggressive male world of generally poor white men excited by political, social, and racial resentments. That world had been diminished by the enlistment of many men in the army during the enthusiastic days of 1861, and Gotham saw significant declines in the number of murders (twenty-nine in 1862) and violent assaults along with the number of inmates in local prisons. By the summer of 1863, however, the world of violence was replenished, in part by the mustering out of eighteen local regiments that had volunteered for two years of service in the first months of the war (there would have been nineteen regiments, but the obstreperous First Fire Zouaves

Citizens welcoming home veterans of New York regiments on April 28, 1863, following the expiration of their two-year term of enlistment. Their torn battle flags contrast
with the captured Confederate Stars and Bars. The expiration of the two-year term
added new pressures for a draft to replace the many veterans who did not reenlist.
From *Frank Leslie's Scenes and Portraits of the Civil War* (New York: Mrs. Frank Leslie,
1894), 464.

Regiment had been dissolved a year earlier, a final insult to one important part of the male world, the city's volunteer fire department).

The ingredients for social violence were there, but it took special
factors to ignite them. The most important spark was the National
Enrollment (Conscription) Act of March 1, 1863. For two years the
metropolis had been able to stave off a draft through a combination
of appeals to patriotism and, increasingly, financial inducements.
Under this system, Gotham used its wealth to complete its quotas by
inducing men from elsewhere to enlist in its regiments. In July, however, the Conscription Act was to go into effect, increasing the threat

of forced service to the men of the city in general, regardless of their feelings about the war.

The idea of a comprehensive draft was nothing new to New York. On August 4, 1862, the *Times* called for a million-man draft and for the conversion of the North "into a vast arsenal of men and munitions of war from which could be hurled with the suddenness and force of thunderbolts, as many separate armies as emergencies may require."[1] A few days later, Archbishop John Joseph Hughes, leader of the Roman Catholic Church in the North, advocated a comprehensive draft as a way to equalize the burdens of war, which he felt had fallen disproportionately on his Irish parishioners. Others also saw the draft as a democratic way to raise manpower.

It was expediency, however, rather than democracy that shaped the Conscription Act. The dominant intention behind the act was to pump new life into the old volunteer system. Under the threat of conscription, it was hoped, men would volunteer to collect enlistment bonuses. In fact, of the 158,000 men whose names were drawn under the act in New York State, only 3,210 were actually drafted; the rest either volunteered or were replaced by substitutes. The result, however, was an imperfect system that grew increasingly dependent on money while further inflaming popular resentments.

The delay in imposing conscription allowed time for feelings against it to fester. By early 1863 the flow of the wounded through the city and reports of battlefield casualties left little doubt that war was a bloody business. The willingness to run the risks of war had been substantially diminished by emancipation, which meant not only the future freeing of masses of black people but their enrollment in the Union army. Although it was pointed out that black men might take the bullets otherwise directed against white men, the argument had little effect on racists, such as the editors of the *Weekly Caucasian:* "Do not these men know that equality as a soldier means equality at the ballot-box, equality everywhere."[2] Such views were played on by the Copperhead spokesmen in their attack on conscription.

Aside from the threat of coerced service in a questionable cause, the Conscription Act had one notable feature that antagonized many people: a provision that exempted from the draft anyone who could pay $300 or hire a substitute. To supporters of conscription this provision made sense. In April the *Times* argued that under the volunteer system the army had been composed of "superfluous material," men who were of no particular use to the community. A comprehensive draft without an exemption provision, however, would take men whom society could not spare, especially those needed in commerce and industry. This explanation, however, had no effect on such men as Fernando and Benjamin Wood, who attacked conscription as class legislation, making for a rich man's war and a poor man's fight. In July, Benjamin Wood's *Daily News,* recently revived after twenty months of silence, declared that "the fact that the Conscription virtually exempts the rich and fastens its iron hand upon the poor alone, is sufficient demonstration of its injustice."[3]

Conscription particularly infuriated New York's large Irish population. In the first year of the war, a large number of Irishmen had volunteered to fight and many had died in defense of the Union. Emancipation and the enrollment of blacks in the military, however, was an outrage for an ethnic group deeply hostile to black people, one that threatened to minimize the contributions they had made. This racist reaction was made even worse by the hiring in New York of black men to replace striking Irish stevedores on the docks; one justification of this practice was the needs of the war. In June, 3,000 mostly Irish strikers were forced to watch as blacks took their jobs under the protection of the police. To add insult to injury, the Irish, being among the poorest in the white population, were the ones most likely to be drafted to fight the war for black freedom.

To make the situation even more tense, the Conscription Act eliminated the earlier draft exemption of the city's volunteer fire department, perhaps a critical factor in the riots. Firemen had already been alienated by what they considered the unfair treatment of the First Fire Zouaves Regiment. While the firemen were only a small part of the male population, they were an organized force, as politicians had long recognized. The hostility of even a few fire companies scattered throughout the city could help ignite the violent potential of the male world. In 1865 the president of the police commission judged that the firemen had instigated and participated in the riots against conscription.

The preparation for the draft further deepened resentments. Lists had to be made of those liable to be drafted, a complicated task that encountered much hostility. Some of the 300 enrollment officers faced threats of violence as they carried out their work. In May a force of twenty-eight men was needed to get the male residents of one boardinghouse to give their correct names. In June nine men were arrested for trying to obstruct the process, and enrollment officers were attacked by a woman with "an immense slingshot." With more hope than fear the *Daily News* reported rumors that "an organized resistance" was being formed in various parts of the city. When the Board of Councilmen learned that the City Park Barrack was being used for the "unlicensed incarceration" of resisters, it ordered—unsuccessfully—that the facility be torn down.[4]

Whatever the extent of the resistance, it was overshadowed in late June by news of the Confederate invasion of Pennsylvania, a threat to the vital interests of the North. In response to a call from the Union government, Governor Horatio Seymour sent eight militia regiments from New York and Brooklyn to help repel the invaders, evoking a great march down Broadway. "The 10,000 men who have gone off to meet the enemy," said the *Tribune*, "were the bone and muscle of society." Overall, the regiments were reserve troops, basically civilians and of little use in battle, but among them was the elite riot-control Seventh Regiment. About 700 of its 1,100 members departed, with the rest remaining behind because of "business engagements." The departure of these regiments stripped the metropolis of its primary defense against large-scale disorder. Confronted with widespread discontent over conscription, Mayor George Opdyke telegraphed Governor Seymour on June 30 to stress the need for a strong military presence in the city. When the governor ignored his advice, Opdyke warned that "it will be imprudent, if not hazardous, to leave the city without at least two or three reliable regiments."[5]

In the end, by the mayor's estimate, New York was left with less than 1,000 men to defend it against what Opdyke feared was "a treasonable and revolutionary spirit among our people." The governor himself contributed to that spirit in an unfortunate speech that he gave in the city on the Fourth of July. After attacking the Lincoln administration for what he saw as a systematic violation of individual rights under the guise of war needs, Governor Seymour issued a warning: "Remember this—that the bloody and treasonable and revolutionary doctrine of public necessity can be proclaimed by a mob as well as by Government."[6] So it was that a partly defenseless city began to implement an unpopular law during a time of extreme discontent.

Things began peacefully. "Many stories have been circulated to the effect that bands, gangs and companies have been organized here and there with the intent of resisting the draft," said the *Tribune* on July 11, "but from what all we can learn no such organizations exist."[7] The situation, however, was soon to change in the Ninth Congressional District, an uptown area with a large number of foreign-born laborers. On the 11th, a Saturday, draft officials began to turn a large lottery wheel ("the wheel of misfortune," said the *Daily News*), which was used to draw the names of those to be drafted. The drawing went smoothly, but it was not completed that day, leaving the rest for Monday. Thus it was that on Sunday men in saloons had the opportunity to study the names of those drafted and to grow even more resentful. Among the names was the captain of the Black Joke Fire Company on West 58th Street; the fire company's members and the captain's friends apparently decided to disrupt the drafting process.

In the early morning of July 13 several mobs of discontented men formed in the city, waiting for something to give them direction. That something came at the Ninth District draft office. There, according to one reporter, about seventy-five names had been drawn "when suddenly the report of a pistol was heard on the street. This seemed to be the signal for an attack upon the [draft] office, for almost upon the instant a perfect shower of brickbats, paving stones and other missiles were hurled from the street and the building." Many of the missiles came from a hose cart hauled to the scene by the Black Joke company. This proved to be the trigger for spreading mob violence. After setting fire to the draft office, the growing mob marched south, meeting with others of a similar temper. By the late afternoon the rioters, frenzied with liquor, were completely out of control. When Police Superintendent John A. Kennedy tried to assert his authority, a mob "beat him, dragged him through the streets by the head, pitched him into a horse pond, rolled him in the mud-gutters, [and] dragged him through piles of filth indescribable," stopping only when they thought he was dead. Kennedy survived, but others were not so fortunate.[8]

By the second day the riot had spread to other parts of the city, as far north as Harlem and as far south as Wall Street. The 86th Street house of Colonel Robert Nugent was burned. Nugent was targeted because, although he had once served in the heroic Sixty-ninth Regiment, he was now in charge of the draft. Rioters were kept from burning the home of Mayor Opdyke on Fifth Avenue, but they did succeed in destroying a gun factory owned by him and his son-in-law. They set fire to the Eighteenth Ward police station on East 22d Street, and, on Catherine Street, they pillaged and destroyed the Brooks Brothers Clothing Store. By the third day, mobs appeared elsewhere in the metropolis and in Brooklyn (where they burned down a new $100,000 grain elevator), Jersey City, and Staten Island. The commercial areas of lower New York were generally quiet, in part because steps were taken quickly to defend them, but efforts were made to attack the East River Shipyards, especially the Webb yard, where the great warship *Dunderberg* was under construction.

The behavior of some rioters was worse than that of savages. A policeman was beaten senseless. While he was unconscious, a woman "rushed forward and with fiendish brutality tried to cut off his ear," only to be stopped by others in the crowd; the ear was sewed on again. There was no such luck for Colonel Henry O'Brien, commander of a hastily assembled military force that successfully dispersed a mob on 35th Street. After clearing the street with the help of two field guns, which left a number of rioters dead or wounded, O'Brien foolishly returned to the scene alone and armed only with a sword and a pistol. He was seized by a mob, beaten, dragged through the gutters, tortured, shot, and finally hung from a lamppost. The rioters might have done the same thing to Horace Greeley, the embodiment of hated Yankee reform, but they could not get to him, although, as Greeley put it, "They must have hurt their throats howling at me." Unfortunately, one innocent citizen was mistaken for Greeley and nearly beaten to death.[9]

Savage attacks against white men were selective. Black men, however, were attacked wherever they could be found. On July 14 the *Daily News* published a short editorial headed "Do Not Harm the Negro," declaring that blacks had been misled by abolitionists. If this was meant to be taken seriously, it had little effect. The *Tribune* noted that one of the most familiar cries of the mob was "Kill the d——d nigger." Racism was not particularly discriminating: Peter Heuston, a Mohawk Indian, was mistaken for a black man and beaten so badly that he later died in Bellevue Hospital. On the same day that O'Brien was killed, two black men were beaten to death and their bodies were hung. At least a dozen others were hunted down and given the same brutal treatment. In one case a mob of 400 men and boys hung their victim from a tree and "not being yet satisfied with their devilish work, they set fire to his clothes and danced and yelled and swore their horrid oaths around his burning corpse."[10]

Reportedly, white longshoremen vented their anger against black strikebreakers by throwing "scores" of black men into the river to drown. Buildings occupied by blacks were attacked and burned, leaving thousands homeless and without employment. One mob set fire to the Colored Orphan Asylum, although in this case brutality was tempered by humanity: A young Irishman by the name of Paddy McCafferty, working with four drivers of an omnibus line, was able to rescue the children and to bring them to the safety of a police station. Many more blacks would have died if they had not fled the city or been able to find refuge at the police headquarters and the almshouse.

During the first day of the riot the mobs were too many and too widely dispersed to be attacked effectively by available forces of order. The Metropolitan Police made an effort to enforce the law, but they were heavily outnumbered, and existing military forces, such as they were, lacked a unified command, some being army regulars and others state volunteers. Wisely, Mayor Opdyke ordered all gun shops closed to keep arms out of the hands of rioters, and by the second day military and civic leaders had begun to put together a defense force. Most of the initial effort was focused on protecting the armories, government storehouses, shipyards, and downtown financial institutions. A warship was anchored at the foot of Wall Street, ready to rake the street with its guns if needed, and a marine artillery unit from the Brooklyn Navy Yard guarded the Sub-Treasury with its stock of gold.

Much of the effort was the spontaneous work of citizens. In the First Ward a group of Irish laborers organized themselves into a force to restore order. They even rescued a black man from a mob. Helping to protect the Wall Street area, said the *Journal of Commerce*, was a "fine corps" of men from the Street Department organized by County Supervisor and Deputy Street Commissioner William M. Tweed. Hundreds of others worked to provide protection against the mobs. At least 400 men were sworn in as special policemen, with badges, clubs, and guns. Largely to protect their property, businessmen, under the lead of the ubiquitous William E. Dodge, formed their own military company to provide night-and-day protection for the Broadway area.

By the third day the forces for order within the metropolis had been sufficiently rallied to enable Mayor Opdyke to declare that the city was winning the battle: "What now remains of the mob are fragments, prowling about for plunder." Then on the fourth day came the return of the Seventh Regiment—the "mob-killing and mob-quelling" unit in the words of the *Daily News*—along with some of the other regiments withdrawn from the city during the Gettysburg campaign. By the fifth day, July 17, the great eruption had virtually ended, exhausted by its own excesses as much perhaps as repressed by the forces of order.[11]

The costs were evident: "Burned buildings, charred furniture, barricaded dwellings, emptied stores, gutted palaces (so to speak), deserted foundries, suspended labor, millions of damage and thousands of loss, greet us on every side."[12] A week after the riot ended, the ruins of the five-story Eighteenth Precinct Police Station, torched by a mob, collapsed on women and children scavenging for wood and coal, killing at least three of them. Initial claims for property damage totaled $1,088,000, of which $17,456 was claimed by black people; eventually, the total claims reached about $2.5 million. The exact number of deaths will never be known because at least some were not reported. Although Police Superintendent Kennedy estimated that 1,155 people were killed, the more likely figure is between 120 and 150.

Even before this destruction ended, New Yorkers tried to explain its causes, generally with copious amounts of partisan bias. On the one side were the defenders of existing Republican policies, who charged that the riots were a conspiracy of rabble-rousers, incited by the Copperhead press. Ignoring the possibility of class preference in the $300 exemption, critics argued that conscription was only a pretext for efforts to sabotage the war effort. In 1865 the highly partisan George Templeton Strong claimed that, with the support of Governor Seymour and also of local Democratic officials, a massive uprising against Federal authority was planned and would have occurred if Robert E. Lee had triumphed at Gettysburg. The riots, said Strong, "were a partial deflagration and explosion of combustible ruffianism that had been stored away for yet worse mischief." Frederick Law Olmsted went further, declaring that the "most dangerous foes of the Republic are in New York City" and proposing that the metropolis be treated like New Orleans or any other occupied city in the South.[13]

Peace Democrats presented a different explanation based on a different set of values. They saw the rioters as protesting against the systematic violation of their rights. A week before the riots began, Governor Seymour in his Fourth of July speech warned Republicans that they might well provoke mob violence "by seizing our persons, by infringing upon our rights, by insulting our homes, and by depriving us of our cherished privileges." Beyond individuals' rights for white men, there was the increasingly common complaint that the policies of abolitionist Republicans excited racial animosities. "By their ridiculous and phrenzied zeal for the negro urging him into conspicuous rivalry to white men," said the *Daily News*, "they have created an antipathy against the race." After the riots ended, the *Herald* also held abolitionists responsible, "having so filled the empty heads of the blacks with notions of equality that many of them have become insolent to white men and women in the streets, in ferry boats, in cars and other places."[14]

Threaded through the arguments of both sides was the often recognized fact that the city's Irish population provided the bulk of the rioters. Orestes Brownson, a leading Roman Catholic intellectual, declared in October that "the rioters were almost exclusively Irishmen and Catholics," but he blamed conniving Democratic politicians for leading poor Irishmen astray and contended that the eruption was not a Catholic but a Peace Democrat riot. For their part, Democrats generally pointed out that these poor Irishmen were the most likely victims of the class bias of the Conscription Act, and the *Irish-American*, a prowar newspaper, attributed the riots to a "spirit of hostility" raised by the attacks of "ultra-Abolitionist journals" on Irish Catholics. On the other side, the anti-Irish snob Strong had his prejudices confirmed to the point that he was willing to "see war made on Irish scum." Although Strong's views were not uncommon, other Republicans conceded that only a minority of the city's Irish people had been rioters or, more generally, were disloyal or lawbreakers. Greeley's *Tribune* noted that during the riots the heavily Irish Sixth and Fourteenth Wards in the city had "not been disgraced by a single outrage, not even upon their colored residents."[15]

Whatever the disagreements about the nature and cause of the riots, nearly everyone soon reached the conclusion that they were not likely to occur again in any foreseeable future. In fact, the remaining war years would see no large-scale violence on the streets even in the face of several threatened drafts: In July the Conscription Act was suspended, only to be resumed a month later. Undoubtedly, the riots released pent-up resentments on the part of many of the rioters, a significant release of social pressure. Beyond this, though, pressures were prevented from again rising to dangerous degrees by what proved to be a radical change in the draft situation. The key change was the decision of the governments of both New York City and Brooklyn to use public money to buy draft exemptions for those citizens who wanted them. Although the result was to corrupt the recruitment process further, the new system not only eased pressures but also helped local Democratic leaders recover from the effects of the riot and to strengthen their grip on city government.

The essential aim was to provide a noncoercive way for the metropolis to meet its quota under the draft. Enforcement of conscription had been temporarily suspended with the outbreak of disorder, but it was evident that the process would be resumed soon. As early as the second day of the riot, the heavily Democratic Board of Aldermen rushed through "an ordinance to relieve the city of New York from unequal operation of conscription and to encourage volunteering."[16] This act promised to buy $300 exemptions for those unable to afford them and to pay $300 to anyone willing to serve as a substitute for one of the drafted. The plan was to be funded with a $2.5 million loan. This scheme was also hurried through the Board of Councilmen, the other house of the legislature, only to encounter the veto of Mayor Opdyke, who condemned it as a sellout to the forces of disorder and treason.

The effect of the veto, however, was simply to shift the decision from the city to the county government. The issue was resolved by the New York County Board of Supervisors, which at that time shared power in Manhattan with the city council. The county's decision was made more palatable to Republicans by the fact that state law guaranteed them equal representation on the board. If there was to be a mass purchase of exemptions, at least Republicans would be in a position to reap some of its political benefits. To satisfy the demands of Opdyke and others that exemptions be limited to needed civic personnel, the Board of Supervisors provided $2 million to enable firemen and policemen to procure substitutes if they were drafted, but the board also added a more democratic provision granting the same privilege to men too poor to buy their own substitutes. The initial $2 million under the board's control was to be paid out of a special bond issue, enabling New Yorkers to get their exemptions without the pain of additional taxation.

To handle the details, the Board of Supervisors established a County Substitute and Relief Committee (soon renamed the Volunteer Committee), which from its inception in early September 1863 was besieged by drafted men seeking relief. Each man received money to pay for a substitute once he had convinced the committee that he could not pay for one himself. The *Tribune*, which favored the scheme, predicted that soon substitutes would outnumber drafted men in the city, and indeed of the first 1,500 men ordered to serve, two-thirds found substitutes. Some of these men used their own money, but many more benefited from the county plan, which by the end of September had furnished 1,042 substitutes at a cost of over $30,000. From then on, the Volunteer Committee was both an active recruiting force and an effective safeguard against conscription.

The Board of Supervisors boasted that they had found a way superior to the draft to furnish men for the Union army. For many New Yorkers anxious to avoid military service, it was superior. It was not long, however, before the scheme became entrapped in a corrupt system dominated by money and bounty brokers. Sensing profits from the draft, the brokers made themselves the middlemen in the exemption business by rounding up men who could be used as substitutes. Soon, the brokers commanded the supply of substitutes, and they expected to be paid. When military authorities in New York tried to insist that any money be paid only to the substitutes and their families, the brokers took their men to other states, threatening to keep New York from meeting its draft quotas without an actual draft. The decision was reversed, and over the next year and a half New York County borrowed over $8 million to fund a corrupt system that produced bounty jumpers and other dubious material for the army and great profits for the brokers.

Whatever the impact on New York's contribution to the war effort, the substitute program was popular at home to the great benefit of the Democratic Party. Although the Republicans on the Board of Supervisors hoped to benefit politically by supporting the scheme, in general they were linked to the unpopular combination of abolitionism and conscription. On the other hand, Democrats could identify with a measure that seemed to both meet the needs of the war and satisfy the needs of their constituents while helping to avert another bloody riot. They received especially strong support from the Irish and other immigrants who had developed an increasingly tense relationship with the great American conflict that surrounded them.

NOTES

1. *Times,* August 4, 1862.

2. *Weekly Caucasian,* January 23, 1863. *Times,* April 25, 1863.

3. *Daily News,* July 11, 1863.

4. *Tribune,* June 2 and 13, 1863. *Weekly Caucasian,* June 27, 1863. *Daily News,* July 13, 1863.

5. *Tribune,* July 2 and 6, 1863. George T. Opdyke, *Official Documents, Addresses, Etc.* (Albany, 1866), 264–65.

6. *Tribune,* July 6, 1863.

7. *Tribune,* July 11, 1863. *Daily News,* July 13, 1863.

8. *Tribune,* July 14, 1863.

9. *Times,* July 15, 1863. Horace Greeley to Mrs. Howe, August 24, 1863, Greeley Papers, New York Public Library.

10. *Daily News,* July 14, 1863. *Tribune,* July 14, 1863.

11. *Tribune,* July 16, 1863. *Daily News,* July 16 and 17, 1863.

12. *Daily News,* July 18, 1863.

13. Frederick Law Olmsted, *Defending the Union,* ed. Jane Turner Censer, vol. 4 of *The Papers of Frederick Law Olmsted,* ed. Charles Capen McLaughlin and Charles E. Beveridge (Baltimore: Johns Hopkins University Press, 1977–), 15.

14. *Herald,* July 28, 1863. *Daily News,* July 16, 1863.

15. *Tribune,* July 20, 1863. *Irish-American,* August 1, 1863. *Brownson's Quarterly Review,* 4:386–87, 401 (1863). Strong, *Diary,* v. 3, 343, 352.

16. "Communication from the Mayor, John T. Hoffman," Document 1, Board of Councilmen, *Documents* (1867), 9.

Chapter Nine

The Ethnic Dimension

By the time of the Civil War, Gotham had established its reputation as the most European of all American cities, a reputation affirmed by the *Times* when it declared in 1863 that "the texture of society in New York is no longer American but European."[1] In 1860 foreign-born residents were 47 percent of the population of New York City and 40 percent of the population in Brooklyn, a total of 497,000 people for the two cities. Most of the immigrants had been born in either Ireland or Germany, but sizable numbers had come from England, Scotland, and France with lesser numbers from Italy, Switzerland, the West Indies, Latin America, and even China. Although in both New York and Kings Counties the native-born population outnumbered the foreign-born residents, many of the native-born Gothamites were the children of immigrants. New York had become in its ethnic and economic character a metropolis of the world.

Ethnic diversity had both strong positive and strong negative effects on the metropolis. On the plus side, foreign immigrants brought much needed money, skills, and labor that contributed to New York's wealth, and even their poverty contributed to the emergence of a middle class among the more established: "The vast influx of foreign population," wrote one observer, "has tended to elevate the occupations of our native working classes by relieving them of the humble forms of labor."[2] Beyond wealth, the immigrants added to the color of metropolitan life, particularly in their special celebrations: The Irish had their St. Patrick's Day, the Germans their singing fests, and the Scots their Caledonian athletic games.

On the other hand, ethnic differences produced fears and resentments that weakened the cohesion of society and poisoned politics. Undoubtedly, the strongest animosities existed between the city's most influential ethnic group, Protestants from New England, and its numerically largest group, Catholic Irishmen. The friction between these two groups was a central element of metropolitan society and politics. In 1860, for instance, Protestants grew uproariously angry when Roman Catholic school trustees in the Fourth Ward fired nine Protestant teachers for insisting on reading the Bible—Protestant version—to their pupils, many of them Catholics. Nativism, which had appeared in the city in the 1830s, remained strong throughout the period, helping to instill in the immigrant population resentments and fears against especially Yankee Protestants.

Although native New Yorkers had mixed feelings about the newcomers, they could do nothing to discourage the flow of foreigners into their city. As the nation's leading port, Gotham was a natural funnel for people coming from many places, and the flow through it was determined by factors beyond its control. The economic uncertainties following the Panic of 1857 had diminished the numbers. By 1860 immigration had started to recover, only to be discouraged by the economic disruptions produced by secession and then war. In 1860, 105,162 immigrants landed in New York City; in 1861 the number was only 65,537.

This decrease in immigration proved to be a temporary aberration, induced less by the war than by the limited employment opportunities of a disrupted economy. By the next year wartime prosperity and the depletion of the labor supply to fight the war were reversing the situation. Confronted with a rising labor shortage, in October 1862 the New York Chamber of Commerce urged a policy to attract skilled foreigners, and Congress did eventually adopt such a policy. By the late summer of 1864 the American Emigration Company, a private firm headquartered in New York, had established a widespread system of agencies in Great Britain and northern Europe intended not only to promote migration but also to persuade workers there to sign contracts to work for American employers.

Critics soon claimed that a major aim of such efforts was to provide foreign-born recruits for the Union military, an aim denied by proponents of the policy. Whatever the intention, immigration did provide a supply of recruits and substitutes that helped protect New Yorkers from the draft. Some immigrants enlisted voluntarily, but others were literally kidnapped by bounty brokers. The year 1863, a time of prosperity as well as of the Draft Riots, saw an increase in the number of immigrants landing in New York, to 156,880, more than twice the total number of the two previous years combined. This upward trend continued for the remainder of the war; in 1865 nearly 200,000 Europeans arrived. Wartime needs and service weakened earlier antiforeign attitudes. In 1862 the Chamber of Commerce justified its call for increased immigration by noting that "the events of the war have so fully proven the patriotism and bravery of our adopted citizens that the largest accessions to their members would be hailed with delight by the loyal American people." In fact, during the first months of the war the metropolis produced something like a multicultural military among the regiments that were enlisted at that time. Virtually every immigrant group had some early representatives in the enthusiastic rush to enlist. New York's small Italian community, many of whose members had fled from the failed revolutions of 1848 and 1849 in Italy, helped form the Garibaldi Guard, named after the great champion of Italian freedom. Five other nationalities helped to complete the Guard as a regiment, which prepared itself for departure to war, reported the *Tribune,* by "singing German, Hungarian, Swiss, Italian, French, and Spanish camp songs." French residents formed the Lafayette Guards, and the Hungarians, Swiss, Dutch, Scandinavians, and British attempted to form similar units.

The numbers involved in these efforts were too small to produce complete regiments, but the city's Scottish population did succeed in forming one of New York's most notable volunteer regiments, the Seventy-ninth Highlanders, whose official uniform included kilts. The regiment suffered heavy losses in the Battle of Bull Run and was dissolved a month later for refusing to obey orders. The Highlanders soon reconstituted and, sustained by enlistments from outside and inside the metropolis, compiled a distinguished war record, participating in the capture of Port Royal and in numerous other campaigns until the end of the war. In 1864, when the Seventy-ninth reenlisted after the expiration of its three-year term of service, the *Times* called it "one of the bravest and most gallant regiments whoever left this City."[3]

The Scots, however, were dwarfed by two other ethnic groups. One group was the Germans. In 1860 there were 150,000 German immigrants in Gotham and surrounding areas, and during the war years their number grew rapidly. Although often scattered throughout the metropolis in places such as Brooklyn and Hoboken, a large number of Germans concentrated in their own community, Kleindeutschland (Little Germany), on the Lower East Side of Manhattan. Little Germany had a strong community life. Germans created their own bank, insurance company, school, newspapers, and theaters. The Society of German Physicians furnished free medical care for the poor, and another society provided relief for destitute immigrants. As a result, few Germans depended on public charity. There were numerous clubs or *vereins* established for cultural, social, and health purposes, including a shooting club, which celebrated its fifth anniversary in 1863 with a shooting festival to raise money for the care of wounded soldiers. In July 1862 twenty-five *vereins* of various kinds participated in a summer festival intended to raise money to establish a German hospital in the city.

Germans won special attention through two public activities. One was in the realm of music, especially singing. The Liederkrantz, a German musical society, promoted various songfests, including an annual *Sommernachtfest* that attracted scores of musical groups and thousands of participants from throughout the metropolis; at one such event in Jones's Wood, the people sang and danced until daybreak. The other notable public activity was physical, in the form of the *Turnverein*, or gymnastics club. The gymnasts not only developed an artful strength through their exercises but also served as a focus of community involvement through their participation in festivals, picnics, and parades. In May 1863, for instance, they entertained 10,000 celebrants at the annual spring festival by going through their various gymnastic exercises. They did much to introduce the idea of physical fitness to America.

The German community generally shared the hostility of the city's Democrats to "puritanic" interference with their individual freedom, especially to efforts to close their beer gardens and theaters on Sundays, which for them was a day of good-natured pleasure seeking. Despite that hostility, Germans impressed the native population as being an orderly people, and they won widespread respect for their consistent patriotism, supporting not only a war for union but also the war for the emancipation of slaves. Their relative lack of connections with the South, their remoteness from American racism, and their strong libertarian instincts inclined them against slavery, even though they had little sympathy for New England abolitionists.

During the first enthusiastic months following the attack on Fort Sumter, Germans were at the front of ethnic participation in the war. Many had served in European wars and were ready to use their experience to form volunteer units. It was estimated that nearly three-quarters of the men in one regiment, so heavily German that the oath of allegiance had to be translated for them, had European military experience. By mid-May 1861 the New York Bible Society noted that, of the thirty-three regiments to which it supplied Bibles, five were German speaking. The Twentieth Regiment (Turner Rifles) was composed of 400 members of the exercise-conscious *Turnverein*. Overall, the German community contributed a large number of men to at least ten regiments, two of which (the Forty-fifth and the Sixty-eighth) served for the duration of the war.

Although many men enlisted in non-German regiments, they preferred to fight with men of their own culture and background. In May 1861 military leaders agreed to form a brigade that they hoped would be commanded by Carl Schurz, a prominent Republican who had military experience in Europe. Although Schurz was not appointed, the German regiments found an early commander in Louis Blenker, a refugee from the revolution of 1848 who had begun the war as head of the Eighth Regiment. Blenker's division in the Army of the Potomac was called the German army, and it received the support of Kleindeutschland, which encouraged enlistment in its units.

Like many other enthusiasts during this early period, the Germans had much confidence in their fighting ability, sometimes too much for the good of all concerned. Colonel John C. Bendix, commander of the Steuben Volunteers, complained that his officers ridiculed "the American sistem of Tactics and Warfare, so much so, that I got completely disgusted with them." Undoubtedly, many Germans agreed with Francis Lieber, a Columbia College professor and strong supporter of the war, who responded to a suggestion that perhaps the new soldiers needed military training by denying that it was necessary: "You can say that the german nation has seen far more war, and the germans have fought in more wars in other countries than any nation on earth." Lieber went on to deprecate the importance of studying tactics. What was important, he said, was bravery and physical endurance: "The german soldier if well led is to the first equal to any, and is to the second superior to any."[4]

The war, however, raised questions about German military

leadership. General Blenker was relieved of his command of the German brigade in June 1862 following a bungled operation against Stonewall Jackson. Even earlier, New York Germans had held a mass meeting in the city to protest the mismanagement of troops under his command, posting large handbills announcing the protest in both German and English in New York City and other places with German populations. Blenker was replaced by a new hero, General Franz Sigel of Missouri. Sigel also became a subject of controversy. When he was temporarily relieved of his command in early 1862, Germans protested, declaring that he was the victim of prejudice. Although they continued to support the Union cause, it was said that they often held back from enlisting until they could be sure that they would "fight mit Sigel." Probably, it was this conviction that led to the formation in the summer of 1862 of a "Sigel Brigade," which brought the enthusiasm of Kleindeutschland to what the *Times* called a fever heat. In early 1863, though, Sigel again was relieved of his command after two of his regiments apparently panicked in battle. Again, the German community protested. Sigel was assigned a new command, only to be relieved one last time when he was defeated at the Battle of New Market in 1864.

Despite these disappointments, New York's Germans generally supported the policies of the Lincoln administration, including emancipation and the draft. In doing so, they intensified the contrast that many native New Yorkers saw between them and the Irish. The two groups occupied, as the *Times* pointed out in 1862, two separate worlds in the city with little contact between them. That separateness was reinforced by strikingly different reputations in which Germans were almost inevitably favored. In the general view, the Germans were the steady, orderly, loyal population whose only vice seemed to be their loud and cheerful Sundays. In contrast, the Irish were often stereotyped as ignorant, dirty, and drunken. Unfortunately for them, existing statistics supported the stereotype because the Irish were heavily overrepresented among the city's poor, illiterate, and prison populations. Long before the Draft Riots, newspaper reports of personal assaults by Irishmen, generally on other Irishmen, often under the influence of drink, created the impression that they were an unusually violent people.

As with other such social stereotypes, the popular view misrepresented the situation. Most of the Irish population was orderly, literate, and self-sustaining, often under adverse social circumstances. In significant part, the negative features of their lives had been imported from their abused and exploited homeland. Likely, Irish social life during the war was further depressed by a dramatic increase in immigration in 1863, when the number of immigrants from Ireland more than tripled over the average of the previous two years. This increase may have been a factor in the Draft Riots in that year. Many of the newcomers were fleeing not simply from poverty but from the threat of outright starvation resulting from crop failures. Because of their initial poverty, a disproportionate number of them fell into the debilitating environment of the city's slums.

Even before the war, though, the Irish had begun to establish themselves as an important part of New York life, proving the hopeful observation of one New Yorker "that New-York energy acts as a solvent to fuse the motley masses that Europe is pouring in on us into a consistent body of valuable and happy freemen."[5] Most began with few useful skills; the men were disproportionately laborers, teamsters, and longshoremen and the women were disproportionately domestics and seamstresses. More than a few, however, began the climb to prosperity and influence. Over 10,000 Irish were employed in the city's clothing trade, most of them in low-skilled, easily exploitable work, but at least a few became employers. Daniel Devlin headed one of the largest clothing firms in the city, employing over 2,000 workers. Second only to Brooks Brothers in the clothing trade, Daniel Devlin & Company was able to take advantage of the wartime demand for military clothing. By 1860 other Irish businessmen had appeared along with a small professional class of physicians, lawyers, and teachers, and Irishmen began to make great strides along the road that brought them the most success, politics and government. Although they were not yet ready to replace such native Protestant bosses as Fernando Wood and William M. Tweed, they were firmly establishing themselves in the lower levels of the Democratic Party.

Religion and church were as important for the Irish as politics and government. Unlike the religiously divided and often secular Germans, the Irish were overwhelmingly Roman Catholic, a characteristic that both further separated them from a still predominantly Protestant society and provided a basis for identity and communal life. They were fortunate to have a strong religious leader in John

Joseph Hughes, archbishop of New York, who for more than twenty years tried to promote the unity and welfare of his people. As their "bishop and chief," Hughes fought to protect their rights and interests, building churches, schools, and other institutions to meet their needs. During the war years the great St. Patrick's Cathedral began to rise on Fifth Avenue, to be completed in 1879.

With the outbreak of war, Archbishop Hughes did nothing to moderate the deep hostility of his followers to abolitionism. In October 1861 he warned the Lincoln administration that should they have "to fight for the abolition of slavery, then, indeed, they will turn away in disgust from the discharge of what would otherwise be a patriotic duty." It was said, apparently with reason, that Hughes did not consider the black race to be part of his flock. He did, however, use his influence to support the restoration of the Union, a conservative cause suited to the conservative instincts of his church. In 1862, Hughes played a larger role, traveling to Europe, where he tried with some success in France and elsewhere to stem what he called a "current of fixed prejudice against us." When on his return to America he was presented with a resolution of thanks for this service from the city council, he closed his response by saying, "The country, as I know it, was one, and I hope I shall never be called upon to recognize it as two."[6]

In the beginning, Hughes's communicants were unsurpassed in their willingness to enlist in the war. Some volunteered perhaps less out of enthusiasm than necessity, army pay being more than many could make in civilian life, but larger motives also played a part. In some respects, the isolation of the Irish made them especially determined to prove that they too were Americans by serving in the war to reunite the nation. With as much hope as truth, one observer said that the war "has silenced forever the charges against the naturalized citizen and the Catholic as being unworthy of citizenship." More than a few men had a second reason, namely, to gain military experience that could then be used in the liberation of Ireland. In 1863 an Irish American bard ended an ode on Irish military involvement with the lines:

> God prosper poor old Ireland too!
> We'll trample on all tyrants laws;
> Hurrah for the old land and the new.

The Irish, said Hughes in 1862, "entered into this war partly to make themselves apprentices, students as it were, finishing their education in this, the first opportunity offered them of becoming thoroughly acquainted with the implements of war."[7]

The heroic reputation of the Sixty-ninth Regiment at the Battle of Bull Run served to sustain these hopes and also to produce two Irish war heroes. One, Michael Corcoran, the commander of the Sixty-ninth, was captured by the Confederates and spent the next year as a prisoner of war, but in 1862 he returned to inspire new enthusiasm for the war. The other was Thomas Francis Meagher, whom the press portrayed as serving with great bravery at the Battle of Bull Run: "He rode a splendid white horse. He lost his cap, and was remarkable in his bare head, urging his men forward." Not all accounts were so favorable: Some other officers of the Sixty-ninth said, as reported by Maria Daly, that he "had just enough sense and elation to rush forward and afterward fell from his horse drunk, and was picked up by the troopers."[8]

Whatever Meagher's deficiencies as a commander, he was an excellent recruiter. In August 1861, as the Sixty-ninth was concluding its three months of service, he took the lead in perhaps the greatest military project of the New York community, the formation of the Irish Brigade. Earlier Irish brigades had been organized to fight in foreign lands, the last winning acclaim for fighting for the Papacy in Italy. In June the *Irish-American* called for a "Division of Irish Americans," which it hoped would spur their countrymen to immortal deeds. The idea of an all-Irish army within the army, commanded by Irish officers and protected by the Catholic religion, had a strong appeal. Before the end of 1861 more than 3,000 volunteers had been organized into three regiments, which formed the heart of the brigade: the regenerated Sixty-ninth Regiment and the Sixty-third and Eighty-eighth Regiments. The months of preparation did much to energize the whole Irish community. Recruiting booths sprung up in every Irish area of the city, and community leaders formed the Irish Brigade Committee to provide support for the volunteers and their families.

Of special symbolic importance was the ceremonial bestowing of identifying flags on each of the regiments, an honor accorded to women. Mrs. Meagher presented the Eighty-eighth Regiment with its colors, making it, as it was sometimes termed, "Mrs. Meagher's

Own." The Sixty-third Regiment received a green banner with the motto "Wounded but not conquered," and the Sixty-ninth had a green flag with an Irish harp at its center. Every banner was an emblem of Irish bravery and Irish life. When the commander of the Sixty-third Regiment accepted his regiment's flag, he announced to his men, "To you I confide this flag. You must cherish it and protect it, and let no traitor's hand pollute its sacred field." For many of the Irish these banners were to be thrust forward in battle and to be protected to the death. When one unfortunate member of the Sixty-ninth abandoned the regimental flag at Bull Run, Daly (who had presented the flag to the regiment a few months before) reported with some relish that he did not dare show his face in the city, and some of his former comrades declared that "he shall be shot if he does."[9]

Later, Father William Corby, a chaplain in the Irish Brigade, described the regiments as "a body of about 4,000 Catholics marching—most of them—to death but also to the glory of their Church and country." In fact, the reckless devotion among the men of the Irish Brigade resulted in heavy casualties. To belong to such an all-Irish unit increased the dangers of military life because, as a writer in the *Irish-American* pointed out, the soldier was doubly driven by concern for reputation "for if he fought as an American citizen, he also fought as an Irish exile." The cost was great. In less than a year after it had marched triumphantly from the city in December 1861, the Irish Brigade had lost so many men in a series of bloody campaigns that one observer declared that it "no longer exists." The three New York regiments of the Irish Brigade were among the sixty-three regiments that were estimated to have lost more than 50 percent of their men, killed or wounded, in a single battle during the war.[10]

The Irish Brigade was able to recover enough to survive until the war's end but as little more than a shadow of its original self. In the summer of 1862, General Meagher appealed for 1,000 men to bring his force up to full strength, but he got less than 250. Part of the problem was that he had to compete for recruits with another major Irish unit, the Corcoran Legion. In August 1862, Corcoran had been released from a Confederate prison to a hero's welcome. Like Meagher, he proved to be a successful recruiter for his command. The *Times* paired him with Archbishop Hughes under the head "the Priest and the Soldier," expressing the hope that Hughes would use his influence to get local priests to devote themselves to supporting the war and predicting that Corcoran would excite the military ardor of his countrymen. Within a few months, Corcoran was able to raise five regiments, many of the men coming from outside the metropolis, and in October his legion had a "grand review." Archbishop Hughes, whose nephew, Tracy Hughes, was on Corcoran's staff, appeared with ten priests to bless the men. "It was," said the *Irish-American*, "a most impressive sight to see over four thousand men kneeling in reverence, under the bright sky."[11]

By 1863 the Corcoran Legion was in the field, but it did little to raise the spirits of the Irish community at home. For months the regiments saw little or no action, and idleness seemed to intensify the habit of drinking among the men, including their officers. The commander of one of the regiments tried to cut off the supply of whiskey to his officers, warning that if that were not done, "I assure you that before four weeks expire there will not be a line officer fit for duty in the Regt."[12] Further demoralization soon followed when in late December 1863, Corcoran died, not from a battlefield injury but from the aftereffects of a fall from a horse. Soon after, the Corcoran Legion was thrown into the bloody conflicts in Virginia under Ulysses Grant and was decimated along with the remnants of the Irish Brigade.

The other chieftain, Meagher, survived but with a much diminished reputation in the community and in the army. He was essentially stripped of any meaningful command in the last years of the war, his Irish Brigade having virtually disappeared. Times for the New York Irish community were not good. As battlefield casualties mounted, requiems and burials in Calvary Cemetery replaced flag presentations and parades. In late 1863, William Smith O'Brien said that he could not "calculate at less than two hundred thousand the number of Irishmen who have already fallen in this horrible warfare."[13] The number was much inflated, but the sentiment behind it was not. It was notable that on January 2, 1864, when the much shrunken Irish Brigade returned to New York, it was welcomed by only a few hundred relatives and friends rather than the thousands of cheering citizens who had sent it off two years before. On the next day, January 3, Archbishop Hughes died, depriving the community of its priestly chieftain.

Not all went badly. In March 1863, on St. Patrick's Day, the Irish found new confidence that the larger world was accepting them when a gunboat, named the *Shamrock* in their honor, was launched into the East River. The same year saw the emergence of a new voice for the Irish community, not a chieftain but a common soldier. This was Private Miles O'Reilly, the literary creation of Charles Halpine, a New York newspaperman who served as a ninety-day volunteer in the original Sixty-ninth Regiment. Halpine published his *Life and Adventures, Songs, Services, and Speeches of Private Miles O'Reilly* in November 1863, raising much popular interest in his fictional creation, an ordinary Irishman with a keen sense of satiric humor and practical intelligence. The public was captivated by O'Reilly's "Song of the Soldiers," which ends with a patriotic stanza:

> By the baptism of the banner,
> Brothers of one church are we!
> Creed nor faction can divide us,
> Race nor language can divide us,
> Still, whatever fate betide us,
> Children of the flag are we.

To underscore his point, Halpine has O'Reilly repeat the words of another man: "I hear people saying that this general is shtrong wid the germans, and that some other general is shtrong with the Irish; but I tell you that there's nayther Irish nor Germans amongst the men who have been atin', marchin', shleeepin' an' fightin' side by side since the summer that was two years ago."[14]

Halpine's work was a much needed reminder for many that the war had bound many New Yorkers and others together in a common cause. In some respects the war served as a great mixing bowl, reducing the sense of difference among ethnic groups and opening the way for their acceptance in society as defenders of the American union, yet the gains were only partial, a poor repayment in Irish eyes for their sacrifices. The last years of the war brought complaints from Irish soldiers that they were being discriminated against, that they were being thrown into battle without regard for their lives. More than a few would agree with the *Weekly Day-Book*, an antiwar paper, when it asked why the Irish community should honor General Meagher when he had "been the means of bringing some thousands of Irishmen to bloody graves." Indeed, the graves were many. In April 1864, Halpine broke from his humorous commentary to take note of the third anniversary of the Sixty-ninth Regiment's participation in the war, observing that in the beginning there had "twinkled a thousand bayonets," but then:

Of the thousand stalwart bayonets
Two hundred march today
Hundreds lie in Virginia swamps
And hundreds in Maryland clay.[15]

To make the situation worse, Irish hostility to a war of emancipation deprived them of much public regard for their sacrifices, especially when it was associated with their part in the Draft Riots. Although Irishmen such as Meagher and Halpine were obvious supporters of the war, their community at large was just as clearly hostile to emancipation, abolitionists, blacks, and President Lincoln. In July 1864, George Templeton Strong gave his opinion that the proportion of men with Irish names in the casualty lists was "extremely small," betraying a common tendency among his class to minimize the Irish contribution. Perhaps the most disdainful dismissal of Irish contributions came from one of the heroes of the war effort, Reverend Henry W. Bellows, who in December 1865 declared in a sermon on the war that "we owed little to the Irish regiments and commanders, and nothing to pontifical good will." [16]

Undoubtedly, however, the service contributed by the Irish in the great war to preserve a nation did strengthen their claims on American society, just as it did for other ethnic groups who fought for the Union cause. Even the disdain and discrimination that continued to confront them did less to drive them into isolation than to intensify their search for a place in America. And they found it, if not in military heroism, then in politics. In the last years of the war, they may have been, in the eyes of such men as Bellows, a disreputable minority but they were also becoming the majority force within the local Democratic Party. That party, too, suffered from an unpatriotic reputation because of the activities of its peace wing, but with war's end, it was to rapidly rebuild its power and reputation to become a force once more in national politics—and the Irish would rise with it.

NOTES

1. Daniel Curry, *New York: Historical Sketch of the Rise and Progress of the Metropolitan City of America* (New York: Carlton & Phillips, 1853), 200.
2. *Tribune,* May 6 and 7, 1861, and October 27, 1863.
3. *Times,* May 17 and 18, 1864.

4. Francis Lieber to C. P. Daly, May 22, 1861, and John Bendix to Daly, August 3, 1861, C. P. Daly Papers, New York Public Library.

5. Curry, *New York,* 321.

6. John R. C. Hassard, *Life of the Most Reverend John Hughes* (New York, 1866), 437. *Times,* September 25 and 26, 1862.

7. *Times,* November 19, 1861. Hassard, *Hughes,* 482. Quoted in D. P. Conyngham, *The Irish Brigade and Its Campaigns* (New York: W. McSorley & Co., 1861), 188.

8. Quoted in Edward K. Spann, "Union Green: The Irish-American Community and the Civil War," in *The New York Irish,* ed. Ronald H. Bayor and Timothy Meagher (Baltimore: Johns Hopkins University Press, 1996), 198.

9. Spann, "Union Green," 198–99.

10. W. Corby, *Memoirs of a Chaplain's Life* (Notre Dame, Indiana: Scholastic Press, 1894), 31. John F. Maguire, *The Irish in America* (New York: D. & J. Sadlier, 1868), 552. Spann, "Union Green," 201.

11. *Times,* August 19, 1862. Spann, "Union Green," 200.

12. James P. McIvor to Captain Grey, December 9, 1863, McIvor Papers, New-York Historical Society.

13. *Freeman's Journal,* November 28, 1863.

14. Charles Graham Halpine, *The Life and Adventures, Songs, Services, and Speeches of Private Miles O'Reilly* (New York: Carleton, 1864), 177–78.

15. *Weekly Day-Book,* March 25, 1865. Halpine manuscripts, New-York Historical Society.

16. George Templeton Strong, *Diary* (4 vols.), ed. Allen Nevins (New York: Octagon Books, 1974), v. 3, 458. *Tribune,* December 8, 1863.

CHAPTER TEN

THE RACE ANGLE

THE ETHNIC DIMENSION of the metropolis was a powerful influence, a unifier and a divider, but ethnicity was far less powerful than race as a determinant of the thoughts and behaviors, the lives and destinies of most New Yorkers. Although a small number of Asians lived in the city, race in 1860 meant the invisible but nearly solid wall that separated white and black Americans. Whatever the name used at the time, whether it was "colored" or "Negro," a comparative darkness of skin or even some identification with that color (because a few "colored" Americans had white skins), race determined the New Yorker's place in society. In what was essentially a caste system, race was destiny. During the war years the system would change radically in some respects, opening the way to a better future for all, but it would survive.

In 1860 the 12,574 blacks in New York City formed only a few tiny islands in a great white sea of over 800,000 people. Their small percentage (1.6 percent) had actually fallen from the 2.7 percent of ten years before, the result not only of the large growth of the white population but an actual decline in the number of black people from 13,815 in 1850. Early in 1861, even before the full census figures were reported, the notably racist *Herald* considered this decline in an article titled "The Negro in the Metropolis." It noted that out of 10,000 black New Yorkers, only 85 held any real estate and less than 80 were skilled workers. To support its claim that indiscriminate and "illegal" sexual intercourse was common, the *Herald* mentioned that nearly 30 percent of Gotham's blacks were of mixed blood. The newspaper made no secret of its belief that black people were inferior to whites, contending that they were made to be slaves and that "negroes in the much heralded condition of freemen are descending in the scale of civilization."[1]

Stripped of the *Herald*'s racism, such statistics suggested a different picture, that of a race subjected to systematic discrimination that had limited its potential. Black people had been freed from slavery in New York in the 1820s, only to face a rising tide of white racism, which was soon compounded by the arrival of a growing number of Irish immigrants who, in their desperate search for opportunity, helped force blacks out of manual labor and skilled jobs. In 1855 only 5 of the city's 3,512 coopers and 12 of its 7,531 carpenters were black. As a general rule, African Americans got the leftovers, a significant number finding jobs as waiters or domestics in the "first-class" houses of prostitution and gambling in the city. Such places provided probably the maximum of integration of the races, or, as a hostile white press saw it, of racial amalgamation. In one notorious disorderly house in the Fourth Ward the police found "negro men occupying the same room with white women and vice versa."[2] In this case, gender prevailed over race; the men were released, and the women were sent to prison on Blackwell's Island as vagrants.

In housing, discrimination again prevailed, forcing even the most respectable blacks into mini-ghettos. In 1862 a tenant, angry at his landlord, tried to sublet his place to a "parcel of niggers," but he was blocked by a court ruling that the area involved was meant for white people: "The social law of the community which assigned the colored population of the community only to a particular part thereof is founded in natural law."[3] As a result, some African Americans lived in small rundown communities on the fringes of the metropolis, but more occupied a few crowded tenements mostly located in the downtown wards of New York City. In the Fourteenth Ward, for instance, a census taker in 1860 found forty-three black families crowded together in one tenement house. The tenants were something of a microcosm of the African American community: thirty-eight domestics, six laborers, eight porters, five tailors, one minister, and one teacher.

The destruction resulting from the Draft Riots made the housing situation even worse. In 1865 one sanitary committee discovered that blacks formed three-quarters of the population on Jersey Street, "a filthy, densely packed, decaying, small-pox ridden narrow lane running from Crosby to Mulberry Street only a block from Broadway." Little wonder that the black death rate was nearly three times that of native whites and even considerably higher than that of foreign-born residents. In the 1850s a health official noted the persistent preponderance of reported deaths over births among blacks and asked whether the statistics were "not an indication of a gradual but certain extinction of this class of our population."[4]

In politics only a few black men could vote because they were subject to a special property requirement. When in 1860 an attempt was made to end this discriminatory requirement in the state constitution, the effort went down to overwhelming defeat, with less than 4 percent of voters in the city supporting it. In public transit, blacks had seemingly won the right to travel on the street railways by the mid-1850s, but in practice they were often expected to ride in the few "Jim Crow" cars set aside for them: In 1860, when Charles Sanders, "a young colored man," insisted on trying to board a whites-only car of the Sixth Avenue line, he was arrested on charges of assault and battery for resisting the conductor's efforts to eject him. Prejudice was not all pervasive. It had not reached many Germans, who had yet to learn the etiquette of the American caste system, and even the Irish often related to their black neighbors as fellow human beings. On the whole, though, discrimination was a persistent reality for every African American regardless of social class or moral worth.

Many whites wondered why a people so abused would remain where they were, especially if their place was in such a deeply racist city as New York. In 1851 a committee of African Americans meeting in New York reported an answer. Hoping to encourage the migration of black people to rural locations where they could establish communities of their own, the committee stressed the negatives of city life, but it also had to admit that it was easier in cities for people to organize themselves, to find some opportunities for education, and to foster the development of leaders and a professional class willing to serve them. In New York, black community life was somewhat organized, especially in the form of the black churches but also through a score of Masonic lodges. There seems to have been some system of mutual support, because few African Americans applied for public charity. "Those who know the colored people of this city," said the *Observer* in 1863, "can testify to their being a peaceful, industrious people, having their own churches, Sunday schools and charitable societies; and that as a class they seldom depend on charity." Other observers made basically the same point.[5]

The African American community was no match for Klein-deutschland in its resources or successes, but some of its members did climb at least a few rungs on the tall ladder of opportunity. Even the *Herald* could count eight physicians, fourteen clergymen, and seventeen teachers in its supposedly benighted population, and this did not include at least a few black businessmen, such as the restaurateur Thomas Downing, who by 1860 had long been famous for his oyster house at Broad and Wall streets in lower New York. Downing and several clergymen, for example, Henry Highland Garnet, pastor of the Shiloh Presbyterian Church, were determined opponents of both slavery and discrimination, as was James McCune Smith, a black physician (whose medical degree was bestowed by the University of Glasgow), pharmacist, and scholar with numerous publications. In 1859, Smith was listed as having $7,700 in property and Downing had $6,800 in property. That was far less than the property of such white entrepreneurs as George Opdyke ($101,000) or even Fernando Wood ($25,000), but at least it was in the same league with such notable whites as Horace Greeley ($7,300).

Much of African American community life focused on the black churches, which both provided a refuge from a troublesome world and initiated most of the feeble resistance to white racism. In the mid-1850s, Elizabeth Jennings, a black teacher and church organist, successfully sued a streetcar company after being ejected from a whites-only streetcar. Chester A. Arthur, later the state quartermaster, was the lawyer who won her case. Soon after, Reverend James W. C. Pennington, a Congregational minister, urged all black people to oppose segregation in any form, getting himself arrested—and then released—for boarding a whites-only car. Such efforts, however, had only a marginal effect because the black community could mobilize only a puny force against entrenched racism, even with the support of sympathetic whites. In September 1860, Greeley asked, "Can anyone doubt that Jesus of Nazareth, if now on earth and in New York, would reject more indignantly and rebuke more sharply our negro-cars [and] negro pews in churches that evoke his name?"[6] Unfortunately, it was difficult to find more than a few traces of Jesus in New York City.

The cause of equal justice had to wait for the time when the Civil War mobilized white hostility to slavery and then to discrimination. The first reaction to the war revealed one of New York's most shameful secrets: the involvement of some of its merchants and officials in the international slave trade. Although the trade had long been illegal, Democrat-appointed Federal officials in the port had winked at the sailing of ships intended chiefly to carry slaves from Africa to Cuba—as many as two ships a weeks, so it was charged in 1860. In March 1861 the *Times* declared that under U.S. Marshal Isaiah Rynders "the Slave-trade has established itself among us as a secure and influential business interest." In the fall of 1861, however, Federal officials began to investigate the matter, and by the end of 1862 the U.S. district attorney for New York (a Republican appointee) claimed that, with the aid of one execution and two convictions, authorities "have broken up the slave-trade at the port of New York."[7]

The trend toward freedom encountered strong resistance, but times were changing under the pressure of the war. In February 1862 the great black leader Frederick Douglass called for emancipation before a large, mostly white audience at Cooper Union in New York, adding an attack on the then Union policy of excluding black men from the military. Although the Lincoln administration was slow to respond, demands that it act against slavery intensified in Gotham and elsewhere. June 1862 brought the formation of the Emancipation League, headed by William Cullen Bryant, whose *Evening Post* had become a strong voice for change. Soon after, a mass meeting at Cooper Union adopted a resolution declaring that the war was "making it impossible to stem the avalanche of emancipation which was sweeping down from the Potomac and Ohio to the Gulf."[8] Lincoln still hesitated in the months that followed, but the stubbornness of the Confederacy in continuing the war left him no choice but to declare emancipation on January 1, 1863. Along with the new commitment to freedom came a decision to recruit black men for the Union military.

The African American community responded to these developments with growing confidence in the future. On September 30, 1862, a large gathering at Reverend Garnet's Shiloh Church on Prince Street was described as being a little impatient with Lincoln's reluctance to commit to emancipation but overall as being grateful and hopeful. Blacks throughout the metropolis joined with white abolitionists at the opening of 1863 to celebrate the "Jubilee of Freedom," packing the large hall of Cooper Union to overflowing. A month later, African American leaders in New York and Brooklyn met to form the American Freedman's Friend Society to provide assistance to free slaves.

Slavery was doomed, but it was evident that white racism in the metropolis remained strong. Although three of the city's most influential newspapers, the *Tribune,* the *Times,* and the *Evening Post,* had come to support the cause of freedom, the popular *Herald* and the Democratic Party press had not. A war for the restoration of the Union, yes; a war to free the slaves, NO! Opposition continued to be strong among the city's Irish population, the result of an amalgam of ethnic, political, and religious considerations. Much of the opposition resulted from the intense hostility of the Catholic Irish to New England "puritans" and "fanatics," whom the Irish believed were willing to foster black freedom at their expense. Hostility to abolitionism was often a test of group loyalty. In 1863, for instance, the Catholic intellectual Orestes Brownson complained that "the Catholic who does not throw his influence on the side of the proslavery party is read out of the pale of Catholic society, especially in the city of New York, where there are more Catholics than in all the seceded states put together."[9]

Hostility to emancipation intensified hostility to free black people. For many whites the black man in slavery was an acceptable being because, as the *Herald* put it, "the condition assigned to him by God is one of servitude," but in freedom, he was a menace. In 1863 the *Irish-American* used the title "Negrophilism and Its Results" to describe an incident in Newburgh where a black man allegedly raped "a young Irish girl" and was lynched by an angry mob. Many believed that abolitionists were encouraging blacks to be insolent in their attitude toward whites, a belief encouraged by a story in the *Herald* that blacks were "known frequently to push white women off the sidewalks and to insult them."[10]

Much racial anger was focused on the workplace, where blacks and whites, especially the Irish, competed for jobs. When it was rumored in the summer of 1862 that men were being fired at the Brooklyn Navy Yard to make way for freed slaves, the commandant of the yard assured whites that "there is not a colored person employed in the Navy-yard, nor has there been since the day I assumed the command, or before." Many whites resented the employment of blacks in jobs that they wanted. In Brooklyn in early August 1862 a mob of men "calling themselves Irishmen" attacked two Lorillard tobacco factories that employed a dozen black men and women, shouting

"Kill the damn naygurs" and "Turn out the negers." Although the workers escaped and the riot was soon suppressed by the police, the riot evoked considerable comment.[11]

The *Herald* used the riot as an occasion again to incite racist feelings, alleging that there was a plot by some abolition-minded "capitalists" to replace white workers with black workers: "The agitators who puff Sambo up with absurd ideas of his importance are to blame." From the other side came a defense of black people combined with new attacks on Irish "ruffians" and opponents of the war as the culprits. A week after the riot, Reverend Garnet made it the subject of a sermon at his Shiloh Church, charging that friends of the Confederacy were fomenting race hatreds to divide the people of the Union. After asking, "Why, in this Christian land, did white people openly hate the negro?" Garnet declared that his people were as industrious and respectful as whites, and he appealed to the what was generally called the better sort of white people to defend them.[12]

Neither Garnet nor the growing number of supportive whites had much effect on reducing racial tensions, and in July 1863 the race volcano exploded with the Draft Riots. Much of the anger was directed against public authorities and the draft, but black people became the prime victims of white rage. At least three were lynched, others were beaten, and their homes were demolished. Refugees crowded into the Central Police Station or fled from Manhattan Island. The loss of property and jobs forced thousands of men and women to depend on some kind of assistance. When a relief station was opened on July 23, an estimated 3,000 people, some of whom were desperately hungry, crowded the street. Although desperate need soon disappeared from public view, blacks often found that their employers were reluctant to rehire them out of fear of further provoking the Irish. One measure of the disruption was the decline of school attendance among black children in 1863 and 1864, leading the superintendent of schools in 1865 to observe that, as a result, educational performance in the city's segregated schools "has very considerably deteriorated."[13]

It was a terrible time, but 1863 also began a significant advance for African Americans. If the riots deprived the Irish of part of their claim to service in the war, they also activated direct white efforts to provide aid and assistance to riot victims. When collections were taken at several churches, the anti-abolitionist *Journal of Commerce* declared that "this poor, dependent race demand the sympathy and fostering care of the white man," but the reaction went beyond a supercilious paternalism. A committee of merchants was soon promising not only relief but also "all the influence we possess to protect the colored people of this city in their right to pursue unmolested their lawful occupations." In August the *Tribune* observed that "our City papers contain an unusual number of applications for colored help," mostly in traditional jobs such as cooks, waiters, and housekeepers and generally at the expense of the Irish. To ensure that their help could get to work, leading citizens protested against racial discrimination on the city's transportation system, sometimes boycotting street railroads that practiced it.[14]

The backlash against racism helped bring about what was probably the greatest single attainment of black men during the war: the right to fight and die for the Union cause. The opportunity to enlist in the military had been demanded by African American leaders since the beginning of the war, but the idea had been resisted by public authorities, who wished to keep the conflict a white man's war for white purposes. In 1861, when a group of black men tried to organize for military drills in their own rented hall, the chief of police warned them that he "could not protect them from popular indignation and assaults."[15] For most New Yorkers the right to carry a gun was to be limited to whites.

Under its new emancipation policies in early 1863 the Lincoln administration dropped its own policy of exclusion and began to recruit free blacks and former slaves for the Union army, but the new policy received a mixed reception in New York. In May 1863 a group of New York Unionists, including Bryant, William E. Dodge, and Henry W. Bellows, formed the Committee for Colored Volunteers. Soon, the committee appealed to Democratic governor Horatio Seymour to support the recruitment of black soldiers, warning that if New York State did not act soon, it would lose its volunteers to other states, making it more difficult for New York to meet its draft quota. Even the appeal to self-interest, however, had no effect. After two months of silence, Seymour announced that he would not authorize a black unit, leading the *Evening Post,* of which Bryant was editor, to protest that the governor's inaction had cost New York State at least one regiment of black soldiers who enlisted elsewhere.

By this time, however, the reaction against the Draft Riots had intensified support for the idea, and the Committee for Colored Volunteers was able to convene a mass meeting and demand action. Again, Seymour was slow to respond, but soon the committee had the support of the Union League Club, which raised what was described as a large sum for the purpose of forming a black regiment. Supported by the wealth and influence of the club, proponents pressured the War Department into granting the authority to raise what became the Twentieth United States Colored Regiment. Only when it became evident that the regiment might be needed to fill the state's draft quota did it receive the governor's reluctant acceptance.

Much attention was given to creating the regiment. In December 1863 newspapers published an advertisement describing a statewide effort to recruit black men for it, offering $10 a month in pay and support for their families when needed. Recruiting agents fanned out through the state and before the end of the month enlisted 700 men, most of whom were sent to New York's Rikers Island for training. Not everything went smoothly, especially when bounty brokers and their tactics entered the picture. When Reverend Garnet visited the regiment's camp, he found at least fifty men who complained that they had been "swindled" into the ranks by the brokers, some being told that they would merely have "to take charge of a horse." [16] A later investigation of 263 members of the regiment revealed that they had received an average of only $80 in bounty money while the brokers appropriated $220.

On March 5, 1864, however, the Twentieth marched into history, parading from the Rikers Island ferry landing on East 26th Street to the Union League clubhouse in Union Square, where it was welcomed by the president of Columbia College "as fellow countrymen, fellow soldiers." After some speeches the regiment proceeded down Broadway to the Hudson River, where it boarded a ship bound for New Orleans. It carried with it a regimental flag presented to it by a long list of upper-class women headed by Mrs. John Jacob Astor. Union League member George Templeton Strong wrote in his diary that this was one of two memorable military marches in New York since the beginning of the war, the other being the gaudy parade of the Seventh Regiment on its way to defend Washington in April 1861. The crowds were smaller and less enthusiastic in 1864, but Strong concluded that "yesterday morning's phenomenon— Ethiopia marching down Broadway, armed, drilled, truculent, and

March 5, 1864, was a day of rejoicing for Gotham's African American community when the Twentieth United States Colored Regiment gathered before the Union League clubhouse to be applauded by some of the city's best citizens. This unit was New York's first black regiment, a sign of a major change in the direction of the war that did not please most ordinary New Yorkers. From *Frank Leslie's Scenes and Portraits of the Civil War* (New York: Mrs. Frank Leslie, 1894), 398.

elate—was the weightier and more memorable of the two." Greeley's *Tribune* also saw progress: "One thousand men with black skins, whose color has been a crime in the eyes of multitudes of whites, now marched freely along streets and avenues past cheering crowds."[17] By mid-July the regiment was in Louisiana.

The Twentieth United States Colored Regiment was soon followed by the formation of the Twenty-sixth Colored Regiment, under the auspices of the Union League Club but recruited primarily from upstate. Before the end of the war both regiments served in battle with heavy casualties. Seemingly, black Americans were winning the acceptance of whites with their patriotism and blood. Maria Daly, whose husband had condemned even the thought of black troops two years before, wrote in her diary that, while she was "very little Negrophilish," she was deeply moved not only by the troops themselves but by the reaction of spectators: "Many old, respectable darkies stand at the street corners, men and women with tears in their eyes as if they saw . . . the beginning of a better state of affairs for them."[18] Undoubtedly, the appearance of black soldiers on city streets did much to hearten the African American community and to raise its hopes for the eventual end of racism.

In some respects, black New Yorkers had reason to be hopeful, because military service did increase public support for equal rights, although, as usual, nothing moved on a straight line. In April 1864, Ellen Anderson, the widow of a sergeant in the Twentieth Colored Regiment, was dragged off a streetcar by a policemen when she refused the conductor's order not to board it. In this instance the policeman was tried for assault before a police board (a white man testified against him), and the railroad company announced that "hereafter colored people are allowed to ride on all cars." When the Confederacy threatened to execute black soldiers who fell into its hands, the conservative *Observer* joined with Republican newspapers in condemning the threat, declaring that Negro soldiers "are entitled to the same rights which the laws of war accord to white or red or yellow men." By 1865 the *Observer* was prepared to advocate the right to vote for black men.[19]

On August 2, 1865, African Americans from throughout the metropolis gathered en masse in Brooklyn to celebrate what had been for decades their freedom day, the anniversary of emancipation in the British West Indies, an act that had helped to initiate the abolitionist movement in the United States. Many listened to William Howard Day of Brooklyn describe his dream for the future:

> I see this Government made one by black and white hands, yielding up a portion of Government control. I see the schools thrown open for the black child as for the white. I see black and white priests ministering together at the altars of religion. I see black men elected to petty and then to higher offices in the State. I see preferment open to the black man, even to the Presidential chair. I see everywhere respect for brain and worth moral and material.[20]

Although the war and military service did bring progress toward a just biracial society, that progress faced a powerful undertow of the old white racism. Even the decision to enlist black soldiers had its racist side, because a strong consideration was that blacks would replace whites in the draft, a consideration that led the *Tribune* to observe that thousands of whites in the metropolis were racists but "will not be so far led away by their pride of blood as to hesitate for one moment to send a colored substitute to the army." Charles G. Halpine, in his "Sambo's Right to Be Kilt," has his spokesman, Private Miles O'Reilly, say that he would not object if "Sambo's body" stopped a bullet directed at him.[21]

It was telling that, when the Twenty-sixth Colored Regiment marched through the city, it marched without the two leading military bands of the city, Dodsworth's and the Seventh Regiment band, both of which refused to be hired for the occasion. Even at war's end there were acts of petty and not so petty harassment. In April 1865 the Common Council barred blacks from marching in Lincoln's funeral procession, only to be overruled by the Metropolitan Police, who provided protection for a black delegation—at the rear of the procession.

Most of the problem could be traced to the still deeply entrenched racism of the local Democratic Party, which seemed to intensify as blacks won the support of the Republican minority in the city. In significant part, the party was falling under increasing Irish influence, and Irishmen continued to be the most antiblack group in the city. In an article on "The War of the Races," the *Times* observed that "a negro is an object which every loyal Irishman desires to kick." The Democratic Party's racism, however, derived not just from the Irish. Benjamin Wood's *Daily News* kept up a stubborn defense of the old order, denying that the principle "All men are created equal" applied to anyone but white men and applauding when a Miss Emma Webb declared at a Democratic Party rally in Brooklyn—in March 1864—that "the negro can only be a happy and useful being when he is subservient to the white race."[22]

Not all Democrats were racists, but the party itself was committed to maintaining as much of the old racial order as possible. In 1864, Fernando Wood, who had been elected one of Gotham's congressmen, attacked the proposed Thirteenth Amendment, which abolished slavery, as a revolutionary act that he could not support. The next year, he voted against the amendment in Congress, being joined in his opposition by the other five Democratic congressmen elected from the metropolis. In the state legislature every Democratic representative from the area voted against ratification of the amendment. In the future the heavily Democratic metropolis would also oppose the Fourteenth and Fifteenth Amendments, which established a constitutional basis for African American rights. The metropolis was still a white man's world devoted to keeping black Americans in "their place." William Howard Day's dream of equality and justice was to be denied and largely forgotten, until it would be reawakened a century later in a new time of rising hope.

NOTES

1. *Herald*, February 2, 1861.
2. *Times*, March 22, 1861.
3. *Times*, March 23, 1862.
4. Citizens Association, *Report of the Council of Hygiene and Public Health on the Sanitary Conditions of the City* (reprint) (New York: Arno Press, 1970), 89. City Inspector, *Report* (New York, 1853), 197.
5. *Observer*, March 3, 1863.
6. *Tribune*, September 21, 1860.
7. *Times*, March 18, 1861, and September 13, 1861. *Herald*, December 2, 1861.
8. *Tribune*, June 17, 1862. *Times*, June 18, 1862.
9. *Brownson's Quarterly Review*, 4:369 (1863).
10. *Herald*, August 7 and 17, 1862. *Irish-American*, July 4, 1863.
11. *Times*, August 5, 1862. *Tribune*, August 6, 1862.
12. *Herald*, August 7, 1862. *Times*, August 13, 1862.
13. New York City Superintendent of Schools, *Annual Report* (New York, 1865), 9.
14. *Journal of Commerce*, July 24, 1863. *Tribune*, August 8 and 11, 1863.
15. Quoted in William Seraile, "The Struggle to Raise Black Regiments

in New York State, 1861–64," *New-York Historical Society Quarterly,* 58:216 (1974).

16. *Tribune,* February 9, 1864.

17. Will Irwin et al., *A History of the Union League Club of New York* (New York: Dodd, Mead, 1952), 25. George Templeton Strong, *Diary* (4 vols.), ed. Allen Nevins (New York: Octagon Books, 1974), v. 3, 411–12. *Tribune,* March 7, 1864.

18. *Tribune,* November 5, 1865. Maria Daly, *Diary of a Union Lady,* ed. Harold E. Hammond (New York, 1962), 278.

19. *Observer,* March 3, 1864. *Tribune,* June 30, 1864.

20. *Tribune,* August 2, 1865.

21. *Tribune,* April 25 and 27, 1865. Charles G. Halpine, *The Life and Adventures, Songs, Services, and Speeches of Private Miles O'Reilly* (New York, 1864), 55.

22. *Times,* November 28, 1866. *Daily News,* March 5 and 14, 1864.

Chapter Eleven

Rebuilding Prosperity

In November 1863, Walt Whitman returned to his New York after a long stint in the military hospitals of Washington and observed a vibrant scene pleasing to his eyes:

> Every where carts & trucks & carriages & vehicles on the go, loaded with goods, express wagons, omnibuses, cars, etc.—thousands of ships along the wharves & the piers piled high, where they are loading cargoes—all the stores crammed with every thing you can think of, & the markets with all sorts of provisions—tens of thousands of people every where (the population is 1,500,000) almost every body well-drest & appearing to have enough—then the splendid river and harbor here, full of ships, steamers, sloops, etc.—then the great street, Broadway, for four miles, one continuous jam, of people & the great, magnificent stores.[1]

The thriving city was far different from the fate that a boastful South had predicted earlier, that Gotham's trade would stagnate and that grass would grow in its streets with the withdrawal of the patronage of King Cotton.

It was also different from the fretful city of two years before. In 1861 the metropolis had been especially hard hit by the breakdown of the Union. Heavily dependent on the South as a market for its goods and on the South's cotton for its export trade, New York experienced a depression that heavily damaged its dry goods, leather, and hardware businesses. The evaporation of Southern patronage led to widespread slashing of prices as merchants tried to get rid of their overstocks. "We hear everyday about 'war' prices," said the *Tribune* in July. "Dry goods at marvelous sacrifices. Clothing at next to no price. Beef, pork and mutton at almost nothing. Everything that you have to sell going for next to nothing."[2] The St. Nicholas

Hotel, a favorite of Southern travelers, slashed its rates in the hope of attracting a new clientele.

The loss of the Southern market was bad enough, but there was something even worse. Northern merchants had been eager to sell to Southerners on liberal credit terms. Now, with secession, these customers reneged on their debts, about $160 million owed to New Yorkers alone. Merchants, said the *Tribune*, had been "outrageously swindled and a good part of them stripped of large fortunes."[3] Despite hopes that the Union army somehow might become a collection agent, most of that money was lost in the whirlwind of war. In the first six months of 1861 nearly 100 of New York's 660 dry goods firms went under. In 1861 the great firm of Claffin, Mellon & Company, which had done a multimillion dollar business in dry goods, failed, chiefly because of its uncollected Southern debts.

There were other wounds, small and large. War deprived the city of access to Southern supplies of wood, including Virginia pine, which people favored as kindling to light their anthracite coal fires. More generally, Gotham was hit by the sudden cessation of the coastal trade with the Confederacy, which involved not only wood but also naval stores and dozens of other products. In November 1861 the number of coastal ships arriving at Brooklyn's wharves was estimated to be only about half of what it had been the year before. By the fall an even more ominous problem was developing in New York shipping: the sharp decline of American-owned ships used in foreign trade, the result chiefly of the rapid increase in insurance rates charged on vessels sailing under the American flag. The outbreak of war and the partly realized fear of Confederate privateer attacks on Union ships brought a mass transfer of ship ownership from American to foreign, especially British, hands. *Hunt's Merchants Magazine* noted with "a painful sense of humiliation" that, although the proportion of American trade carried in American ships versus foreign ships had been more than 2 to 1 in 1860, it had changed to nearly 3 to 1 in favor of foreign ships by December 1863.

The economic gloom of the first six months of 1861 soon began to dissipate as the metropolis found new sources of goods and profits. By the end of 1861 it was becoming evident that the industrial and agricultural North was far more important to New York's future than the South. The *Railroad Journal* estimated that the entire cotton crop was worth less than 7 percent of the value of Northern industrial production, and industrial values, with the important exception of cotton textiles, rose rapidly with the war. From the beginning military spending had eased the depression, especially in the clothing and shipping industries. This easing was given a great stimulus in August when the national government succeeded in getting the first installment of a $150 million loan from the nation's banks, the larger part from Wall Street. Coming soon after the defeat at Bull Run, this loan assumed a legendary significance, an act of financial heroism that enabled the Union to take the road to eventual victory. From it, said a New York banker in 1862, "an army and navy arose as if by magic. The nation was saved."[4]

War spending particularly benefited the clothing industry, whose profits from the manufacture of military wear largely compensated for the decline of the dry good trade. Although the depression wiped out many of the smaller firms, big clothiers such as Brooks Brothers and Devlin & Company prospered in filling large government orders. In 1864 about half of the 90,000 workers in the clothing industry were employed in fulfilling government contracts. New York's important boot and shoe industry—about 490 firms employing 4,000 workers—benefited from massive government purchases. By early 1864, Colonel D. H. Vinton's New York Clothing and Equipage Depot had more than a half-million boots on hand along with more than a million items of clothing. The mass production of clothes and footwear stimulated ancillary industries, most notably the production of sewing machines. In 1862 the I. M. Singer Company employed 400 men to produce thousands of machines at its "beautiful fire-proof" factory on Mott Street.

Firms specializing in drugs and chemicals also prospered, especially by meeting the rapidly growing army need for pharmaceuticals. Quinine imports increased more than ten times to help protect the army against the diseases of the Southern climate. Reportedly, some of the quinine found its way to the Confederate army through Louisville, likely as part of a larger trade: In November 1862 the trade journal for the chemical industry said that "it is very probable that the rebel army as well as our own is supplied from our market."[5] Whoever was buying, chemical manufacturers, such as Charles Pfizer and Edward R. Squibb, prospered. In 1863, Squibb, who had begun his business five years earlier, outgrew his laboratory and built "a large and elegant building" in Brooklyn to meet the growing demand. Between 1860 and 1870 the chemical industry of New York City and Brooklyn grew from 11 firms employing 114 men to 44 firms employing 869 men, and the value of their chemicals and drugs rose from $560,000 to $4,550,000.

Although Gotham was not an important producer of armaments, some of its entrepreneurs did engage in the profitable but dangerous business of producing cartridges for the army, generally employing female labor. In response to wartime demand, a young chemist by the name of L. M. Dornback began to manufacture guncotton in Williamsburg, only to be killed when a barrel that he was packing with the guncotton exploded. The Badger Iron Works in the city received a government contract to produce shot and shell, including the 15-inch shot used in the largest naval cannons. In addition, there was at least one notable gun maker in the person of the seemingly omnipresent George Opdyke. When he was mayor, Opdyke succeeded in getting a contract to produce 10,000 carbines. To manufacture them, he purchased lathes and other equipment from the city's machine shops. Various problems delayed production, but by mid-1863, Opdyke's factory had produced more than 1,000 carbines—before it was burned down by draft rioters.

Such metal-working operations were dwarfed by New York's mammoth machine-building industry on the East River. In 1860 ten machine-building firms employed nearly 3,000 workers, and by 1863 the number had more than doubled. The businesses produced marine steam engines and boilers along with various metal fittings. The engines were often immense, with cylinders more than 8 feet in diameter and with a force of as much as 6,000 horsepower. The Continental Iron Works in Greenpoint, the builder of the *Monitor,* employed powerful machines in its work, including huge shears that could cut through 1-inch-thick iron plates and power punches, drills, and planers. With the assistance of similar equipment, in February 1863 the Morgan Iron Works completed nine large maritime engines, and a rival, the Neptune Iron Works, was building a dozen more. Other major firms, such as the Fulton and Allaire works, also generated a large demand for men and materials. By April the ironworks and machine shops of New York were employing 7,500 men directly, not counting those in ancillary industries. Overall, the expansion of the East River works was a major cause of New York's prosperity.

Chemicals, clothing, ships, and engines were only some of the many goods produced in what was, by the value of its product, the Union's largest manufacturing city, but manufacturing continued to be overshadowed in the metropolis by commerce. New York's greatest glory in the past had been its overwhelmingly dominance as the nation's importer, making it vulnerable to the secession of the South, its principal market for foreign imports. Soon enough, however, wartime adjustments proved that Gotham was not dependent on the cotton kingdom. Imports of cloth and clothing were particularly hard hit by the loss of the Southern market, falling to less than $44 million in 1861, but other imports increased to meet wartime demands. To meet what *Hunt's Merchants Magazine* termed "the enormous increase in the consumption of wool by the army," for instance, New York's wool imports increased from 31,000 bales in 1861 to nearly 89,000 bales in 1862 and continued to grow, reaching almost 116,000 bales in 1864.[6] Even with these additions, the overall value of imports remained below the level of 1860, but nonetheless the metropolis was able to increase its share of the nation's total foreign trade from 58 percent in 1858 to 64 percent in 1865.

The cause of this apparent paradox was a spectacular increase in New York's export trade. In 1862 the outward flow of American products through the metropolis was the largest ever recorded up to that time, increasing in value by more than 50 percent, from $95,468,000 in 1860 to $149,180,000. Some of these gains resulted from the natural growth of Northern industry. In 1861, *Hunt's Merchants Magazine* noted that New York was exporting a growing number of American-made sewing machines to Europe and to the rest of the world: "The machines made here are cheaper, more handsome and more complete than those of English makers."[7] Much more of the increase, however, resulted from the wartime disruption of the shipment of Midwestern agricultural commodities down the Mississippi River. With the "Father of the Waters" obstructed by Confederate control, this trade flowed to New York at the expense of New Orleans, a close competitor of Gotham in the export trade before the war. By 1862, for instance, the number of swine sold in New York nearly doubled, leading to a great increase in pork packing and bacon making in the city.

The greatest increase came in breadstuffs (wheat, corn, and flour). The diversion of the Mississippi River traffic came in conjunction with two other favorable developments: bumper crops in the West and crop shortages in Great Britain and elsewhere in Europe. In the year ending on September 30, 1862, New York exported 1,883,134 barrels of flour, 21,269,000 bushels of wheat, and 12,636,000 bushels of corn, far ahead of its nearest rival, Philadelphia. New York grain dealers responded to this flood by developing a more efficient way to load produce from canal boats onto ships bound for Europe. This new method included the port's first floating grain elevator, which reportedly could screen, weigh, and transfer 5,000 bushels of wheat per hour. All told, grain dealers built seven elevators in the early war years, a step toward efficiency so great that it provoked a strike of the port's 2,000 grain shovelers, who declared that the elevators did two-thirds of their work and so "must be suppressed."[8] The defenders of the elevators argued that their greater efficiency would bring more trade to the port, creating more jobs, but this weighed little against worker fears that they would lose the fifty cents per hundred bushels that they earned with their grain shovels.

The last years of the war brought a substantial drop in grain exports, in part because of improved harvests in Europe, but by then New York had found at least one new major export, petroleum. Ever since the first successful oil well had been drilled in western Pennsylvania in 1859, petroleum production had increased rapidly, and so had the public demand for oil, especially for the purposes of lighting and lubrication. In 1864 the *Tribune* pronounced petroleum a "new staple" of the economy, so quickly were consumers becoming accustomed to using it.[9] During the war the United States began to export substantial amounts of oil to Europe, beginning the world's petroleum revolution, and most of the exports went through New York. In 1862 the metropolis exported over 6,880,000 gallons of oil, three times the volume from Philadelphia. The next years brought a rapid increase from 19,545,000 gallons in 1863 to 21,326,000 gallons in 1864, by which time special tankers had been devised to carry the oil to England.

The volume of exported oil was not the whole of the petroleum arriving in New York, because the metropolis itself consumed a large amount: In 1863 the city exported 489,000 barrels but another 314,000 barrels was used locally. The sudden presence of a flammable substance soon made itself known, especially when New Yorkers began to refine it into kerosene for domestic consumption. In April 1862 a small "kerosene oil factory" exploded in Brooklyn, killing three men, and a few months later 15,000 barrels of oil and kerosene stored in Williamsburg caught fire and exploded, setting off an inferno that some claimed would have destroyed a good part of that city if the wind had not contained it. Other fires and explosions followed, leading fire insurance companies to demand that the government intervene to control the areas where petroleum could be refined and stored. This in turn brought protests from local businessmen, who claimed that they had invested more than $1 million in the oil business.

The debate evoked what might have been the first scientific testimony on a business issue. In June 1862 a professor from the New York Medical College gave his opinion that petroleum was not as explosive as people thought, if it were handled carefully. In any case, he said, "This petroleum was the most important raw material introduced to the service of men during the last century, and they would have it, though it was as dangerous as gunpowder. But it was not."[10] Eventually, the industry agreed to move out of populated areas, but as late as February 1865, it was estimated that 40,000 barrels of oil were stored below 50th Street.

Petroleum was only part of a changing mix of products that flowed into and out of the metropolis. The growing volume of the overall trade brought substantial profits to those engaged in transportation. The increase of trade from the West especially benefited New York State's great Erie Canal. In late 1862 the *Times* estimated that the total receipts on the state's canal system for grain alone was about $4 million before cold weather limited traffic, making the system "very profitable." The increased traffic led to proposals that the canal be enlarged, in part to facilitate the movement of gunboats and other military traffic.

Long before the end of the war, though, it was evident that the biggest winners were the railroads, especially the two lines competing for the western traffic, the New York and Erie Railroad and the New York Central Railroad. Between 1860 and 1864 the annual tonnage carried on the Erie and the Central lines increased by about 75 percent. The Hudson River Railroad, which connected the Central line with the metropolis, saw a 60 percent increase in its freight tonnage, much of it military hardware from the Cold Springs armory and the important Troy ironworks; part of the armor and machinery for the *Monitor* came from Troy. The New Jersey railroads serving the metropolis from the South also prospered. The New Jersey Railroad benefited especially from its position as a major troop carrier between New York and the Virginia killing fields; it boasted that it could carry 10,000 troops a day. The coal- and iron-carrying New Jersey Central Railroad experienced a growth of net income from $95,000 in 1861 to $774,000 a year later, much of it from supplying Gotham's machine and shipbuilding industries.

So it went. The prosperity of the railroads in turn contributed to the vitality of the New York Stock Market. The market had fallen after the first defeat at Bull Run, but it soon recovered. By August 1863 the *Herald* could declare with its usual brashness that "the advance of stocks since the beginning of the war is the most wonderful fact in the history of finance." The *Herald* estimated that stock prices had increased by an average of 300 percent, citing as an example Erie Railroad stock, which had skyrocketed from 5 to 125 points. Prosperity also encouraged stock market speculation and manipulation, preparing the way for the multimillion dollar misdeeds of the Robber Barons and their allies after the war. Daniel Drew, the notorious speculator who viewed the war only as an opportunity to make money, bribed military men to provide him with advance information on actions that might influence stock prices. Speculators such as Drew contributed to periodic market falls and panics on Wall Street, but overall there was little doubt over the fundamental soundness of the Northern economy and the expected benefits for the metropolis. New York, wrote George Templeton Strong, had become the "grand, commercial money-making center of the universe."[11]

Gotham did not keep its prosperity to itself. In late 1862, when New Yorkers learned that the workers of Lancashire, England, faced starvation as a result of the Civil War's disruption of the cotton textile industry, they were quick to act, in part out of charity but also to persuade the English to support the Union cause. In December numerous merchants, including Opdyke, William E. Dodge, and Robert B. Minturn, formed the International Relief Committee, which in less than two weeks raised close to $120,000 in cash along with a large quantity of goods. In January 1863 the committee sent the ship *George Griswold* to England loaded with 12,800 barrels of flour along with substantial quantities of bread, pork, and beef. Over the next two months, six more shipments were made, helping to activate similar efforts in England itself. The English were not the only ones to benefit from what one Englishmen called a "bright spot in America." At virtually the same time, New Yorkers such as Opdyke and Horace Greeley joined with local Irish leaders to send money and food to Ireland in response to news of an impending famine there.

In other ways the prospering city reached out to a larger world. The war produced significant advances in the telegraph industry. In part to accommodate the ever increasing demand for war news, the Independent Telegraph Company laid a line under the Hudson River in 1863, using a waterproof cable manufactured by the Bishop Gutta Percha Company in the city. It was an accomplishment that eliminated an important gap in Gotham's ability to communicate "by lightening" with the rest of the nation. Soon after, New York businessmen launched a multimillion dollar effort to lay a cable across the Atlantic (the first attempt before the Civil War had failed). The promoters argued that merchants would have almost immediate knowledge of European prices, an advantage that alone would compensate them for the expense of the cable. The new effort, in cooperation with British investors, succeeded in 1866, making New York a vital part of a worldwide telegraph system of more than 250,000 miles.

Perhaps the best index of wartime vitality was a human one. The compilers of *Trow's New York City Directory* boasted that their 1863 directory contained more names than ever before—153,186—indicating that the city's population had grown, even though many New Yorkers were away at war. They attributed the increase to the city's central role in the new economy, in trade, finance, and manufacturing alike. In November 1863 the *Observer* said that Gotham was never so full of people, the result not only of wartime prosperity but also of wartime misery, as there was an "influx of population from the South" of people seeking refuge from the war. Much of this growth escaped the census taker because it often involved a floating population. New York's hotels and boardinghouses were filled with transients. At one point in 1863 the city's biggest hotels, the Astor, the St. Nicholas, the Metropolitan, and the Fifth Avenue, with rooms for a total of 3,500 guests, were reported to be so full that cots and mattresses were laid out in their public rooms to accommodate the overflow. The situation continued into 1864, even though the hotels raised their rates to $3.50 a day, more than the daily wage of the average New Yorker.

Prosperity, prosperity. Dodge noted that good times had benefited, among many others, hundreds of churches by enabling them to pay off their debts. The *Scientific American* reported in 1864 that prosperity had produced a spurt of inventions; 218 patents were listed in its May issue alone. All told, New Yorkers could sneer at King Cotton's prophecies of doom, sometimes to note that it was the South that was being ruined by the war. The *Journal of Commerce* set the refrain: "Aye, New York, without the South, the city that was to be ruined, depopulated, utterly blasted by the loss of the Southern trade! Look at her seated between two noble rivers forested with masts. . . . She has learned how to prosper without the South." The *Times* agreed, declaring that "the merchant has learned that the trade of 300,000 planters of mixed wealth was of slight importance when compared with 20,000,000 free and energetic people."[12]

The war was good for the metropolis as a whole, but was it good for everyone? There was no doubt that those in a position to make money made money—businessmen, government contractors, railroad owners, hotel men, and others—but what about New York's vast majority of working men and women? Their situation was not so clear, but there is no doubt that it involved a disturbing growth of class consciousness and social tensions.

NOTES

1. Walt Whitman, *Correspondence* (2 vols.), ed. Edwin H. Miller (New York: New York University Press, 1961), v. 1, 180.

2. *Tribune,* July 15, 1861.

3. *Tribune,* May 9, 1861.

4. *Hunt's Merchants Magazine,* 49:291–92 (1863).

5. *American Druggist and Chemical Gazette,* 6:173 (1862).

6. *Hunt's Merchants Magazine,* 48:146 (1863).

7. *Hunt's Merchants Magazine,* 46:210 (1862).

8. *Times,* July 6, 1862.

9. *Tribune,* February 3, 1864.

10. *Tribune,* June 16, 1862.

11. George Templeton Strong, *Diary* (4 vols.), ed. Allen Nevins (New York: Octagon Books, 1974), v. 3, 450. *Herald,* August 24, 1862.

12. *Journal of Commerce,* November 2, 1861. *Times,* May 22, 1863.

CHAPTER TWELVE

WEALTH AND ITS EXCEPTIONS

IN OCTOBER 1862 the *Herald,* having forgotten its earlier prophecies of wartime doom, gloated over developing wartime prosperity:

> Wall Street is giddy with excitement. . . . Every man you meet is rich, and will be richer tomorrow. . . . Such a rapid increase of business and such a sudden influx of wealth no one has seen in this country before. . . . Our importers of silk goods and our leading jewelers are selling their finest goods at the highest prices. The carriages of shoppers surround Stewarts in such numbers as to make Broadway impossible. . . . The theaters are crowded nightly. . . . Princely residences are building on Fifth Avenue . . . men make seventy-five thousand dollars in a week, and spend it as if they were determined to get rid of it in a month.[1]

The newspaper wondered whether this prosperity was not an illusion that might soon dissipate, but what it depicted was only the beginning of a wartime boom.

The ways to wealth were numerous, although generally limited to the fortunate few. The prewar metropolis was known for its social extremes, with a high percentage of its measurable wealth concentrated in the vaults of a small minority, and this gap probably widened during the war. At the top urban landowners, such as the Astor, Goelet, and Rhinelander families, saw their wealth increase with no effort on their part as prosperity elevated rents and land values. Those with stock in private corporations often reaped huge profits. Numerous others got rich on government war contracts, generally honestly but sometimes in ways that justified the tag attached to them by critics, "the shoddy aristocracy."

Although the early years of the war put a damper on the exuberant materialism that had characterized high society, it was not long before the conspicuous display of wealth returned, revealing itself on such traditional staging grounds for fashion as Broadway and in the theaters. By 1862 the rich had discovered the carriage paths of the new Central Park to display themselves—in handsome equipages in the summer and in elegant sleighs in the winter. The same tendency appeared at the summer resorts, for example, Saratoga upstate and Long Branch, New Jersey, which was only two hours away by steamboat. The early stage of the war reduced patronage at both places, but by August 1862 the *Herald* noted that they were crowded with people—many of them parvenus enriched by government contracts—eager to present a gaudy display of silks and diamonds. The next season in 1863 started slowly because of public anxiety regarding General Robert E. Lee's invasion of Pennsylvania, but after the Union victory at Gettysburg "the watering places filled up rapidly and an immense amount of money was spent"—in delightful isolation from the devastation of the Draft Riots.[2]

As they had been in the prewar years, women's fashions especially attracted the public eye as significant reflections of society. In what proved to be a misplaced faith in American character, the *Herald* predicted in the fall of 1861 that the rich would choose a more sober form: "Our ladies will wear gingham dresses, instead of silks and satins." The more sober wealth of New York, that associated with the reform world, did make periodic efforts to down the demon of fashion in support of men who, as one woman put it, "are being murdered by the vile cutthroats of the South."[3] The simplicity movement, however, did little more than attract the already converted. In September 1862, when the fashionable returned from their summer haunts, the *Times* fashion reporter observed that women were able to buy dresses with "new and elegant designs and combinations" and that "bonnets have undergone a complete revolution" and were selling for three times what they had cost earlier. "The extravagance of the so-styled beau monde knows no bounds," grumbled the *Herald*. "Ladies now sweep along Broadway with dresses which cost hundreds of dollars."[4]

Although the war was benefiting the rich, it did not notably intrude on their lives. Generally protected by their wealth from conscription, the rich could and often did ignore the war, even while they profited from it. Although those who read the newspapers could hardly insulate themselves from awareness of the bloody war, the rich found a convenient refuge from that awareness in the culture that they commanded around them. The New York theater, for instance, after producing a few plays with war themes in the early months of enthusiasm, presented virtually nothing of that sort for the remainder of the conflict. What theatergoers got was escape into conventional romance and comedy; their only exposure to conflict was in the plays of Shakespeare. Similarly, in their homes, they surrounded themselves with paintings on familiar themes, chiefly landscapes and portraits. In the world of the rich, the war, so increasingly productive of death and devastation, was little more than distant thunder.

The great conflict had a more mixed effect on the lives of the poor. New Yorkers had long lived with the striking contrast between the city's conspicuous wealth and its massive poverty displayed in its emerging slums. The socially degraded Five Points area, only a few blocks north of City Hall in the Sixth Ward, was as well known as Fifth Avenue. The war did not eliminate poverty, a reality that the populist-oriented *Daily News* was ready to emphasize in March 1864: "There has been much boasting of late by the public journals of the prosperity of the North, but they point only to the costly mansions, the gay equipages of those who have profited by political convulsion, not to the cheerless abodes where industry prolonged its vigil till dawn to earn the pittance that barely suffices to keep soul and body together."[5] The rising number of war widows and orphans added to the problem.

If the war often bore down harshly on the poor, however, it also brought some amelioration of their condition. In 1861 the Association for Improving the Condition of the Poor (AICP), the city's primary antipoverty agency, noted that the economic disruptions of the times brought a level of unemployment higher than any year since the Panic of 1857. By 1862, however, the AICP reported a nearly 25 percent decrease in the number of those seeking relief, from 44,569 to 33,461. The next year also brought a reduced need for assistance; the managers of municipal poor relief joined the AICP in reporting a substantial decline in the needy during the winter. Referring to the last days of 1863, the *Tribune* declared that "no closing year for half-a-century has seen less absolute want, less distress for means."[6]

This change resulted from several wartime influences. One was the decline of immigration in the first two years of the war, and another was the new employment generated by a reviving economy, but the strongest influence was the Union army. Many of those who had no adequate job to support themselves and their families were able to enlist for the benefits and the pay. "We all know," claimed one antiwar newspaper in 1862, "that of the 50,000 men in the army from this city, at least 40,000 of them went because they had no employment at home."[7] The regularization of army pay and the institution of an effective allotment system ensured that much Federal money found its way into the hands of New Yorkers. In addition, poor families of soldiers benefited from much public spending, especially from enlistment bonuses and relief payments. In the last years of the war the number of needy people again began to grow, largely because of the increasing numbers of immigrants, discharged handicapped soldiers, war widows, and, significantly, refugees from the South. Still, a reliable estimate placed aggregate relief costs in 1864 at 20 percent less than the average for the previous ten years.

Often obscured by the glimmer and the extremes was a highly diverse society of many occupations and overlapping classes. The state census of 1865, for instance, revealed a broad middle class in New York and Brooklyn: 746 bankers and bank officials, 26,180 clerks, copyists, and accountants, 706 clergymen, 1,698 lawyers, 1,747 physicians, and 2,203 teachers, 262 actors, 555 artists and designers, and 359 music teachers, many of them musicians. This did not include thousands of petty businesspeople, for example, grocery store and butcher shop proprietors and hotel, boardinghouse, livery stable, and saloon keepers. Although teachers and others on fixed incomes seem to have done poorly, most of this varied middle class probably benefited from wartime prosperity.

An even larger spectrum of skilled and semiskilled workers included more than a few who were also independent proprietors. Among many worker occupations numerous groups had more than 1,000 members, as reported by the census of 1865: blacksmiths, boot and shoemakers, bookbinders, butchers, cabinetmakers, carpenters, coopers, hatmakers, machinists, painters, ship carpenters, and tailors. Below them was an even larger number of carters, drivers and coachmen, laundresses, dressmakers and seamstresses, and the largest group of all, laborers (33,000) and servants (35,000).

The war generally was good for male workers, creating new opportunities for employment while removing competitors into the military. By November 1863 an observer noted that "labor in every department, from the lowest to the highest, was never more in demand."[8] Because of enlistments in the navy, for instance, shippers found it difficult to get seamen and dockworkers, even at high wages. Confronted with a labor shortage, employers turned to hiring boys to do the work of men, a practice that produced a disturbing decline in male attendance in the public schools. On occasion, businesses employed women in previously male roles, although this was not enough to satisfy those who proposed that women be employed so that men could be released for the war.

Good times, however, brought at least one bad effect: inflation, which was intensified by government issues of paper money. The change in the currency brought one especially painful episode for many ordinary people. In the summer of 1862 a jump in the price of gold and silver led to a virtual disappearance of small change in the city. As would-be speculators hoarded gold and silver coins, retailers began to issue their own small change in the form of paper, the notorious "shinplasters." By July this unbacked paper money had grown to at least fifty varieties issued by grocers, butchers, barkeeps, and others, some of whom grew indignant when a customer refused to receive it as change. The situation especially affected people of small means, some of whom were compelled to walk to work when they lacked the coins needed for streetcar fares. The episode was long remembered, but by the end of the year, it had largely vanished after Congress banned shinplasters and authorized the post office to issue its own small notes.

Far less easy to resolve was the rapid increase in the price of basic necessities. The rise began in the fall of 1862 and accelerated during the boom of the following year. By the end of 1863 the price of eggs had increased from 15 cents a dozen in 1861 to 25 cents, the price of potatoes went from $1.50 to $2.25 a bushel, and the price of coal went from $5 to $10.50 per ton. Not all prices increased as much. Rents, which had fallen sharply in 1861, rose more slowly, softening the blow, but overall, consumers faced increases of 20 to 100 percent or more while wages lagged behind. The faculty of Columbia College, for instance, complained in 1864 that their real income had been reduced by 10 percent.

The effects were widespread. People on fixed incomes were the most affected, but it was the wage-earning working class that stepped into the spotlight. Before the war, labor unions had been so few and so weak as to be hardly noticed. By October 1862, however, the combination of inflation and labor shortages activated men in a variety of trades to organize unions to bargain collectively and, when bargaining brought no results, to withhold their labor. It was an inchoate situation that produced a hodgepodge of efforts. Over the next year, demands for higher wages and at least threats of strikes came from ship caulkers, horseshoers, boat builders, coppersmiths, wheelwrights, cabinetmakers, stage drivers, and many others. During November 1863 alone, more than twenty different trades struck for higher wages. The largest strike involved 7,000 machinists at the East River ironworks and elsewhere, who demanded a 25 percent increase in wages. Employers resisted, claiming that they had already raised wages by an average of 48 percent, but the strikers prevailed with the help of financial support from machinists in other parts of the country.

Like the machinists, hard-to-replace skilled workers often were able to get increases to $2.50 or more per day. Strikes by the less skilled, however, tended to be less successful and also more violent, chiefly because employers had the option of replacing strikers with new workers. A strike of laborers at the Secor shipyard in Jersey City, a major supplier of ironclads for the navy, turned violent when Secor hired new laborers, who were promptly attacked by the strikers. These attacks led the employers to call for a squad of marines from the Brooklyn Navy Yard to maintain order. A strike of firemen for the Manhattan Gas Works also turned violent when the gas company replaced some of its Irish strikers with German workers. Strikes by the drivers on the street railroads brought in the police to protect replacement workers, many of whom were herded to City Hall to get the licenses they needed to drive the horse cars.

The worst tensions developed out of the strikes of longshoremen, both because they were especially vulnerable to the use of strikebreakers and because their refusal to work often delayed military shipments. In March 1863 a strike on the East River docks became violent when employers hired black replacement workers, who were promptly attacked by enraged strikers. In June another strike, this time for $2.00 a day plus an extra 50 cents for work after 7 P.M., led to more replacements and more violence, until a strong force of police restored order and work continued. Employers advertised for 1,000 workers to work at $1.50 a day, and when this was not enough, the government intervened by using a force of deserters imprisoned on Governors Island to help with the loading of ships. In May 1864 another strike tied up a large quantity of ordnance and supplies for the Army of the Potomac, leading Quartermaster Stewart Van Vliet to propose that men from surrounding military posts be employed to load the ships.

Violent strikes intensified a growing tendency to identify labor actions as disruptive of the war effort. Employers were little disposed to allow labor to interfere with their profits, and they received widespread support. In March 1864 the New York State Senate considered a bill to revive the old legal doctrine that a strike was a criminal conspiracy to be suppressed by public authorities. Labor responded to the bill with force. Early in April, members of thirty trade associations paraded up Third Avenue to Tompkins Square to demonstrate their opposition and to applaud when one speaker declared that if the bill became law, it would take "3,000 of an extra force of police, and a standing army" to enforce it. A similar meeting in Brooklyn produced a charge that "the capitalists of New York" had sent agents with plenty of money to Albany to lobby the bill through the legislature.[9] Labor organized its own lobbying effort, sending a delegation to Albany, and, with the support of Democratic legislators, the bill was buried in committee.

The unfolding situation in 1863 and early 1864 seemed headed for the violent capital-labor conflicts that were to erupt in the 1870s and later, but in 1864 conditions began to ease. Strikes continued, including one by the stonecutters working on the construction of the new county courthouse (soon to become infamous as the Tweed courthouse). Even the "colored waiters" organized to demand increases in pay, along with longshoremen, carpenters, plumbers, piano makers, and others. By July, however, the wave of strikes was ebbing. The last half of the year also brought an easing of inflation in most basic necessities. Butter fell by 10 cents a pound, flour by $1.00 a barrel, and coal by $2.00 a ton, as reported by the *Tribune*. As a result, conditions improved at least for skilled workers, most of whom had been able to get wage increases.

Any improvements among skilled male workers, however, simply deepened the contrast with the plight of the most exploited class, ordinary working women. The war did bring gains for many women, especially those in the higher levels of society, but for most women it was at best a mixed blessing. The departure of men to war did open up some new employment opportunities. In his *Women of New York*, George Ellington said that women were often employed as clerks in cigar stores and other retail establishments, although men continued to monopolize the counters of the more fashionable stores. Fundamental change, however, was slow to come.

By far, most of the women, generally single or widowed, were employed in the traditional needle trades, where they found themselves trapped in a world dominated by often exploitive contractors. Of all working groups, women were the most easily exploited because of their numbers and desperation. In 1863, Virginia Penny, a careful observer of women at work, said that in New York there was always a surplus of single women seeking jobs: "Their flattened chests, pale faces, and scanty wardrobe tell too plainly of the competition of labor among girls in that great city."[10] In general, women outnumbered men in the cities, and the war increased this surplus—to 20,000 more women in New York by 1865, according to one estimate. These workers had to compete with sewing machines as well as with each other in the garment industry.

In a world of free enterprise, women were the cheapest commodity available. "They must take what they can get or starve," wrote one woman. Even with work, starvation was often only a few days away. In one case a wife and mother abandoned by her husband said that to keep her family from starving, she labored "day and night" for more than a month to make fifty-two pairs of boots, for which she was paid $14.10 cents, less than $3 a week at a time when skilled workmen were getting $12 or more. Thousands of women, said a reporter, "whose husbands, fathers, and brothers have fallen on the battle field, are making army shirts at six cents apiece."[11]

To make the situation even worse, desperate women were sometimes hired to work without pay until they learned the trade and then were fired when they thought they were qualified, outright fraud by the powerful against the defenseless. Little wonder that working women turned to charities or to prostitution for support. Of 260 "vagrants" sent to the Work House in January 1864, 220 were women, many of whom had been arrested for prostitution.

By 1864 inflation had made the lot of such women even worse, and they had far less chance than men of striking for higher wages. In one of the rare instances when seamstresses joined to demand a modest increase, they were refused and were forced to return to work or starve. In 1864 many agreed with the words of "The Song of the Workingwomen":

When you free the slave that is chattel
The joy of freedom is loud
But the prayers that comes from woman
When she asketh bread for toil
Is met with a clamor inhuman
"Make an eager rush for spoil
Work! Work! Work!" This is the answering cry
"Our wives are fond of jewels, and widows were made to sigh." [12]

What to do? One answer was to open up new avenues of employment. In 1863, Penny estimated that at least 100,000 men in the metropolis occupied positions that women could fill just as well. The *Times* urged men who occupied such jobs to find other lines of work, including the army, but few store clerks and others heeded the message. Even when women did find employment in better jobs, they discovered that they were paid less than men, one reason they were hired in the first place. The city's nearly 1,200 female schoolteachers, for instance, received about half the salary of men. In a lecture delivered before the YMCA, William C. Prime, editor of the *Journal of Commerce,* presented statistics that seemed to prove that women were underpaid relative to men even when performing equally as well, and he urged all those present to join in sweeping away these inequalities.

By 1864 the combination of low wages, inflated prices, and employer fraud had raised some recognition of the need for action. In March, Judge Charles P. Daly, an Irish American sympathetic to labor, chaired a mass meeting at Cooper Union that launched the Workingwomen's Protective Union, which was intended to procure legal protection from fraud, to raise wages, and to shorten the hours of labor for women. In September 1864 the Protective Union persuaded thousands of women to sign a petition to Secretary of War Edwin Stanton asking that the government set the wages for women engaged in contract work to a level commensurate with the cost of living. The Protective Union also opened an employment office and attempted to persuade employers that women could be profitably employed as wood engravers, typesetters, cigar makers, and telegraphers. By 1866 the union could claim to have found jobs for more than 6,000 women. On the whole, however, it had little essential effect on either the thousands more desperately seeking work or the overall circumstances of employment. In the coming peace as well as during the war, working women were left to deal with the demands of the marketplace from a position of weakness.

Four years of war had some significant effect on the lives of virtually all New Yorkers, but the war altered only slightly, if at all, a class-organized social order, one that distributed the wealth of the wartime boom far more to the advantaged few than to the ordinary many. New Yorkers were generally aware of this situation but did little, in part because they were often distracted by what appeared to be more serious threats to their lives and interests.

NOTES

1. *Herald,* October 9, 1862.
2. *Herald,* September 2, 1863.
3. *Herald,* October 19, 1861. *New York Times,* May 17 and 22, 1864.
4. *Times,* September 23, 1864. *Herald,* September 3, 1864.
5. *Daily News,* March 23, 1864.
6. *Weekly Caucasian,* June 21, 1862.
7. *Tribune,* January 1, 1864.
8. *Hardware Reporter,* November 1863.
9. *Daily News,* April 1 and 6, 1864.
10. Virginia Penny, *The Employments of Women* (Boston, 1863), 103–4.
11. *Times,* September 4, 1864.
12. *Daily News,* March 22, 1864.

CHAPTER THIRTEEN

A THREATENING WORLD

THE METROPOLIS WAS to a significant degree a self-contained world that bred a strong sense of insularity among many of its people, but insularity did not mean insulation from the troubles of the larger world. Overall, Gotham's attitudes were sharply divided by fundamental cultural and social differences. In the Democratic Party, among the mass of ordinary people, the common view was that the metropolis was not only the center of the world but also a world in itself, with its center at the intersection of Broadway and the Bowery. It was a view shared by many Democratic politicians. For individuals connected with New York's commerce and finance, however, New York was an integral part of a much larger world centered in the North Atlantic and including most of the globe. What happened in London or Paris or on the sea was of great importance, generally for the good but also as a reminder of ever-present dangers.

In fact, the metropolis was oriented toward a larger life, its great harbor an open door to seemingly innumerable influences. In 1861, for instance, the New York Submarine Company was at work removing Coenties Reef, a major obstruction to navigation in the East River, when its engineers and diving bells were suddenly diverted to military uses in North Carolina. Throughout the conflict, New York Harbor literally contained one great powder keg, the naval magazine at Ellis Island, which continued to receive gunpowder from entering ships for storage until the end of the war.

Massive war shipments of men and materials stressed Gotham's already overworked and tired wharf facilities. In March 1863 the Committee of Wharves, Piers, and Slips of the Board of Aldermen warned that, because of poor construction, the city's decaying docks were threatened by storms, rot, and worms. They might have added fire, for wooden docks and crowded conditions contributed to the greatest disaster in the history of the waterfront. In December 1863 a hay barge, the *Cora Campbell*, was set on fire by its cook's stove. The fire spread rapidly to other hay barges and ships, destroying about 30 vessels and heavily damaging piers 51 to 54 on the Hudson River. Most of the cargoes lost in the fire were intended for the military.

Some people accused rebel agents of starting the fire. The charges were never proven, but they were evidence that the open, busy harbor was a subject of anxiety. New York was the place, said the *Times*, "at which the rebels would seek to obtain supplies and materials for the war. There is no doubt that they have a large number of spies and agents in our midst."[1] At the beginning of the war the primary concern was to prevent valuable cargoes from reaching the Confederacy. In 1861 the Metropolitan Police purchased a fast tugboat for use as a floating police station to help control outgoing traffic. Seabound vessels were subject to search by guard ships stationed at the ocean and Long Island Sound entrances to the harbor. Much of the surveillance took place before the ships sailed. In August 1861 two detectives from the U.S. Marshal's office, disguised as longshoremen, discovered that shoe-making machinery was being secretly loaded for the South. The ship was seized. A month later a Confederate agent was arrested at the Fifth Avenue Hotel just as he was completing a transaction to buy machinery for the rifling of cannon.

The Battle of Bull Run and the prospect of an extended war began a long period of anxiety over possible attacks from outside. On paper the harbor was well defended by numerous forts: the Narrows by Forts Hamilton, Lafayette, Richmond, and Tompkins (the first two in Brooklyn and the last two on Staten Island); the inner harbor near the city by fortifications on Governors Island, the major command center for the U.S. army; and, finally, the entrance from Long Island Sound by Fort Schuyler at Throgs Neck. These and lesser forts mounted 1,100 cannon, a seemingly impressive number. Mere numbers of artillery pieces, however, were not enough to satisfy anxious city leaders.

In June 1861 a special committee of the Chamber of Commerce investigated the situation and reported that the forts were in poor condition. The chamber's call for action produced results; in July, Congress appropriated $60,000 for the improvement of Forts Richmond and Tompkins and $100,000 each for new fortifications at Sandy Hook and Willets Point. In September, Colonel Richard Delafield, the army engineer responsible for the defense of the harbor, reported that the Federal government would add 242 heavy guns to the forts, "making collectively, a greater number of guns for the defense of this city than exists in most of the fortified harbors of Europe."[2]

This additional gun power, however, was not enough to calm anxieties, and anxiety became near panic when March 1862 brought the news of the devastation caused by the Confederate ironclad *Merrimack* in Hampton Roads, Virginia. Although the *Monitor* soon put an end to that particular threat, the next years brought nightmare visions of huge armored vessels steaming past impotent forts into the harbor and up the East River, there to blast Wall Street and the rest of the city into oblivion. In September 1862, Secretary of Navy Gideon Welles wrote in his diary that "men in New York, men who are sensible in most things, are the most easily terrified and panic-stricken of any community. They are just now alarmed lest one ironclad steamer may rush in upon them one fine morning while they're asleep and destroy their city."[3]

What could be done? There was no shortage of ideas. One person suggested that big guns be installed on revolving towers built on supports sunk into the harbor, and another proposed that some of the city's tugboats be converted into heavy rams. Chester A. Arthur, then the state's engineer-in-chief, recommended that a large iron chain be stretched across the Narrows, and a writer in the *Scientific American* opted for a large reservoir of petroleum that could be poured into the channel and set on fire at the approach of an enemy fleet. The most popular proposal was to fight iron ship with iron ship, stationing an ironclad at the entrance of the harbor. This last idea seemed to offer hope for the completion of the *Stevens Battery*, the giant ironclad designed by Edwin Stevens, which in theory could fire more than a ton of death-dealing shot in a single broadside. The ship, however, never received the Federal money needed to finish it.

In the end, anxious New York had to depend largely on the strengthening of existing fortifications. Fortunately, the harbor had an able defender in Colonel Delafield, an army engineer and native New Yorker. Before he became engineer-in-chief of the army in 1864, Delafield applied his talents to improving the firepower of the forts. In November 1862 what the newspapers described as an immense quantity of cannon and artillery materials was landed at Governors

Island to be distributed among the forts, and men were given some training in handling them. In 1864 thirty powerful 15-inch guns were installed at Fort Hamilton, some mounted on revolving carriages that enabled them to fire at any point in the Narrows and the bay. The defense of the harbor seemed to be complete, at least against wooden ships. There was some doubt about the ability to resist ironclads, but by that time it was apparent that fears of an attack by some ironclad monster would not be realized, although early 1865 did bring a rumor that the Confederacy had acquired an ocean-going ironclad in Europe that could threaten the harbor.

Overall, the greatest damage to the city was done by wooden ships and at a distance. From the beginning of the war, merchants had anticipated attacks on their shipping by Confederate privateers. Their concern was justified. Although the Union navy became strong, most of its strength was absorbed by the blockade, leaving the merchant marine to fend for itself on the oceans. The sea route to California by way of the Isthmus of Panama did receive some special protection because of the importance of California gold, but most ships on the high seas were vulnerable to rebel attack. Initially, merchants hoped that the blockade, by preventing Confederate ships from leaving port, would provide an effective defense, one reinforced by Union occupation of much of the Carolina coast.

By 1863, however, it was evident that the Confederacy had been able to counter this strategy by acquiring ships in England. This new threat hit home especially hard in March when reports arrived that the English-built raider *Florida* had sunk the New York–owned merchant ship *Jacob Bell,* with a loss of over $1 million. The English-built *Alabama* proved even more devastating than the *Florida,* destroying more than $6 million in ships and cargoes in a 21-month period before it was sunk by the USS *Kearsage* in June 1864. This victory, though, was followed by the appearance of an even closer threat in the form of the raider *Tallahassee,* a converted English-built blockade runner that had slipped out of Wilmington, North Carolina, in August 1864 on a raiding mission along the northeastern coast. Before it slipped back into port in September, it destroyed at least twenty-six ships, some of them off the entrance to New York Harbor. In the process, the *Tallahassee* also accumulated about 200 prisoners, who were eventually released on Long Island.

These attacks did little to disrupt New York's overall trade with

Europe. In fact, 1864 saw a slight increase in steamers entering the port. By spreading fear, however, the raiders evoked large increases in insurance rates for American-owned ships and the mass transfer of ownership of vessels to foreign flags. New York shipowners demanded action, but what could be done? For a time, they considered treating the privateers as pirates, for whom the penalty was death, but this idea was rejected when the Confederacy threatened to retaliate against Union prisoners of war. The shipowners demanded that the navy be deployed on the high seas, only to be told that the blockade came first and that most Union vessels were too slow to catch the raiders anyway. The owners proposed that private ships be authorized to attack rebel vessels so that the New York port itself might put an end to depredations through its own initiative, but again there was no action.

Not everything failed. The Chamber of Commerce sent protests to Great Britain and appealed to the boards of trade of London and Liverpool for support, and by 1864 the British ended the construction of vessels for the Confederacy. Ultimately, though, nothing could reverse the decline of the American merchant marine. At a time when the world was rapidly converting ocean shipping to steam, New York, so productive in building steamships for other nations, fell far behind. It was said in 1864 that not a single steamer on the Atlantic Ocean was American owned.

These dangers, real and imagined, were only part of the threatening world that intruded on Gotham's sense of insularity. From the beginning of the war the city confronted threats from within. Its extensive prewar contacts with the South created the materials of subversion. In an inverted way the threat was illustrated by the departure of the city's street commissioner, Gustavus W. Smith, on a purported sick leave soon after Lincoln's election in 1860. What happened to Smith, an engineer educated at West Point? The answer came the next year when he surfaced in the South as a major general in the Confederate army. The deputy street commissioner, Captain Mansfield Lovett, a classmate of Smith's, also left New York to join the Confederacy; he, too, became a major general. The prominence of these two men in local politics led the *Herald*, always ready to smell a plot, to charge that earlier they had tried to ignite "a sudden revolution, in favor of the South, whenever the rebel troops shall have passed the Potomac and occupied Maryland and Pennsylvania."[4]

Smith and Lovett were not the only cases of desertion from important posts. In 1862, Columbia College's professor of physics, Richard S. McCulloh, disappeared, finally to send a letter of resignation from Richmond with the declaration that his heart belonged to the South. Suspecting that he was being paid to use his skills in the rebel cause, the Columbia College Board of Trustees refused to accept his resignation and instead expelled him from his professorship. McCulloh became a brigadier general in the Confederate army.

Who knew how many other rebel sympathizers remained in the city? In September 1861 the police arrested one man for trying to persuade others not to volunteer for the war and took into custody another man for attempting to ship cannons allegedly to secessionist North Carolina. Two months later, the police seized Morris Meyer, the son of a wealthy Mississippian and the owner of a boot and shoe store on Broadway, on suspicion of having carried on a "treasonable correspondence with parties in Mississippi." Later, two Irishmen who had urged their countrymen not to join the Union military were arrested, forced to swear support for the Union cause, and paraded "bound ironclad together" through the recruiting booths in City Hall Park. There was some special concern over the strategic Brooklyn Navy Yard where, according to the *Times*, there were "squads of traitors" who openly cheered at rebel victories.[5] To root out these sympathizers from the largely Democratic workforce, the yard required all employees to take an oath of allegiance or lose their jobs.

The nation's leading port attracted various Confederate agents anxious to circumvent the blockade. In May 1863 the president of an Atlanta bank was imprisoned on charges that he had chartered a vessel and loaded it with supplies to be sent to the Confederacy by way of Mexico. Early the next year an even more serious case unfolded with the arrest of Louis Benjamin of New York on similar charges. Investigation revealed that he had bribed A. N. Palmer, the private secretary of the collector of the port, to get the necessary clearances. A further investigation by the collector, Hiram Barney, raised strong suspicions that numerous clearances to Mexico, Nassau, and Havana involved shipments intended for the Confederacy. The U.S. Marshal arrested at least two other New Yorkers involved in the case.

Some of the seemingly endless number of schemes involved women. In 1862 the police arrested Mary Ann Clernand, alias

Mrs. Onderdock, on suspicions that she was a spy. She was sentenced to prison, but then, on the intercession "of some prominent persons," she was paroled, only to be arrested a year later for shoplifting in Stewart's Department Store. Also in 1862, Police Superintendent John A. Kennedy ordered the arrest of Mrs. Isabel M. Brinsmade as a possible spy. She was jailed until some outraged New Yorkers got her released, charging that Kennedy had arbitrarily declared her "a spy who ought to be hung." In 1864 the War Department closed the Ladies Kitchen, which had been set up to minister to the needs of sick and wounded Confederate soldiers at the prisoner-of-war camp on Davids Island, on the grounds that it was being used to smuggle supplies to the Confederacy. The women, according to the *Tribune*, "came with their pockets and baskets full of percussion caps and other instruments" to be smuggled home by released prisoners.[6]

If the charges were serious enough, those suspected of aiding the Confederacy were likely to be sent to the "Bastille of the North," Fort Lafayette in New York Harbor. Situated less than a mile from Fort Hamilton on a shoal and surrounded by water at high tide, Fort Lafayette was more military prison than fortification. It was an elite establishment, holding important Confederate political and military leaders along with blockade runners, spies, and rebellious opponents of the war. One of its occupants, James W. Wall, said that, when he was there, the fort held over 400 prisoners—men imprisoned often without knowing the charges against them. In December 1861 the Metropolitan Police advised prisoners at Fort Lafayette that authorities "will not recognize any one as an attorney for political prisoners, and will look with distrust upon all applications for release through such channels."[7] The message was clear. Fort Lafayette was a symbol for New Yorkers of arbitrary arrests and denial of rights, but, probably because of its elite character, it also was rated by some of its prisoners as the best military prison in the country.

Threat of imprisonment at Fort Lafayette or anyplace else did little to deter the use of the city for rebel purposes. New York was too open and the stakes were too high for anything to be secure. In December 1863, for instance, Confederate agents boarded the steamer *Chesapeake* at New York and hijacked the ship as it neared Cape Cod on its voyage to Portland, Maine. After dropping off the passengers in St. John's, Newfoundland, they set out under the Confederate flag, toward Wilmington, North Carolina; pursuing Union ships were able to recapture the steamer.

Such incidents fed local concerns over the growing influx of Southerners into the city in the last years of the war. Many were Southern Unionists fleeing from the persecutions of the Confederacy, but the loyalty of the newcomers was not guaranteed. In November 1864, a year in which there appears to have been a flood of refugees, the *Times* complained that "they put no check on their tongues, habitually insulting the Union cause and rejoicing in Confederate victories."[8] In an effort to deal with the problem, military authorities began to register the names of the Southerners and to require that they take an oath of allegiance on penalty of being treated as a suspicious person. The problem was that there was no way of knowing who all the refugees were. The *New York Sun* warned that there was an organized scheme to channel the newcomers away from hotels, where they would have to sign registers, to sympathetic boardinghouses, where they could escape notice.

This floating population of possible subversives fed concerns over Confederate plots directed against Gotham. In the first months of the war in 1861 rumors of various schemes had circulated, including one rumored plot to disrupt the city's water supply by destroying the Croton Aqueduct at the High Bridge where it crossed the Harlem River. For a time, public concern seemed to lessen, but in the last months of 1863, in part because of the Draft Riots, fears again mounted. Later, some New Yorkers charged that the great fire on the Hudson River waterfront had been started by "rebel emissaries" to destroy the hay needed by the horse-drawn Army of the Potomac. September 1864 brought rumors that rebel agents had arrived from the South to arrange for the destruction of the steamers operating on Long Island Sound.

This rumor proved unfounded, but then came a report with more tangible consequences. On November 2, 1864, Secretary of State William Henry Seward issued a warning of a conspiracy to set fire to Northern cities on the evening of the important presidential election, November 8. On November 6, John Decker, chief engineer of the New York Fire Department, placed his men on alert to suppress any fires. Nothing happened on the scheduled date, but in late November, rebel agents did make an effort to torch the city. Despite concerns about thousands of Southerners supporting such a plot, the actual plotters proved to be less than a dozen men, but they had a serious plan. R. A. McDonald, the proprietor of a "carriage repository" on Broadway, was reported to be the ringleader; others were newly arrived rebel agents. Their intention was to set fire to major hotels, Barnum's Museum, important public buildings, and ships at the wharves in the hope of igniting the whole city—in retaliation for the recent burning of Atlanta. Their weapons were 144 four-ounce bottles of "combustible liquid," compounded out of phosphorous, designed to spontaneously burst into flame and begin the fires.

It was an ingenious plot, but from the beginning it did not go well. The chemist responsible for preparing the liquid at a secret laboratory off Washington Square was slow to complete his work, forcing both a delay and a cutback in the scope of the operation. Finally, on November 25 the plotters found rooms at various hotels and other places to deposit small carpetbags filled with paper, rosin, and the combustible liquid, and soon fire bells were clanging over much of the city. Barnum's Museum, Wallack's Theater, and the St. Nicholas, Astor House, and ten other hotels were set on fire, but the incendiary devices were slow to produce intense flames and the fires were discovered quickly enough to prevent serious damage. The *Times* reported that the worst damage was at the St. Nicholas Hotel, and that was no more than $2,000. Later, the *Scientific American* concluded that the "fiendish attempt" had been well planned with one important exception: The plotters had not used materials with enough oxygen to bring the initial flames to maximum intensity.

The scheme produced little panic but a quick response. The fire and police departments acted swiftly, reducing the extent of the damage, and soon came the pursuit of the plotters. In a meeting of the County Board of Supervisors, William M. Tweed submitted two resolutions, one to provide a $5,000 reward for the capture of the plotters and the other to create a "Secret Service Fund" in the police department to be used to ferret out comparable plots in the future. The Association of New York Hotel Owners offered rewards totaling $20,000 for the apprehension of the arsonists.

Within a few days a special team of New York detectives pursued suspected plotters as far as the Canadian border. By January 1865 four alleged arsonists had been arrested. One of them was Robert Cobb Kennedy, a Confederate army officer and nephew of Confederate leader Howell Cobb. Captured near the Canadian border, Kennedy admitted that he had set fire to Barnum's Museum and a hotel, and in March he was executed at Fort Lafayette.

The great incendiary plot did not end Confederate efforts to strike at the city. April 1865 brought reports of a scheme to set off a yellow fever epidemic by shipping in bales of infected clothing gathered from the fever wards of hospitals. The purported author of this attempt at germ warfare (before the germ theory of disease was proven) was Dr. Luke P. Blackburn, a Southerner who had fought yellow fever epidemics in the South before the war. The clothes were intercepted and burned, and Blackburn was arrested in May in Montreal, only to be released by Canadian authorities. Even after the war ended, there were reports that rebel agents operating out of Canada had concocted plans to poison the Central Park Reservoir with arsenic and to disrupt the city's water supply by blowing up Croton Dam, using "small torpedoes" shipped to the city in barrels of flour.

Attempted sabotage was by no means the only wartime concern of New Yorkers. By 1863 they were becoming engrossed in a far more complicated danger—internal division and discord—that threatened to imperil the future of both the metropolis and the nation. This discord found its most threatening form in the politics leading up to the presidential election of 1864, when local Democrats tried to turn back the logic of the war in favor of making a peace that would have restored the past. The effort failed, but it would have important consequences for the future.

NOTES

1. *Times,* May 13, 1861.
2. *Tribune,* September 12, 1861.
3. Gideon Welles, *Diary* (3 vols.), ed. Howard Beale (New York: W. W. Norton, 1960), v. 1, 123.
4. *Herald,* October 11, 1861.
5. *Times,* November 20, 1863.
6. *Knickerbocker,* 60 (1862). *Tribune,* October 19, 1863.
7. Quoted in John A. Marshall, *American Bastille: A History of Illegal Arrests and Imprisonments of American Citizens During the Civil War* (Philadelphia, 1869), 717.
8. *Times,* November 30, 1864.

CHAPTER FOURTEEN

THE POLITICS OF WAR AND PEACE

BY 1864 THE patriotic enthusiasm of the months before the Battle of Bull Run had vanished, replaced with grim determination on the one hand and smoldering resentments on the other. The cleavage of opinion regarding the objectives of the war was deep. Was it to be the old Union restored to what it had been, or was it to be a new nation without slavery and with a substantial free black population? By 1864, Republicans largely identified with the dream of the new nation. In heavily Democratic Gotham, they were a distinct minority, but they had a disproportionate share of wealth and social influence along with the backing of New York's most influential newspapers. Moreover, they benefited from a deep division among Democrats over the means to restore the old Union: Was it to be through compromise and peace or through the continuation of the war to victory without an abolitionist objective?

So long as War Democrats prevailed—and in New York they included politically powerful Tammany Hall—the metropolis was unlikely to withdraw its support from a war that brought it so many economic benefits. However, as the Draft Riots demonstrated, the opposition to both emancipation and Republican "tyranny" was a potent political brew that could be tapped in support of peace. The peace movement had the support of some socially influential Democrats, including August Belmont, the wealthy international banker and chairman of the state Democratic Party. Belmont, linked to the great European Rothschild banking house and married to the daughter of Commodore Matthew Perry, lent money and reputation to the movement. The movement also had the halfhearted support of Governor Horatio Seymour.

The boldest peaceman, though, was Fernando Wood, whose friendship with the South and hostility to President Lincoln and abolitionism remained constant throughout the war. Although Wood had been defeated for mayor in 1861, he soon won a seat in the U.S. House of Representatives, where he established a reputation as a critic of existing war policy and a friend of state rights, voting 85 percent against policies friendly to the administration and 100 percent against anything favorable to black people. Near the end of 1863, Wood submitted a resolution to send a peace commission to Richmond to negotiate an end to the war. In early June 1863 he convened a convention for "peace and reunion" in support of the idea that the only way to end an impossible war was through compromise with the seceded states. Resorting to two of his favorite themes, the former mayor claimed that the war was an act of aggression not only by New England abolitionists against slavery but by bank and railroad interests against the economic system of the South, an idea that was to have a long history after the war.

Wood could still count on the support of many of his old political friends and of a portion of the New York press, especially his brother Benjamin's *Daily News*, resuscitated from its suppression early in the war. The *Daily News* reappeared in June 1863 with the claim that four of every five New Yorkers rejected force in favor of "conciliation and concession." Also advocating a policy of concession were the *Express* (published by another congressman, James Brooks), the *Journal of Commerce*, the *Freeman's Journal*, the *Metropolitan Record* (which called itself a "Catholic Family" newspaper), and the *World*.[1] The *World* had been founded before the war as a Republican newspaper, but it had been purchased by a syndicate of Democratic investors who turned it into an anti-administration paper. In March 1863 the paper declared that a "second uprising" was underway, fueled by popular resentments raised by the war. So it seemed in the metropolis, where Peace Democrats gathered strength not only in New York City but in Kings and Richmond Counties in New York and in Hudson and Bergen Counties in New Jersey.

In response, Republicans and War Democrats mobilized their forces. Democrats such as James T. Brady and Leonard Jerome, a grandfather of Winston Churchill, formed the Loyal League Club, which declared its "unconditional support of the Government," only to add the qualifier "[in] all its Constitutional efforts to suppress the rebellion." For their part, Republicans looked to the Union League Club to rally wealth and talent in favor of the war. The Republicans created the Loyal Publications Society to serve as their principal propaganda agency. By 1864 the society had distributed 400,000 copies of its pamphlets. In May 1863 women, including Susan B. Anthony and Elizabeth Cady Stanton, organized the Woman's National Loyal League, pledging their loyalty to the government "in so far as it makes the war a war for freedom." The league declared that "there are Ten Thousand Woman in our City able and willing to give time and effort to the National cause."[2]

The supporters of the war effort, Republicans and their allies among War Democrats, chose patriotism as the basis for their campaign, attacking Peace Democrats as Copperheads, insidious enemies of the cause of freedom and allies of the treasonable Confederacy. In this view, the Copperheads were, if nothing else, responsible for lengthening the war by encouraging the rebels to believe that their rebellion might succeed. In July 1863 the Unionists received support from two distinct events: the Union victory at Gettysburg, which challenged the peace argument that the war could not be won without compromise, and the Draft Riots, which challenged the claim that peace advocates were the true conservatives.

Whatever they said, however, supporters of the war effort faced an uphill fight against a combination of partisanship and outright hostility to a war to abolish slavery. Republicans created a Union movement with the hope of establishing an alliance with War Democrats, but Democrats, peace and war, were suspicious of Republicans, especially seeing them as abolitionist radicals. Politically powerful Tammany Hall, although it supported the war, stayed away from any association with Republicans. On the state level, Unionists faced Governor Seymour, who was more interested in protecting the rights of his state than in supporting the war.

Then, in December 1863 the city elected C. Godfrey Gunther, an outright advocate of peace, as its mayor to replace the retiring George Opdyke. Although Gunther ran as a political reformer, as mayor he soon made his mark as a peace advocate and enemy of the Lincoln administration. He was an early member of the Anti-Abolition Rights Society, a small but not insignificant group of Democrats who declared their opposition to the alleged tyranny of the war government and their support for "the supremacy of the white race." The *Times* denounced him as representing "the cold-blooded Copperheadism of the day," and he seemed to confirm this charge when in late September 1864 he vetoed a resolution to illuminate public buildings in celebration of Union victories in the South. In a veto message, Gunther said that he could not celebrate what he saw as victories for emancipation and for revolutionary change: "I yield to no man in my attachment to the Union as it was, and the Constitution as it is," but he could not "rejoice over victories which, whatever they may be, surely are not Union victories."[3]

"The Union as it was, and the Constitution as it is"—that was the popular slogan of the peace movement. Increasingly, the last part of that slogan came to mean a defense of constitutional rights against an allegedly despotic regime. The arrest and imprisonment of New Yorkers on obscure charges of disloyalty raised cries of protest and defiance. In December 1862, New York County District Attorney A. Oakey Hall, soon to be a leading figure in the Tweed ring, directed a grand jury to look into the possibility of using the state's kidnapping laws to punish those responsible for illegal arrests. In 1864 protests were inflamed by what looked like threats to freedom of the press. In August, Federal agents arrested John Mullaly, editor of the *Metropolitan Record,* on charges of inciting resistance to the draft. Two months earlier, General John A. Dix, commander of the Department of the East, ordered the arrest of the editors and proprietors of the *World* and the *Journal of Commerce* for publishing a forged presidential proclamation declaring a new military draft. In response, Governor Seymour ordered District of Attorney Hall to arrest Dix for kidnapping. After some hearings the case was dropped, but not before it had deepened the chasm separating the supporters and the opponents of the Lincoln administration.

"The Union as it was"—by 1864 that slogan meant the effort of Democrats to reverse the course of history through a compromise with the slaveholding South that would overturn the Emancipation Proclamation and assure Southerners that their "peculiar institution" would be protected. The idea had immense appeal to New York Democrats anxious to restore the old prewar alliance with the South that had enabled the Democratic Party to rule the nation as well as the city. It also had an especially powerful appeal to the Democrats' largest ethnic constituency, the Irish.

By 1864 the Irish had lost most of their enthusiasm for fighting in the war, but they had not lost their loathing for Yankee reformers and abolitionists. One Irishman charged that reformers supported emancipation because they expected the votes of freed blacks to cancel out the influence of Irish voters. Moreover, he said, black freedom threatened the very existence of the Irish race: "The four millions of Negroes must either become our equals and amalgamate with us, or remain in slavery." In 1864 an Irish priest charged that the administration carried on the war in the hope that "every Irishman should perish by rebel hands."[4]

Irish opposition in New York and other major cities threatened to defeat Lincoln's bid for reelection in 1864. During the summer of that year, antipathy to the administration reached new heights. By then, the Union had created a powerful military machine, but the defeat of the Confederacy seemed far off. Even many Republicans came to have doubts about Lincoln and considered nominating someone else. The Republican Party, temporarily reorganized as the Union Party, eventually did renominate the president with Andrew Johnson as his running mate, only to see Lincoln's popularity fall even further in the late summer when a series of military failures threatened to prolong the war. It was a time of rising pessimism among many Republicans. "The great experiment of democracy may be destined to fail a century sooner than expected," wrote George Templeton Strong of the times. "So much for traitors, demagogues, and lunatics. All in the South and half of the North are absolutely demented."[5]

By September, it seemed that a united Democratic Party might well defeat Lincoln in the November presidential elections, producing an unprecedented change of leadership and policy during wartime. The Democrats, however, were deeply divided between their war and peace factions. Many Democrats thought that they had an ideal candidate in General George McClellan, former commander of the Army of the Potomac. McClellan's excessive cautiousness had led to his ouster as commander, but this only strengthened his appeal to anti-Lincoln Democrats. In November 1862 the general had been given a hero's welcome in New York, and in January 1863 he and his wife took a house on West 31st Street, a step that he said was "doubly pleasing from the fact that it makes us citizens of New York & fixes our residence in the midst of so many kind friends."[6] Actually, McClellan spent most of his time in Orange, New Jersey (after the war, he was elected governor of that state), but he remained the special hero of most Gotham Democrats. In March 1864 important

Democratic politicians, such as Samuel J. Tilden and Belmont, began
a campaign for McClellan's nomination, and in August, they organized a mass rally, complete with fireworks and booming cannon, to
declare him New York's favorite son.

Both Fernando and Benjamin Wood, put off by McClellan's continued support for the war, tried to head off his nomination by promoting the candidacy of Governor Seymour, only to be blocked by
Seymour's refusal to run. At the Democratic National Convention,
they and other Peace Democrats were able to put a plank in the party
platform calling for peace through compromise, but they could not
prevent McClellan's nomination for the presidency. Instead, they
were forced to see the Democratic Party celebrate the nomination in
New York with bonfires along each river and a Tammany Hall bril-
liantly illuminated by gaslight.

From the beginning, there were serious problems with the
McClellan campaign. Although the general pleased all Democrats by
opposing emancipation, he displeased Peace Democrats by repu-
diating their plank and advocating the continuation of the war until the rebellion was crushed. As a result, the peace movement
split. Benjamin Wood refused to support the candidate, whereas
his brother, Fernando, reluctantly went the other way. In mid-
September, Benjamin Wood got together with the editors of the *Metropolitan Record,* the *Day-Book,* and the *Freeman's Journal* and with
other Peace Democrats to consider forming an independent party,
but nothing was done. At the other extreme, War Democrats were
uncomfortable with the peace plank, and some decided to support
the Lincoln administration. Still, there was no doubt that the combination of McClellan's popularity and Lincoln's unpopularity ensured a decisive Democratic victory in the metropolis.

Although both sides recognized that a Democratic victory in the
city was inevitable, they were, as in 1860, concerned about the size
of the Democratic vote: Democrats wanted to run up a large enough
vote to overcome Republican majorities in much of the rest of New
York State, whereas Republicans hoped to nullify the impact of the
city vote by keeping it as small as possible. Because New York State,
with the greatest number of presidential electoral votes, could well
turn the election, the size of the city vote had immense consequence
for national policy and for the future. By electing McClellan, a pro-
foundly racist city could possibly overturn emancipation and pro-

long slavery. "We must save the Government from the Copper-heads," wrote Horace Greeley privately, "for we see no difference between their triumph and that of the outright rebels."[7]

Both sides ran predictable campaigns with their usual practices for exciting enthusiasm. The *Herald* said that they resorted to the firing of guns to such an extent that "nervous old ladies now take the precaution of stuffing their ears with cotton before venturing into the vicinity of City Hall Park." Democrats launched their campaign on September 1 with a mass meeting at City Hall. In opening the meeting, Judge Charles P. Daly, a strong supporter of the war, expressed confidence that, under McClellan, peace could be negotiated with an exhausted South—without emancipation. Daly said that he disliked slavery as much as Lincoln but thought that "under our system of government it was a domestic institution which could not be meddled with." Another speaker was more blunt, declaring that, although he was a War Democrat, "he was not for a war for the nigger, which could never be successful." The meeting passed a series of resolutions supporting the Union but condemning the "imbecility" and tyranny of the administration.[8]

Throughout the campaign, Democrats portrayed themselves as conservatives fighting to preserve the old nation against revolutionary change. Extremists within the party openly attacked Republicans on racist grounds as planning to force an "amalgamation" of the races. In general, though, conservatism was phrased in less offensive terms: "The good men of all parties will unite on McClellan," predicted the *Journal of Commerce*. "The army will love him as of old with faithful affection, will sustain him. The nation, under his lead, will emerge from the trial of blood into peace. The Union will be restored. The Constitution will be reestablished."[9] What they meant was that with peace, slavery would be maintained and the Negro would be put in his proper place, leaving him, as before, no threat to the white race.

Each side claimed the sacred name "Union" for itself, but the supporters of the Lincoln-Johnson ticket had the better claim to being the Union Party, a coalition of Republicans and War Democrats supporting a man from Illinois and a man from Tennessee. In New York, Unionists generally defended administration policies as the only way to end the war and restore a permanent union. Although they often soft-pedaled the racial implications of emancipation, they identified the war as a great fight for human freedom worth its costs in human suffering. More aggressively, they depicted McClellan Democrats as Copperheads and defenders of slavery who only prolonged the war by encouraging the South to believe that, by persisting, it could eventually force a compromise.

Both parties recognized that there were important uncertainties. One was the disposition of the ethnic vote. The Irish could be expected to vote heavily for McClellan, but the Unionists hoped to win the support of most Germans, who generally were hostile to slavery, a point that differentiated the two ethnic groups. They feared, however, that poorer Germans might unite on a class basis with the Irish to vote against Lincoln, because there was widespread hostility among workers to administration policies. This was connected with a second question: How many immigrants, both Irish and Germans, would be naturalized in time to vote in the election? Because immigrants were inclined to support the Democratic Party, Unionists were concerned that the Tammany Hall naturalization machine would work overtime, legally and illegally, to create as many as 25,000 new voters in favor of McClellan.

A third factor was a new provision that allowed soldiers in the field to vote in the election. Previously, Governor Seymour had blocked legislation to that effect, but the provision had been approved in a popular referendum by a 2-to-1 majority early in 1864. Although General McClellan had once been popular with his troops, it was believed that most soldiers would vote for the administration as a patriotic duty. As a counter to that prospect, some Democrats were caught trying to vote the names of dead soldiers, using a list of casualties allegedly provided by the governor's office. The Democratic Party, "political ally of the Rebellion," screamed a Republican paper, "has resorted to a crime without parallel."[10]

An even more disturbing concern was that an election in the city might not even take place, because rumors circulated of a plot to ignite an uprising even more threatening than that of 1863. The *Times* reported a claim that "a secret organization existed in the State of New York whose avowed object was to accomplish the defeat of the Union ticket by force, if necessary. They had purchased arms in large quantities, and had secret meetings for the purpose of drill." The *Tribune* estimated that hundreds of boardinghouses in the city were occupied by Southerners and run by Southern women, some with husbands in the Confederate army. It warned that such people "act the part of Rebels. They are the bitterest of our enemies."[11] Although there was little chance of a massive uprising, memories of the Draft Riots brought an unprecedented military occupation of the city in the days immediately before the election.

The occupation came without fanfare. It involved 6,000 troops, including selected units from the Army of the Potomac sent to the city on "special duty." The commander of the force was General Benjamin Butler, who had carried out the occupation two years before of New Orleans, where his harsh policies led Confederates to contrive the sobriquet "Beast" for him. Whether deserved or not, that reputation was an asset in this case. Arriving in early November amid threats of assassination, Butler set up his headquarters on the first floor of the Hoffman House, a new hotel on Broadway and 25th Street, where he soon announced that his mission was to safeguard "constitutional liberty, which is the freedom to do right, not wrong."[12]

To ensure a quick response to any attempted uprising, Butler installed a telegraph office that connected him to Washington, DC, to every city in New York State, and to every police station in Gotham. There would be no repeat of the delayed response to the rioters of 1863. Although he kept his troops out of sight, Butler prepared them for action, stationing a strike force on Governors Island, from which they could be easily landed at the Battery. Commandeering three ferryboats, he equipped them with artillery and stationed them where they could defend Wall Street and the Croton Aqueduct along with other strategic locations.

Butler withdrew from the city on November 15, soon after the election. Whatever the necessity of his presence, he helped to ensure that the voting was one of the most orderly in New York history. In the weeks before the election both parties had activated their vote-getting machines: "The political meetings here in New York & Brooklyn are immense," wrote Walt Whitman. "I go to them as to shows, fireworks, cannon, clusters of gaslights, countless torches, banners & mottoes." A few nights before the election, all the Union clubs of the city held a grand parade with thousands of men "illuminated by lanterns and torches." Many voters recognized the significance of the election, agreeing with Strong that the results "are to determine the daily life of millions and millions who are to live on this continent for many generations." *Hunt's Merchants Magazine* said that so deeply engrossing was the interest in the election that it "checked all disposition to do business." [13] When Strong went to his polling place, he had to stand in line for nearly two hours before he could cast his ballot.

There were 124,587 registered voters in Gotham a week before the election—the largest number of potential votes in Gotham's history, with more being enrolled in the last days of the campaign. Unionists hoped that Lincoln would get at least 35,000 votes in the city and would lose by less than 20,000. Their hopes were bolstered by a series of military victories in the South, culminating with General William Tecumseh Sherman's capture of Atlanta. They were disappointed. When the votes were counted, Lincoln had 36,737 votes, over 4,000 more than in 1860, but he was swamped by a flood of ballots. More than 110,000 votes were counted, about 15,000 more than in any previous election, and of these ballots, McClellan had 73,709 votes, a gain by the opposition of 11,000 since 1860. The president carried only one of the city's twenty-two wards, the silk-stocking Fifteenth Ward around Washington Square.

Unionists cried fraud, and there probably was fraud in the heavily Democratic downtown wards, but it also seems that the Unionists failed to win most of the immigrant and working-class vote. They were especially disappointed in their hopes of winning the German vote. Germans were not happy with administration policies, especially with the treatment of their heroes, for instance, General Franz Sigel, but the primary reason may have been local: their identification of Republicans with "puritanic" hostility toward saloons and beer gardens. Unionists did better in Brooklyn's Kings County, where many Republicans resided, but they lost there, too: McClellan won 25,716 votes and Lincoln took only 20,858. Overall, it was evident that Gotham was decisively not Lincoln country.

In New York State as a whole, however, not even a 41,000 vote majority in the metropolis could overcome a heavy Republican vote upstate, and Lincoln won the state by 7,000 votes, ensuring his reelection and the completion of emancipation. Once again, Gotham was reminded of its political difference from the rest of the state, and this sense of difference was soon deepened when a Republican-controlled legislature imposed new state-appointed health and fire commissions on New York City and Brooklyn.

Democrats, however, were to retain their hold on New York City. Part of their success lay in their leaders' achievement in protecting citizens from forced conscription. Men such as Tweed found ways to buy the men needed to meet enlistment quotas and therefore avoid a draft. The results of these efforts were not pretty, and they again served to underscore the city's isolation, but they did allow thousands of New Yorkers to avoid service in an unpopular war, and most of them voted for the Democratic ticket.

NOTES

1. *Weekly World*, March 28, 1864.
2. "The Constitution of the Loyal Union League," C. P. Daly Papers, New York Public Library.
3. *Times*, July 14, 1864. *Tribune*, October 1, 1864.
4. G. B. B. to James McMaster, May 31, 1864, McMaster Papers, Notre Dame University. Father B. A. Reilly to C. P. Daly, January 30, 1864, Daly Papers, New York Public Library.
5. George Templeton Strong, *Diary* (4 vols.), ed. Allen Nevins (New York: Octagon Books, 1974), v. 3, 483.
6. George B. McClellan, *The Civil War Papers: Selected Correspondence, 1860–1865*, ed. Stephen W. Sears (Boston: Tichner & Fields, 1969), 535.
7. Horace Greeley to W. O. Bartlett, August 30, 1864, Greeley Papers, New York Public Library.
8. *Herald*, September 27, 1864.
9. *Journal of Commerce*, September 1, 1864.
10. *Independent*, November 1, 1864.
11. *Times*, November 16, 1864. *Tribune*, November 8, 1864.
12. Quoted in Edward G. Longacre, "The Union Army's Occupation of New York, November 1864," *New York History* 65:146 (1984).
13. Walt Whitman, *Correspondence* (2 vols.), ed. Edwin H. Miller (New York: New York University Press, 1961), v. 1, 243. Strong, *Diary*, v. 3, 509–10. *Hunt's Merchants Magazine*, 51:445 (1864).

CHAPTER FIFTEEN

THE MANPOWER BUSINESS

EVEN AT ITS most insular, Gotham could not completely forget the war. The news of battles, of victories and defeats, tempted the attention of optimists and pessimists alike. George Templeton Strong managed to reflect both extremes in his diary entries regarding the conflict. As a New Yorker, he was especially interested in the eastern front, reacting with joy to the great Union victory at Gettysburg, not the least because the victory ensured the safety of New York's companion cities to the south, Baltimore and Philadelphia as well as Washington, DC. In 1864, Strong took hope for a quick end to the war from General Philip Henry Sheridan's victories in the Shenandoah Valley and from General William Tecumseh Sherman's dramatic conquests in Georgia. There were also, however, eastern Virginia and Richmond, where the great Army of the Potomac had so often failed. The supercautious George McClellan, the "Virginia Creeper," had been replaced by the more aggressive Ulysses Grant, but the results seemed the same, inconclusive battles with General Robert E. Lee—at Hanover Court House, Spotsylvania, Petersburg—battles without an apparent end.

One thing was assured: the stream of casualty reports following each battle, a reminder to New Yorkers that war was a bloody thing. Strong came from a segment of society largely able to avoid military duty, but in May 1864 he noted that a college classmate, Tom Cooper, had been killed in one of Grant's bloody battles. Not all casualties had names. In 1865 the state census noted that dozens of New Yorkers had been killed at Spotsylvania but that their bodies had not been found for many months: "The exposure to the weather for more than a year had rendered every trace of identification impossible."[1] Unlike in 1861, the war was not something that encouraged the men of Gotham to high hopes of military glory.

How could the manpower be raised to sustain a bloody war? By 1863 the primary responsibility for maintaining the military had shifted to the national government, especially in the form of periodic drafts to supplement volunteering. At no time during the war, however, was there anything so simple as a national system of recruitment. The whole business also involved state and local governments, creating innumerable opportunities for not only jurisdictional conflicts but also partisan suspicions and resentments. The recruiting business probably achieved its greatest complexity in Gotham, which had by 1864 devised a system that, through exemption payments and bonuses, virtually guaranteed that few of its citizens would be compelled to serve against their will.

This system grew increasingly dependent on money to buy the people needed to fill New York's draft quotas. At a time of rapidly declining patriotism in the metropolis, the most reliable way of procuring manpower without a draft was an appeal not to a sense of duty but to economic self-interest. In the last twenty months of the war, Gotham spent close to $10 million on bonuses paid out to 116,382 men, who were credited to its quotas. This might seem as though the city actually provided that many men to the war, but the real number was considerably less, because many of the men actually came from elsewhere. In August 1863 the *Tribune* estimated that of 36,000 volunteers furnished by the city, nearly 10,000 were "country recruits," and the proportion seemed to grow over the next year. The special military census conducted as part of the state census of 1865, though incomplete, tends to confirm the suspicion that Gotham did far less than its fair share in meeting national manpower needs. The entire metropolis, with more than 25 percent of New York State's population, contributed only 18 percent of the 123,000 enlistments reported by the census and less than 10 percent of the 5,422 men killed in action.

It seems, then, that most New Yorkers were protected from the draft, thanks especially to the system run by the New York County Special Committee on Volunteering. The most prominent and hardest working member of the Volunteer Committee was County Supervisor Orison Blunt. Aside from his deep commitment to the war effort, Blunt was useful because he was a Republican who could deal most effectively with a Republican-controlled national government. Much of the real power in the committee, however, rested in the hands of two stalwarts of Tammany Hall, William M. Tweed and Elijah Purdy, veteran Democratic politicians. The committee had the responsibility of meeting Gotham's draft quotas under Federal rules, which exempted males under 20 or over 45 years of age along with alien residents who had never voted, the physically disabled, and veterans honorably discharged after two years of military service. Those who were eligible to be drafted could get themselves exempted if they furnished a substitute to do the fighting for them.

The goal of the Volunteer Committee was to avoid a draft entirely by filling the established quota for the county through volunteers and substitutes, with the inducement of substantial bonuses provided by the Federal, state, and local governments. In New York County in 1864 the total bounty was $677 ($777 for veterans who reenlisted), $300 of which was provided by the county. This was roughly the equivalent of the average worker's annual income. The committee paid the county's share of the bounties from money derived from several bond issues for which the county was liable. Initially, the sale of Bounty Fund bonds was slow, but bankers and other investors soon recognized that the issues not only provided interest income but also helped to protect their employees and themselves from the draft.

The Volunteer Committee ran its recruitment business out of an office on the second floor of a building on Broadway opposite City Hall Park. There, they frequently dealt with bounty brokers. Sensing that great profits could be made from a share of the bounties, the brokers took the initiative to find recruits anywhere they could. In late 1863 a reporter for the *Tribune* climbed up the stairs to a long room where the committee did its work. He found it conducting the required physical examinations as quickly as possible with little concern for possible defects. The reporter noted that a black man was accepted, with half of his bounty going to a white man. Among other recruits were three veterans who received the maximum bonus and also, significantly, a farmer from upstate who was credited to New York's quota.

In late December 1863, Blunt was confident that "the recruiting business in this city will be crowned with such success that there will be no need of another draft."[2] Although more drafts were to come, in one sense, Blunt was right, because the committee was able to protect New Yorkers from conscription. Success, however, had heavy costs, not only in money but in the corruption of the recruiting system. This system was put under great stress in 1864, when the continued need for manpower was intensified by the expiration of the three-year terms of many of the volunteer regiments formed in the patriotic days. The generally shrunken and battered look of these returning units reminded the public of the dangers of military service. The Sixty-sixth and Fifty-ninth Regiments brought back only about 130 men each, and two largely German regiments recruited in the city returned with barely 200 men each. In Brooklyn the Fourteenth Regiment, which had fought every battle in Virginia from Bull Run to Spotsylvania, came back in late May to an enthusiastic welcome complete with fireworks, but it returned with only 140 of the 1,100 men who composed it in 1861.

Many of these veterans reenlisted, but others did not, and 1864 brought three separate draft calls, each of which Gotham was able to meet—but at great cost in money and in the increasing corruption of the system. In its struggles to avoid conscription, New York did get one highly favorable decision: The city was allowed to count naval recruits at the Brooklyn Navy Yard as enlistments helping to fulfill one of its quotas. The manpower needs of the navy were smaller than those of the army, but they were still considerable, especially in a major port city such as New York. In April 1864 the sailings of some ships were delayed because of a shortage of hands, and the Volunteer Committee advertised for 5,000 recruits for the navy and marines, offering a navy bounty of $200 and a marine bounty of $300 to qualified males sixteen years and older.

Soon a flood of new recruits threatened to overwhelm the training ships in Brooklyn Navy Yard—5,000 in one month alone—and the men were shipped off to their duties as quickly as possible. The Volunteer Committee wanted to count these men as helping to fulfill Gotham's draft quota regardless of where they had come from, and, to the great relief of New Yorkers, draft officials agreed, going so far as to include all navy recruits since the beginning of the war. The importance of this decision became apparent when the fulfillment of Gotham's 23,170-man quota under the September 1864 draft call was itemized: There were 733 enlistments, 1,821 substitutes, and 19,477 navy credits.

With the navy credits used up in this fulfillment, the Volunteer

Committee confronted the question of where to find the men to meet future draft calls. In August, New York County began to consider the idea of sending agents to the South to recruit Southern blacks. The county board, however, rejected the idea on the grounds that recruiting Negroes "would demoralize the army." The *Tribune* charged that Democrats, by ignoring thousands of black recruits, "will be held personally accountable for the draft of just so many [white] men."[3] Gotham, however, had already found a better and more accessible source of recruits, namely, the increasing number of white immigrants. In July 1864 a new recruiting station was opened near the immigrant landing depot at Castle Garden for this purpose. A month later, Provost General James B. Frye claimed that both New York and Brooklyn were using immigrants to fill a large share of their draft quotas.

Whatever men were enlisted, the Volunteer Committee continued to depend heavily on bounty brokers to provide them. Animated by a power greater than patriotism, namely, the profit motive, brokers scoured the landscape looking for men to enlist, expecting to get a substantial share of the bounties paid to them. "A large class of volunteers can only be secured through the agency of runners and brokers," said the *Times* in December 1863. "They have their agents all over the country, who pick up the men and pay their fares to this city."[4] Some New York brokers, handling large volumes of men, made small fortunes of $50,000 to $200,000 each. The profit motive governed. When in August 1864 the demand for substitutes in Brooklyn temporarily declined, the brokers took their men to "other markets," with the result that the price of substitutes skyrocketed from $500 to as much as $1,500.

Brokers were often ruthless in their efforts to build their stocks. Men were sometimes drugged and then kidnapped from ships and saloons; the naive were persuaded into believing that they were being hired for some kind of civilian employment; immigrants were enlisted even before they were landed, often receiving no more than one-third of the bounty due them—anybody who could be enlisted at a profit was fair game. In one case three young men not yet even sixteen years old were induced to come to New York from out of town with promises of jobs, only to be drugged, enlisted, and sent into the rifle pits of the Union army in Virginia. In another case fourteen men were induced away from Long Island by offers of jobs as teamsters, only to be enlisted without receiving a cent of bounty money.

The public soon became aware of the abuses in the broker system. In December 1863 draft authorities attempted to control the situation by insisting that bounties be paid only directly to the enlistees. They soon learned how dependent they were on the brokers when the number of enlistments suddenly fell, because brokers took their men elsewhere. Increasingly, New York County found itself in a rivalry with virtually every other county in the Northeast to find the men needed to forestall the draft. Recruiters from other places looked on Gotham as a place to help meet their quotas, leading the Volunteer Committee to complain that "so bold the evil doers, that men are constantly taken from under our very noses."[5] On the whole, however, New York was generally able to outbid other communities, protecting its citizens from the draft literally by buying outsiders through the broker system.

Overall, efforts to meet the draft became a vicious competition that corrupted much of the recruiting system, because recruiters were persuaded to overlook the abuses of the brokers and to enlist anyone presented to them, including the unfit. One critic claimed that "cripples, old men, mere boys, men laboring under incurable diseases, and soldiers previously discharged for physical disabilities form a great part of the recruits enlisted in this city." Early in 1864, Blunt and Tweed protested that the fault lay with some Federal draft officials who seemed willing to certify any man as fit for service. It was rumored that city authorities were giving some men who had been arrested for crimes a choice between jail and enlistment. Little wonder that military men began to complain of the "trash"—the drunks, criminals, imbeciles, and handicapped—that cities such as New York were dumping into the army. One general noted in 1864 that some of his regiments had an unusually high rate of desertions and blamed it on the men having been "either deceived or kidnapped, or both, in the most scandalous and inhuman manner in New York City."[6]

These results were not surprising in a system where profit had replaced patriotism, but even worse was the problem of bounty jumping, that is, the desertion of recruits after they received bonuses. Later, Provost General Fry was to say in regard to the metropolis that "there is no doubt that the authorities have paid bounties to a large number of men who have subsequently deserted and indeed who never had any intention of serving."[7] Given the way that men were enlisted and the conditions that they faced in the army, it was inevitable that some enlistees would literally take their bounty money and run, deserting at the first opportunity. New York City was a hiding place for thousands of deserters. In February 1863 the army launched a brief campaign to catch them; its patrols arrested bounty jumpers, many of them found in brothels and gambling houses, at the rate of a dozen a day.

Such sporadic efforts, however, did little to resolve the problem. In November 1863 it was estimated that nearly 6,000 deserters roamed the city, and the situation grew worse. To prevent instant desertions, officers stripped some new recruits naked to make sure that they were not concealing civilian clothes under their uniforms, but nothing prevented some men from making careers out of getting a bounty and then disappearing. In August 1864 army detectives arrested one George Coffin on charges that he had enlisted at least twice and deserted. When Coffin attempted to escape, the detectives shot and seriously wounded him, leaving him in the hands of military authorities. Early in 1865, James Develin, a bounty jumper, was executed at Governors Island. Develin made the mistake of abandoning his wife for another woman, and the spouse informed on him.

In the metropolis, it was inevitable that bounty jumping would become an organized system to make money. Early in 1865, Private Miles O'Reilly (that is, Charles G. Halpine) published a humorous book titled *Bounty Swindling as a Fine Art, and Bounty Jumping as One of the Exact Sciences,* but for many there was nothing funny about the system. In one case, it was determined that of one group of seven recruits sent from New York to the army, four were soon shot for attempting to desert. Reportedly, thirty men deserted from the city's Sixty-first Regiment in a single night. Authorities estimated that more than 3,000 professional bounty jumpers were in the city, and the men often organized into small groups to be sent anywhere money was to be made from enlistment bonuses. Those who enlisted for a share of the loot were given some assistance in deserting so that they could sign up again. Because many recruits were first sent to either Hart or Governors Island, guards there were bribed by the brokers to allow bounty jumpers to escape back into Manhattan.

By early 1865 the bounty system had become such an outrage

that Colonel Lafayette C. Baker, head United States detective, was sent to New York to deal with the problem. After investigating the situation, Baker concluded that he had discovered "the vast machinery of bounty-swindling" in the city. To disrupt that machinery, he and his men set up a "decoy recruiting station" in Hoboken and, after convincing the brokers that the station was legitimate, he sprung the trap, arresting 17 brokers and about 200 jumpers, many of whom were members of one of the city's volunteer fire companies. The brokers were imprisoned at Fort Lafayette, and at least some of the jumpers were sent to the front. Baker also arrested several officials, including the assistant chief clerk of naval recruiting at the Brooklyn Navy Yard, who had conspired with a broker to provide hundreds of forged enlistment papers. There were so many forged papers that Baker concluded that most of the navy enlistments that had enabled New York to meet its draft quota the previous September were fraudulent. Baker was not averse to a little showboating. Soon after hearing that a broker was threatening him with personal violence, he visited the broker's office, where he was attacked, "but the Colonel," reported one newspaper, "snatched his pistol from its holster and knocked the ruffian to the pavement."[8]

Baker's operations were good drama, but they may have compounded the city's difficulties in meeting what turned out to be the last draft call of the war. Early in 1865 the Volunteer Committee learned that the county would have to raise an additional 21,000 men. In February, Tweed and Blunt were able to persuade Washington to reduce the quota by one-fourth, but that still left 15,000 men to find after having scraped the bottom of the manpower barrel in 1864. Although the county doubled its bonuses to attract recruits, it enlisted less than 3,000 men before it ran out of money. Some of those who did enlist were purported to be professional thieves who planned not only to be bounty jumpers but also to steal from other recruits. In mid-March the draft was actually begun in the city, the first since the bloody days of July 1863, but it proved to be meaningless, because it was becoming apparent by that time that the Confederacy would soon collapse. April brought the capture of Richmond, followed quickly by Lee's surrender, and the war was over.

The Volunteer Committee raised 95,655 men to meet all calls under the draft, saving many New Yorkers from enforced service in a war they did not want to fight. The cost was high, not only in dollars but also in the quality of the men supplied, manpower that may have done as much to weaken the army as to strengthen it, but the end of the war brought new esteem to members of the Volunteer Committee. Tweed, who had been elected president of the Board of Supervisors in late 1864, could expect the gratitude of many New Yorkers, especially among his fellow Democrats. If the efforts of the Volunteer Committee encouraged corruption, at least it was the kind of corruption that Tweed could understand and soon would use himself to buy his way to power.

NOTES

1. New York State, *Census* (Albany, 1865), 729.
2. New York County Board of Supervisors, *Reports of the Special Committee on Volunteers* (New York, 1866), 251.
3. *Tribune,* August 10, 1864, and January 19, 1865.
4. *Times,* December 31, 1863.
5. *Proceedings of the Board of Aldermen,* 93:227–28 (1864).
6. *Times,* January 10, 1865. *Tribune,* February 14, 1865.
7. James B. Fry, *New York and the Conscription of 1863* (New York, 1865), 46.
8. *Observer,* March 16, 1865. *Times,* February 14, 1865.

Chapter Sixteen

Victory and Beyond

In the early months of 1865, as the Volunteer Committee scrambled to find ways to head off the draft, New Yorkers were already anticipating the ending of a war that a year earlier had seemed without end. In particular, General William Tecumseh Sherman's dramatic victories in Georgia and South Carolina changed the look of the future. In mid-February 1865 news of the fall of Charleston, cradle of the rebellion, evoked a "Monster Metropolitan Celebration" with parades, cannons, flags, music, and speeches. "In no part of the country but New York," puffed the *Herald*, "could such an evidence of national strength be presented, because New York is the heart of the Republic—the mirror that reflects its power, military, naval, commercial and intellectual." In early April the news first of the capture of Richmond and then, a few days later, of General Robert E. Lee's surrender at Appomattox set off even more booming demonstrations. "It is impossible to describe the enthusiasm, the frenzy of the demonstrations," said the *Journal of Commerce* of the Wall Street area. "Cheers succeeded cheers in tremendous volleys. Men threw their up their hats and waved their handkerchiefs in an ecstasy of gladness."[1] Coming full circle, the mood in April 1865 resembled the great patriotic effusions of four years earlier, with victory falling just a day short of the anniversary of the attack on Fort Sumter.

Patriotic fervor, however, quickly changed to gloom with President Lincoln's assassination at the hands of John Wilkes Booth, an actor known to many New York theater lovers. Lincoln's death brought him the united support that he had been denied in life; even the Irish community mourned. The city spent most of the next week preparing for the arrival of Lincoln's body on its way home to Springfield, Illinois. On April 24 the martyr's remains were transported across the Hudson River from Jersey City in a ferryboat draped in black. Mayor C. Godfrey Gunther issued a proclamation urging that all business cease, and the funeral procession moved up Broadway before silent masses of onlookers. The only sounds were the solemn tolling of church bells and the muffled thump of the drums for the dead. Heading the procession was New York's favorite, the unscathed elite Seventh Regiment. After resting in state at City Hall, Lincoln's body was sent on its way, again with the Seventh heading the procession.

Lincoln's death broke the escalating mood of joy, but it did little to slow the rapid dismantling of the war machine that the metropolis had helped to build. Early in May, City Hall Park, the site of army barracks and recruiting stations, was plowed and replanted to return it to its former grassy state. In the same month over 600 workers at the Brooklyn Navy Yard lost their jobs as a result of cutbacks in the navy, a prelude to a massive cutback of over 2,000 men in December. As quickly as possible, the government sold off its accumulated war materials, much of it in New York. In the early summer, it auctioned off hundreds of army mules, many from Sherman's army, some of which were bought for plantations in the West Indies. In July the government began the sale of horses from its stables on Tenth Avenue to farmers, cartmen, and streetcar companies. A few weeks earlier the government had auctioned off five steamers and two schooners with more ships to follow. By June government ships sent to New York for sale had become so numerous that they obstructed the channel to the navy yard.

Along with liquidation of the government's war stock came the winding down of the volunteer agencies set up to minister to the needs of soldiers. In July the Woman's Central Relief Association terminated its work, having exemplified the ideal of rational organization where, as a male observer put it, "volunteer work has had all the regularity of paid labor." Its members had hoped to continue, but the need for their efforts had vanished. "They hope we may work together again," wrote Louisa Lee Schuyler, their leader. "God's hand has been very visible throughout the work."

God's hand was also evident in the work of the New York Soldiers' Depot, which closed down in April 1866 after feeding and housing nearly 150,000 soldiers in its four years. The greatest of the agencies, the United States Sanitary Commission (USSC), closed its books in 1868 after spending over $4 million to improve the health of the army. *The Nation* said that the USSC "represented the American people more fully and fairly in their best and noblest mood."[2] It was certainly the noblest contribution made by New York to the war. The most deeply wanted demobilization was of the Union army itself. Numerous regiments had returned to the city before 1865 on completing their three-year obligations; many had been met with little fanfare if not absolute indifference. Now, however, the units were returning from a victorious war and to a grateful public. After the grand review of the Union armies in Washington, DC, in mid-May, scores of regiments descended on New York, many on their way home to New England or upstate. In June an estimated forty-five regiments from New England passed through the city. A British observer said that the arrival of troops in New York "was incessant," many of them coming by ships and many more by ferry from the railroad depots on the New Jersey side of the Hudson. Among the returning city units was the Second Fire Zouaves, who unlike their ill-disciplined brethren in the First Fire Zouaves, fought with distinction throughout the war; 2,000 men served in the regiment over its four years of service. Throughout the summer, military units continued to move into and through the city. One of the last was the Forty-second Infantry Regiment, formerly the Washington Grays New York Militia, which arrived in early September with 568 men, having been involved in thirty-three engagements since the summer of 1861.

These dispersed arrivals prevented a grand march like the one that had been held in Washington, DC, but the city did use Independence Day to celebrate its military heroes. The Fourth of July saw a great military parade with thousands of flags and the booming of cannon. Most of the marchers were actually members of militia companies who had little if any acquaintance with the battlefield, but the parade had a dramatic centerpiece in the recently returned Irish Brigade. It marched under its old colors, "shattered and torn by whistling bullets and bursting shell." It had fought at least twenty battles and marched up Broadway with only about one-third of the numbers with which it had gone to war in 1861. Headed by their commander, Colonel Robert Nugent, riding on a coal black horse, the marching men "looked strong and hardy; their faces, bronzed by the exposure of years, were wreathed with smiles and bestowed with tears as cheer upon cheer rent the air."[3] A historian of the

Brigade was to say, rightly, that its sacrifices for the cause of the Union significantly reduced popular prejudice against the people it represented. It was a great day for the Irish.

Performing a role it had played many times before, the elite Seventh Regiment marched in front of the Irish Brigade with twenty-six drummers and Grafula's Seventh Regiment Band. Although it had not tasted the bitterness of a single battle, the Seventh was to shine in the public eye long after the battlefield units had dispersed into history. Early in 1866 the Seventh celebrated its bloodless defense of Washington in 1861 with a grand reception at the Academy of Music. It was one of the fashion events of the year: "The beaux and belles of the metropolis," wrote the social reporter for the *Tribune,* "are of the qui vive to prepare themselves with sufficiently elaborate toilettes for the distinguished occasion." Some months after sponsoring this "blaze of beauty," the Seventh felt that it should take an excursion to Paris at a cost of $30,000, a bit of inflated self-importance that the *Times* condemned as absurd: "The Seventh regiment is in no sense a representative regiment, either of our regular army or our volunteers."[4] With its precision drills and handsome uniforms, however, the Seventh was well equipped to win acclaim in the halls of fashion and to pose a threat to all those tempted to disturb the public order.

The ordinary members of the ordinary city regiments experienced a different fate. Some returned home not to receive just rewards but to be robbed. Pickpockets and sharpers did their work as usual, but the end of the war also brought more organized crime, probably spawned by gangs of bounty jumpers. In September 1865 the *Tribune* reported that "gangs of ruffians" had acquired small steamboats with which they offered to transport soldiers discharged from the service at Hart's Island. Anxious to return to their homes, soldiers were eager to pay a small fee to be taken to the city, but once away from land, they were beaten and drugged so that the thieves could rob them. In one case the captain of the boat delayed landing so that the thugs could complete their work, robbing the soldiers of the Twenty-sixth Colored Volunteers of hundreds of dollars each.

The biggest problem faced by most returning veterans was the usual one of finding work. For many the transition was not difficult. "Yesterday they were soldiers," said the *New York Sun* in August. "Today they are industrious and hardworking civilians." Many others, however, were left to look for any job they could find. "Their old places have been filled," said the *Tribune*. "Many of their employers are either dead or broken or somehow out of business; some of the boys have been swindled out of their hard-earned wages; some have fooled them away; and here they are, without money or work."

The heads of poor families were especially desperate, because their dependents no longer had the relief payments and pay allotments that had sustained them during the war. As a result of the change, said the manager of the Patriot's Orphan Home, "hundreds of children are to-day shivering and hungry in our streets, picking rags and gathering cinders."[5] Unemployed veterans probably were largely responsible for a startling increase, by more than one-third, of arrests made by the police in May, June, and July 1865.

The unemployment problem had been anticipated. As early as December 1864 the ever active William E. Dodge had joined with other New Yorkers to establish, under the auspices of the USSC, the Bureau of Employment for Discharged Soldiers and Sailors. By April 1865 the bureau was registering veterans for jobs and urging employers to provide descriptions of available openings. Not to be outdone, in January a number of New York officeholders, including County Supervisor William M. Tweed, started the Metropolitan Employment and Relief Agency for Soldiers and Sailors at 136 Canal Street. The success of such efforts was limited. The Metropolitan Employment Agency claimed to have found 942 jobs for 1,325 applicants in ten months of effort, but it confessed that applications had increased faster than the number of available jobs; among the jobs it did find was one for a few men to dig guano on an island in the West Indies.

Much of the work of the two agencies came to focus on finding places for handicapped soldiers. With the end of the war these men were released from the care of military hospitals to make their own way. At the end of May the superintendent of the Howard Street Soldiers Depot estimated that at least 1,000 such veterans in the city were without homes: "I am daily compelled by want of room, to turn away from the Depot soldiers with one leg or one arm." Soon after its formation the Bureau of Employment urged employers to recognize that those whom the war had left "unfit for their previous calling and disheartened by their misfortune, are entitled to our special sympathy and generous aid." It went on to emphasize that this was not charity, because the "severe drill of army life has made them useful and reliable." The bureau suggested that men who had lost an arm, a hand, or a leg could still perform as "confidential clerks" or in other positions of trust.[6]

The response to the bureau's appeals, however, was limited. Up until the end of May the bureau had found jobs for slightly more than half of the 1,566 men who had registered with it, but the proportion was less than one-fifth among the 252 applicants who were handicapped. To meet the growing need for jobs, the Bureau of Employment decided to act more directly, organizing a Soldiers Messenger Corps, which stationed handicapped veterans at various points in the city to deliver letters or parcels. The Metropolitan Employment Agency soon followed by creating a Soldiers Advertising Corps, which used the handicapped to hand out advertising fliers or to carry signs; the agency touted the scheme as "one of the best and cheapest advertising mediums."[7]

All such efforts, however, fell far short of resolving the problem. In January 1866 the superintendent of the Five Points House of Industry, S. B. Holliday, reported an extraordinary increase in the number of men who came to the mission for a meal; most of them were veterans, some of whom were handicapped. Later in the year, the *Journal of Commerce* said that hundreds of handicapped soldiers were compelled to beg or starve, citing as an example "one poor fellow" with one arm, one leg, and one eye seen begging on the ferryboats. Many others scraped out a bare living selling "toys and trinkets about the streets."[8]

Fortunately both for the veterans and for society, most of the men returned to find jobs in what proved to be a thriving economy. Postwar prosperity was a surprise to more than a few observers. Nearly everyone expected that the end of wartime spending would disrupt the economy. "For three years," said the *Tribune* in April 1865, "a vast population in New York has been employed incessantly, at high wages, in various branches of manufacture and supply for the army. These will be rapidly discontinued. There is coming a period of depression that will suspend enormous workshops and break up establishments that now employ thousands."[9]

It soon became apparent, however, that the nation was in better shape than expected, emerging from the war with an abundance of money and with relatively limited private debt. In 1864 the Union government spent more than $1 billion, and much of that money found its way to New York. By the beginning of May 1865 the *Tribune* was changing its tune, noting an "enormous" trade in goods to meet consumer demand, a demand spurred by the money brought back by returning soldiers. By late August the same newspaper reported that, because of high consumer demand, times were never more prosperous, and in December it noted that more than a million men once in arms had been "restored to productive labor."[10] Prosperity continued into 1866, sustained in good part by the dry goods and clothing trade for which the city was famous.

Good times did not prevail in every part of the metropolitan economy. Shipbuilding began to feel the effects of government cutbacks in the summer of 1865, as did the equally significant engine-building industry. Some government work in these businesses continued for a time, and peacetime construction took up part of the slack; the Etna Iron Works, for instance, was engaged in building the giant engines for the great ironclad warship *Dunderberg*. On the whole, however, the industry declined. Symbolic of the change was the departure in July 1867 of the *Dunderberg,* "the most formidable and the fastest iron-clad ever constructed," for Europe. It was sold to the French government despite public protests.[11]

The effects of the decline of this important industry were overshadowed by the revival of trade with the South. The metropolis recovered from the loss of its Southern trade thanks to wartime spending, and now it hoped to compensate for the decline of that spending by renewing its business ties with the people of the old Confederacy. A combination of self-interest and benevolence impelled New Yorkers to provide economic aid to impoverished Southerners. During the war, they organized efforts to help Southern Unionists burdened not only by poverty but also by Confederate intolerance, and with victory in sight such efforts were broadened to include everyone. Sherman's capture of Savannah in December precipitated a movement to provide relief for the people there, to "show the southern people," said the *Times,* "that we cherish no malice, and are ready to extend the hand of fellowship."[12] By May 1865 the Savannah Relief Committee had sent three shiploads of supplies southward; the first ship, the *Rebecca Clyde,* sailed under a white flag with a dove holding an olive branch. A similar effort was made to help the people of Charleston, South Carolina.

A broader effort to help the South began even earlier when a group of New York businessmen, professionals, and clerics formed the American Union Commission (AUC) in June 1864, installing Reverend Joseph P. Thompson as president. Modeled after the USSC, the AUC's stated aim was to aid people who lived in areas desolated by the war "in restoring their civil and social state upon the basis of industry, education, freedom, and Christian morality." Its ultimate aim was to establish a "true Christian civilization" in the South, erecting a "new temple of liberty" on the ruins of the old slave culture.[13] The principal work of the AUC was practical relief. In 1864 it sent bundles of donated clothing and blankets to Arkansas, Tennessee, North Carolina, and Florida, adding stoves to its shipments to Memphis and Newbern, Tennessee. It also provided assistance for the thousands of Southern refugees who streamed into New York at the end of the war, renting a large building on 24th Street to house the women and children. To accommodate them in transit, the AUC placed thirty beds on two steamers working between New York and Southern ports.

Organizations such as the AUC expected a rather quick recovery of the Southern economy now that it was freed from the incubus of slavery. New York businessmen expected to be very much involved in what some called the economic reconstruction of the South, supplying the capital, commercial talent, and markets. New York's eagerness to provide relief for the people of Savannah was mixed with thoughts of making that port city an entry point for the restoration of economic relations. The first results were promising. By mid-February 1865 a "cotton fleet" of twenty-seven vessels carrying 11,000 bales of cotton from Savannah entered New York Harbor; the cotton was valued at $6 million, with more soon to come. Before the end of 1865 one million bales had been discovered in the South, much of which came to New York—a fact illustrated by the outbreak of several fires in warehouses packed with cotton, leading a few to wonder whether unrepentant rebels had packed the bales with incendiary devices. Between September 1, 1865, and April 1, 1866, New York received more than 710,000 bales of cotton and exported nearly 395,000.

Along with the renewal of the cotton trade came the restoration of steamship routes between New York and Southern ports, made possible by the repeal in the summer of 1865 of government restrictions on trade with the South. By July a growing number of Southern merchants were coming to New York to restock their stores, reviving the important dry goods trade of years gone by. Although the New York commercial houses hoped that the Southerners would repay their presecession debts, they showed an even greater eagerness to extend more credit to accommodate the buyers. Optimists believed that the South would be an even more profitable customer than before, because its purchasing population now included 4 million freed men. A new market was sure to develop, wrote a correspondent for the *Times,* from the love of finery that he thought was so evident among the women in the freed population.

Reviving the old trade, however, required that the South's wartorn economy be revived, a job in which New Yorkers expected to participate—at a profit. The lands of the former Confederacy were a new frontier for capital and skill. In September the *Tribune* called the Southern states "a vast field for emigration," noting, among other opportunities, the chance to grow fruits and vegetables for sale in Northern cities. In October came the formation of the American Land Company in New York with the announced intention of promoting the "grand work of the social and economic reorganization of the South" by facilitating the sale of Southern lands to Northern investors. Six months later, a group of investors, including Chauncey M. Depew, formed the American Planting and Loan Company, capitalized at $2.5 million, to provide loans "to the impoverished cotton and sugar planters of the South to grow and get their crops to market." The investors expressed the confidence that their money, along with the elimination of slavery, would turn the South into the "Garden of the World" that nature had intended it to be.[14]

This initial optimism, however, soon collided with the reality of a South more impoverished and debilitated by war than had been recognized originally. The cotton crop in 1866 fell below expectations, threatening to deepen poverty. With the autumn of 1866 came reports of Southern stores being overstocked with goods they could not sell because their customers had no money. Southern merchants continued to buy their goods in New York, but they bought less and chose cheaper goods than before. Although the South would continue to provide both markets and materials, it would not regain its prewar importance for the metropolis.

The war, though, had brought a new economic order dominated

by Gotham and embracing the industrializing North. The lessening importance of cotton for New York was counterbalanced by a new king born during the war, petroleum. Wall Street found a source of wealth in the sale of stock in a growing number of petroleum companies formed to exploit the oil fields of Pennsylvania, West Virginia, and Ohio. In 1864 a meeting of the new Petroleum Stock Board was attended by representatives from over fifty firms. Many of the companies seemed so profitable that they attracted hordes of investors; the price of one company's stock tripled in a week. To accommodate the "petroleum fever," brokers in early 1865 formed the Petroleum Stock Exchange in a building on Broadway; it had more than 350 members. At its opening, said a reporter, enthusiasts depicted the new industry as "mounting the throne of the defunct King Cotton, and swaying the sceptre of commerce over the universe." Apparently so: In the first three months after the exchange was opened, reportedly 138 new companies were formed. "The savings of actors and actresses waned or enlarged on fountains of oil," said the *Tribune*. "Green grocers, butchers, and candlestick makers became interested in petroleum." [15]

It was a new world, but it was an old world as well. Although the metropolis had changed during the war, it had not escaped the past. Much of prewar politics and local government remained, as did old social and environmental patterns. The end of the war opened the way for a new wave of physical development and for numerous improvements, but the new gains were mixed with old habits, old interests, and old evils. So it was that the Civil War gave way to the corruptions of Boss Tweed and, eventually, to a new era of racism fostered by a revived alliance between the New York Democratic Party and the South.

NOTES

1. *Herald,* March 7, 1865. *Journal of Commerce,* April 5, 1865.
2. *Independent,* November 20, 1866. Louisa Lee Schuyler to Angie, July 11, 1865, Schuyler Papers, New-York Historical Society.
3. *Times,* July 6, 1865. *Irish-American,* July 15, 1865.
4. *Tribune,* January 22, 1865. *Times,* October 16, 1866.
5. *Tribune,* July 22, 1865. *New York Sun,* August 4, 1865. *Observer,* November 30, 1865.

6. New York State Soldiers Depot, "Circular," May 30, 1865, Daly Papers, New York Public Library. Bureau of Employment, "Circular," Daly Papers, New York Public Library.

7. *Tribune,* November 16, 1865.

8. *Journal of Commerce,* November 6, 1866. *Commercial Advertiser,* March 1, 1867.

9. *Tribune,* April 11, 1865.

10. *Tribune,* May 1, 1865, August 31, 1865, and December 12, 1865.

11. *Commercial Advertiser,* July 5, 1867.

12. *Times,* January 6, 1865.

13. *Observer,* July 27, 1865. American Union Commission, "Proceedings" (manuscript), May 9, 1865, and June 29, 1865, New-York Historical Society.

14. *Tribune,* September 2, 1865, October 2 and 11, 1865, and April 24, 1866.

15. *Tribune,* July 12, 1866. *Times,* February 2, 1865.

EPILOGUE
A World Restored

IN JUNE 1865 the poet and editor William Cullen Bryant confessed to a friend that he had nothing to say about the just completed war that in any way equaled its "terrible grandeur," and most Americans probably felt the same way. The Civil War was too great, too cataclysmic an event for them to fully understand in their lifetimes. As a military event the war could be understood as a bloody and/or glorious calculus of battlefield victories and defeats, but it was far more than a military event. It was a great moral event, leading a racist society reluctantly to abolish slavery and to make some commitment to a new version of human equality. In addition, the war was a political event, originating from political decisions that led to national disunion and requiring political decisions to complete the work of uniting the nation along new lines.

One who did think he understood the war in its totality was Horace Greeley. Writing in 1866, in the preface to his history of the war, *The American Conflict,* Greeley said that if the Confederacy had established itself, Democrats in the loyal states would soon have initiated a movement to join it, placing these states under the control of a "dominant Slaveholding oligarchy." This prospect, he said, had been defeated by the great Union victories in the summer of 1863, making sure that the nation would be the land of the free and not the land of the slave. Greeley saw New York Democrats as among the leading supporters of the slave movement. Regarding the Draft Riots, he wrote that he "had seen the rebellion resisted and defeated in this City of New York (where its ideals and critical aims were more generally cherished than even in South Carolina and Louisiana)."[1] His partisanship distorted the real situation and ignored Gotham's great contributions to the Union cause, but he was not entirely wrong in seeing the city as the South's greatest Northern ally in the turmoil that had begun in 1860.

New York proved to be an even more important ally for the defeated South after the war, again primarily through the agency of the Democratic Party. Although the Democratic Party had been shaken by the war, it survived to dominate New York politics for most of the next century. From the beginning of the peace, local Democratic leaders were active in restoring the old political ties with the South that had enabled their party to dominate the national scene before the war. With the restoration of old ties came the restoration of old values, most notably white racism and resistance to outside interference. The war forced a racist nation to abolish slavery, and the brief period of radical reconstruction afterward brought a reluctant commitment to racial justice, but much of the old hostility to "puritan" reformers, abolitionists, and free black people survived in Gotham.

Overall, the Democratic Party was a conservative party determined to resist what it believed were the efforts of abolitionists to revolutionize the existing world, and the party became more conservative with the growing political influence of the city's Irish. In 1865 a Democratic mass meeting that included William M. Tweed and other Tammany Democrats declared that anything similar to racial equality would drive ordinary white men down to the level of blacks, creating "a mixed, degraded caste of laborers."[2] It was no surprise when in 1868 a proposal to give black men equal voting rights in New York State was defeated in a popular referendum by a heavy vote against it in the city.

Southern white leaders recognized that Gotham was their natural ally in their battle to escape the domination of the victorious North. The war had hardly ended when they appeared in the city, many staying at the New York Hotel, a favorite place for Southern visitors before the war. In October 1865 two former Confederate officials, Vice President Alexander H. Stephens and Postmaster General John H. Reagan, arrived to discuss politics with local Democrats. Numerous ambitious Southerners migrated to the metropolis in search of opportunity. They received a ready welcome from Democrats. Several former Confederate officers found their way into the local Democratic Party, including those early deserters from the New York Street Department, Gustavus W. Smith and Mansfield Lovett, who returned to the city. Thomas L. Snead, a member of the Confederate Congress, became managing editor of the *Daily News* even before 1865 ended. In the mid-1870s, Tammany mayor

William H. Wickham appointed the former private secretary of Jefferson Davis, Burton H. Harrison, as his secretary.

These and an uncounted number of other Southern migrants reinforced the Southern leanings of the New York Democratic Party. Hoping to revive their national influence, local Democrats strove to restore the old alliance between New York and the South that had dominated prewar politics. In 1868 they took a great step toward that goal by persuading the national Democratic Party to hold its presidential nominating convention in New York at the new Tammany Hall recently erected on 14th Street. The convention aspired, in the words of one Democratic politician, to work a "new birth of the old Union," nominating former Governor Horatio Seymour, an opponent of Republican policy during the war.[3] In the election, Seymour was defeated handily by General Ulysses Grant in the electoral college, but he lost the popular vote by less than 310,000 and might have won if most of the former Confederate states had not still been under Republican control.

Eight years later, in the presidential election of 1876, hopes of giving a new birth to the old Union were realized through the fate of Samuel J. Tilden, a New York Democrat and a persistent critic of Republican policies. Although Tilden's position during the war was obscure, *The Nation* likely was right when, in 1866, it charged that he "has always held that slavery was a divine institution, that any State had a right to secede, and that . . . the war was a gigantic crime."[4] In 1876 the national party nominated Tilden for president. In the election, he carried New York State with the votes generated in New York City by Tammany Hall, and nationally he outpolled his Republican opponent, Rutherford B. Hayes, by 250,000 popular votes. In the end, Tilden was defeated by a questionable count of the electoral vote, but as a condition for acquiescing to this count, Southerners were able to negotiate an end to Northern interference in their internal affairs. Over the next two decades a coalition of New York and Southern Democrats helped lead the nation away from its reluctant commitment to racial justice and equality, leaving the South free to enact in the 1890s a substitute for slavery in the form of racial segregation and white domination.

And so the old Union was restored to the satisfaction of New York Democrats. Although Tammany Hall confronted a strong reform movement at home, it generally dominated local politics, using its strength to support a party receptive to white immigrants but, at best, indifferent to the rise of Jim Crow racism. In 1928, Tammany was able to nominate one of its own for the presidency in the person of Al Smith. As the first Roman Catholic ever nominated for the presidency, Smith encountered a bigotry accumulated over decades of religious conflict, a new version of the old conflict between the Irish and American puritanism. In the South, however, religious bigotry was trumped by an even stronger racial bigotry against blacks, and the man from the streets of New York won the electoral votes of most of the states that had formed the old Confederacy. Unfortunately for Smith, he carried only those states, losing even his own state of New York, another victory of upstate over the metropolis.

After 1928, Tammany began to lose its power, and the world around it began to change, Eventually, the cause of racial justice would revive. It would be years, however, before African Americans would begin to see once more the vision raised by the Civil War, a vision so eloquently expressed by William Howard Day in 1865 when he declared, "I see black men elected to petty and then to higher offices in the State. I see preferment open to the black man, even to the presidential chair. I see everywhere respect for brain and worth."[5] The nation would wait until 1963 to hear a new African American leader proclaim, "I have a dream," a dream reclaimed from nearly a century of neglect. By then, a new America was rising to replace the old, and a new Gotham had risen to work toward restoring the promise of the Civil War, helping to create a new birth of freedom and a new Union stronger than the old.

NOTES

1. Horace Greeley, *The American Conflict* (2 vols.) (Hartford, 1867), v. 2, 7–8.

2. *Tribune,* October 19, 1865.

3. *The Nation,* 6:48 (1868).

4. *The Nation,* 3:202 (1866).

5. *Tribune,* August 2, 1865.

BIBLIOGRAPHICAL ESSAY

FEW BOOKS HAVE been able to do justice to the complexity and scope of Gotham's history. A work that does just that is Edwin G. Burrows and Mike Wallace's mammoth *Gotham* (New York: Oxford University Press, 1999), which takes the city's history up to 1898 in no less than 1,200 pages. Unfortunately, the book is at its weakest on the Civil War, probably because so little has been written about this period of New York's history. The only notable exception to that oversight before the writing of *Gotham at War* is Ernest A. McKay's *The Civil War and New York City* (Syracuse, NY: Syracuse University Press, 1990), which provides many important details but is weak in relating the war to New York as a city.

Numerous secondary sources provide insights into significant aspects of Gotham's past. Edward K. Spann's *The New Metropolis: New York City, 1840–1857* (New York: Columbia University Press, 1981) sheds much light on the society and government of the city immediately before the war. Similarly, Robert G. Albion's *The Rise of New York Port* (New York: Scribners, 1939) is a classic study of the commerce, trade, and maritime industry of New York before 1860. The best source for Gotham's politics before and during the war are two books by Jerome Mushkat: *Tammany: The Evolution of a Political Machine* (Syracuse, NY: Syracuse University Press, 1971) and *Fernando Wood: A Political Biography* (Kent, OH: Kent State University Press, 1980). Also useful is Sidney D. Brummer's *Political History of New York [State] During the Civil War* (New York: Columbia University Press, 1911).

There are no notable general studies of Gotham's military involvements, with the exception of McKay's *The Civil War and New York City,* although many details can be gleaned from such older works as James Grant Wilson's (ed.) *The Memorial History of the City of New York* (4 vols.) (New York, 1893) and Frederick Phisterer's *New York [State] and the War of Rebellion* (Albany, 1912). The first months of mobilization receive some attention in John Austin Stevens's (ed.) *The Union Defense Committee of the City of New York* (2 vols.) (New York, 1885).

Few accounts of city regiments have much value, but two notable exceptions are D. P Conyngham's *The Irish Brigade and Its Campaigns* (London, n.d.) and John F. Carroll's *A Brief History of New York's Famous Seventh Regiment* (New York, 1960). Much can be found regarding the draft situation in New York in two works by Eugene Murdock: *One Million Men: The Civil War Draft in the North* (Madison: State Historical Society of Wisconsin, 1971) and *Patriotism Limited: The Civil War Draft and Bounty System* (Kent, OH: Kent State University Press, 1967).

One aspect of New York's Civil War history, the Draft Riots of 1863, is the subject of three books: Iver Bernstein's *The New York City Draft Riots* (New York: Oxford University Press, 1990), Adrian Cook's *The Armies of the Streets* (Lexington: University Press of Kentucky, 1974), and James McCague's *The Second Rebellion* (New York: Dial Press, 1968). Each of these books provides a detailed account of the riots, but they all have the same weakness: exaggerating the significance of their subject by not adequately investigating its context.

Another aspect of Gotham's character that has been given much attention is ethnicity. The general subject is well covered in Robert Ernst's *Immigrant Life in New York City, 1825–1863* (New York: King's Crown Press, 1945), although one wishes that Ernst had not ended his book in the middle of the war. New York's Irish population has received considerable attention, most notably in Florence E. Gibson's *The Attitudes of New York Irish toward State and National Affairs, 1848–1892* (New York: Columbia University Press, 1951) and in Ronald H. Bayor and Timothy J. Meagher's (eds.) *The New York Irish* (Baltimore: Johns Hopkins University Press, 1996), which includes one chapter specifically devoted to the Civil War, Edward K. Spann's "Union Green: The Irish Community and the Civil War." New York's German population is well portrayed in Stanley Nadel's *Little Germany: Ethnicity, Religion, and Class in New York City, 1845–80* (Urbana: University of Illinois Press, 1990). Unfortunately, there is no corresponding study of Gotham's small African American population during the period.

The involvement of New York women and others caring for sick and wounded soldiers is partly covered in several sources. For women, L. P. Brockett's *Women's Work in the Civil War* (Philadelphia,

1867) is especially useful, as is Virginia Penny's classic study, *The Employment of Women* (Boston, 1863), which provides insights into the wide variety of work involving women. For notable contemporary glimpses of the United States Sanitary Commission, see the commission's own *A Succinct Narrative of Its Works and Purposes* (reprint; New York: Arno Press, 1972) and Henry W. Bellows's article titled "The Sanitary Commission" in *North American Review*, 98:153–94 (1864).

These and similar secondary sources provide much information, but collectively they leave many gaps in the story of Gotham's involvement in the Civil War, forcing a heavy dependence on more original primary sources. Some of these involve unpublished manuscripts. Although numerous manuscript collections were used here, only a few made notable contributions, namely, the Peter Cooper Papers at Cooper Union, the Charles Patrick and Maria Daly Papers at the New York Public Library, and for supplies of military matériel the records of the United States Quartermaster Corps in the National Archives, both in Washington, DC, and in New York City.

Printed primary sources are also important. Two collections of government documents provide insights into municipal involvement in the war: the *Documents* and *Proceedings* of the two boards of the New York City Council and the *Reports of the Committee on Volunteers* published by the New York County Board of Supervisors. Among other primary sources, George Templeton Strong's great four-volume *Diary*, edited by Allen Nevins (New York: Octagon Books, 1974), is essential, and Maria L. Daly's *Diary of A Union Lady*, edited by Harold E. Hammond (New York: Columbia University Press, 1962), is often useful. Several published collections of private correspondence have been especially helpful: *Defending the Union*, edited by Jane Turner Censer, the fourth volume of *The Papers of Frederick Law Olmsted* (Baltimore: Johns Hopkins University Press, 1986); George W. Whitman's *Civil War Letters*, edited by Jerome M. Loving (Durham, NC: Duke University Press, 1975); and Walt Whitman's *Correspondence* (2 vols.), edited by Edwin H. Miller (New York: New York University Press, 1961). Whitman also wrote and published a striking poetic account of the war in his "Drum Taps," now published as part of his *Leaves of Grass*.

The most essential sources of information, however, have yet to be mentioned, namely, the various periodicals published during the Civil War period. Some were specialized magazines, most notably *The Scientific American* for technological information and *Hunt's Merchants Magazine* for commercial news. More important than these are New York's daily newspapers. These papers were often biased and frequently careless in their reporting, but collectively they furnish a detailed day-by-day journal of Gotham's political, social, and economic life. Even their biases are useful as reflections of essential differences among New Yorkers. The *New York Times* and the *New York Tribune* provide insights into Gotham's Republican minority, whereas numerous other newspapers, headed by the *New York Daily News*, reflect the diversity of the dominant Democratic Party. No account of a city can be written without the extensive use of the daily press.

Index

Labor unions, 150–51
Ladies' Home for Sick and
Wounded Soldiers, 78
Leland, Charles Godfrey, 89
Lieber, Francis, 111
Liederkrantz, 110
Lincoln, Abraham: and elections,
2–4; 169–74; in New York, 8–9;
funeral of, 132, 187–88
Lincoln, Mary Todd, 78
Longshoremen, 96, 100
Lorillard tobacco factories, 126
Lovett, Mansfield, 159
Loyal League Club, 166
Loyal Publications Society, 167
Lynch, James, 86

Machine building, 36–37, 138, 150
Manpower, 21, 60, 177–85
Marshall, Charles H., 25, 40
McCafferty, Paddy, 100
McClellan, George (general), 169–
70, 174
McCulloh, Richard S., 160
McDonald, R. A., 163
McDowell, Irvin (general), 86
Meagher, Thomas Francis (general), 28, 57, 117–18
Meat supply, 52–53, 139
Medical Purveying Department, 48
Meigs, M. C. (quartermaster general), 48
Memphis (ship), 34
Merrimack (ship), 38, 157
Metropolitan Employment and
Relief Agency, 191–92
Metropolitan Police, 83, 132; and
arms shipments, 9–10, 156; and
Lincoln assassination plot, 8–9;
and riots, 66, 100
Metropolitan Sanitary Fair, 81–82
Meyer, Morris, 160
Middle class, 148
Military: contractors, 49–50, 54;
draft, 62, 94–95, 103; enrollments, 96–97; health, 75; hospitals, 71, 77, 79–80; inventions,
51; pay, 58–59, 148; recruitment,

21–22, 26, 33, 58, 61–62, 88, 94–
96, 178–85; relief, 45–54, 59–60;
spending and supply, 45–64, 59–
60, 137; training, 17–18, 27, 57–
58, 63–67; transport, 67–69, 77
Minturn, Robert B., 25, 142
Monitor (ship), 36, 38–39
Monitor-class ships, 40–42
Montauk (ship), 40–42
Monticello (ship), 9–10
Montgomery (ship), 10
Morgan, Edwin E. (governor), 46,
68, 62
Morgan, George D., 47
Morgan Iron Works, 36–37, 138
Mott, Valentine, 73
Mozart Hall, 84
Mullaly, John, 168

Narrows, the, 31, 156
National Enrollment (Conscription) Act, 94–96, 102–3
Naval Recruits, 180–81
Navy, 33–36; recruitment, 181,
184
Neptune Iron Works, 137
New Berne (North Carolina), 34
New England Soldier's Relief Society, 76–77
New Englanders, 2, 14, 83–84, 108,
168–69
New Orleans, 31, 139
New York Bible Society, 64, 111
New York Chamber of Commerce,
25, 38, 69, 108–9, 156
New York Christian Alliance, 64
New York Christian Commission,
64
New York City Council, 85–88,
103, 132
New York City Joint Committee on
National Affairs, 88
New York Clothing and Equipment
Depot, 48–49
New York County Board of Supervisors, 103–4
New York County Special Committee on Volunteering, 178–82